SŁOWIACZEK

D1194716

THE POWER OF FEELINGS

Nancy J. Chodorow

The Power
of Feelings

Personal Meaning in Psychoanalysis, Gender,
and Culture

YALE UNIVERSITY PRESS

NEW HAVEN & LONDON

PUBLISHED WITH ASSISTANCE FROM THE FOUNDATION
ESTABLISHED IN MEMORY OF AMASA STONE MATHER
OF THE CLASS OF 1907, YALE COLLEGE.

DESIGNED BY REBECCA GIBB.
SET IN ADOBE GARAMOND TYPE BY
KEYSTONE TYPESETTING, INC., ORWIGSBURG, PA.
PRINTED IN THE UNITED STATES OF AMERICA.

Library of Congress Cataloging-in-Publication Data
Chodorow, Nancy.
The power of feelings : personal meaning in psychoanalysis, gender,
and culture / Nancy J. Chodorow.
p. cm.
Includes bibliographical references and index.
ISBN 0-300-07959-1 (cloth)
ISBN 0-300-08909-0 (pbk.)
1. Psychoanalysis.   2. Subjectivity—Psychological aspects.   I. Title.
BF175.C53   1999
150.19′5—dc21   99-21260
                                                            CIP

A catalogue record for this book is available from the British Library.

The paper in this book meets the guidelines for permanence and durability of the
Committee on Production Guidelines for Book Longevity of the Council on
Library Resources.

10 9 8 7 6 5 4 3 2

For Rachel and Gabriel, again

CONTENTS

ACKNOWLEDGMENTS

A project as long in the making as this one incurs many debts of appreciation and gratitude, and I hope I can remember them all. Barbara Laslett and Barrie Thorne read and commented extensively on a first draft many years ago and have been strong supporters all along. Robert Wallerstein read the entire manuscript when it was close to completion and gave me invaluable advice as well as invaluable encouragement. Peter Loewenberg, Carter Wilson, and Victor Wolfenstein offered comments and unswerving enthusiasm. Sherry Ortner helped enormously in my early attempts to untangle the history of anthropology. Jean Briggs, Robert LeVine, and Robert

Paul gave careful, critical readings to the anthropology chapters at a later time. Elizabeth Abel found my title in a conversation we had when I was just beginning this work. She and Janet Adelman see qualities in my writing that always encourage me to continue. As I presented various chapter drafts or prepared them for publication, I received useful comments from Peter Goldberg, Maureen Katz, Maurice Marcus, Arnold Modell, Owen Renik, and the Study Group for Semi-Baked Ideas. I am, finally, grateful to the San Francisco Psychoanalytic Institute, which provided not only the opportunity for psychoanalytic training and clinical practice but also supportive colleagiality, friendship, and community along the way. Undergraduates Laura Torres and Daniel A. Caeton helped with the bibliography.

I am extremely grateful for fellowships from a number of organizations that supported my writing: in 1991–1992, the American Council of Learned Societies and the University of California, Berkeley, Chancellor's Humanities Research Fellowship, and in 1994–1995, the National Endowment for the Humanities and the Guggenheim Foundation. Yearly small grants from the Committee on Research of the University of California at Berkeley enabled me to upgrade my computer and obtain other necessities for writing and research.

Earlier versions of several chapters have been published as articles in the *Psychoanalytic Quarterly* (Chapter 3), *Signs* (Chapter 4), and the *Journal of the American Psychoanalytic Association* (Chapter 5). I thank the publishers for graciously permitting me to draw on this material.

Chapter epigraphs are from the following sources: Introduction, Erikson (1950), 403; Chapter 1, Klein (1952), 48; Loewald (1960), 254; Chapter 2, Gussow (1996), B6; Chapter 3, Steiner (1995), 442; Chapter 4, Freud (1937), 235; Chapter 5, M. Z. Rosaldo (1984), 141; R. Rosaldo (1989), 16; Chapter 6, Briggs (1991), 151; Chapter 7, Erikson (1959), 29; Chapter 8, Donington (1990), 3; Loewald (1960), 251.

This book is dedicated to my children, Rachel and Gabriel. They have been great supporters (and occasionally clear-eyed critics) of this project and have given me more in every way than I can ever sufficiently acknowledge.

THE POWER OF FEELINGS

Introduction

I have nothing to offer except a way of looking
at things.

ERIK ERIKSON

CHILDHOOD AND SOCIETY

THIS BOOK IS A CONTRIBUTION TO OUR UNDERSTANDING OF
individual subjectivity. It is an argument for the existence of an irreducible realm of psychological life in which we create unconscious personal meaning in the experiential immediacy of the present. Psychoanalytic understandings that begin from clinical concepts—unconscious fantasy, transference, projection, and introjection, all of which assume that affects or emotions help to constitute internal pictures and stories and shape psychic reality—best describe this realm. Psychoanalysis is first and foremost a theory about the creation of personal meaning in the clinical encounter. This encounter illumi-

nates the power of feelings, the ways that powerful unconscious inner realities and processes shape, enliven, distort, and give meaning and depth to our experience. Psychoanalysis tells us why we feel deeply about certain things, certain experiences, and certain people and why these powerful feelings are part of a meaningful life.

In *The Power of Feelings* two major concerns, and one overarching theoretical stance, weave through the text. First, arguing that meaning as we experience it comes always both from without and from within, I elaborate a theory of meaning. Meaning is an inextricable mixture of the sociocultural and historically contextualized on the one hand and the personally psychodynamic and psychobiographically contextualized on the other. I argue further, drawing from particular psychoanalytic approaches and from an appeal to the clinical encounter in general, that experienced meaning, as this overlaps and combines the individually idiosyncratic and the cultural, is situated and emergent in particular encounters and particular psychic moments for the individual. Some constructions of meaning may be more likely than others, but neither the intrapsychic nor the interpersonal past, on the one hand, nor the culturally given, on the other, fully determines meaning and experience in the immediacy of the present.

Second, a focus on psychoanalysis as a theory about the creation of personal meaning in the immediate present leads me to be concerned, in a thematic rather than direct way, with a tension that confronts case method in general and clinical method in particular. I investigate how we can reconcile an apparently incompatible method and theory: on the one hand, a clinical method that is directed to unraveling, and that documents incontrovertibly, the particularistic uniqueness of each individual psyche and life history and each analytic pair in the unfolding of the treatment and, on the other, a theory that purports to explain and describe how the psyche functions in all humans. In other words, all theories about human functioning, including psychodynamic theories, but also sociocultural theories, by definition make generalizing or universalizing claims, or claims about what is essential to being human. Many but not all of these theories also investigate the particular case, whether this case is historical, ethnographic, biographical, or clinical. That such a tension also resides within psychoanalysis leads to problematic theorizing and has been the focus of just criticism of psychoanalysis from without, even as some of these critics face similar, and similarly unacknowledged, problems in their own fields.[1] Here, I try to develop a theoretical understanding that can both recognize individual clinical uniqueness and make general claims about psychological life and the relations between psyche and culture.

Throughout, I tend to adopt a both-and rather than an either-or theoretical stance in response to the tensions and contradictions I address. I have always been a theoretical synthesizer. Accordingly, although some readers will probably find a Kleinian flavor to the psychoanalytic theorizing in this book—that is, I consider personal meaning in terms of unconscious projective and introjective fantasy—I also range freely across whatever psychoanalytic theory seems apt, drawing heavily on Hans Loewald in particular. I do not worry that Kleinian theory, British Independent object-relations theory, Loewald, Erikson, and others are usually seen to be incompatible, and I do not take a strong stand for or against one-person or two-person psychologies. Similarly, with regard to social and cultural theory, in my sections on gender and culture I am quite critical of the cultural determinisms found in much academic social science and the humanities, as expressed most recently in poststructuralism-postmodernism, and I argue in my conclusions for forms of psychic wholeness that are distinctly modern. Yet I am also critical of psychoanalysis for its pretheoretical cultural assumptions, universalizing, and essentializing, and I put forth, in these same chapters about gender and culture, views on the multiplicity, partiality, instability, tensions, and contradictions in meanings of gender, self, and identity that are clearly influenced by poststructuralism and postmodernism.

Both-and infuses my approach to specific questions. In Chapter 2, for example, I challenge the view that current transferences and current psychic reality come from the past, but I also hold that psychic reality is created from birth on, so that the past is drawn into the present. In Chapters 3–7, I argue that meaning is both cultural and personal at the same time. In Part 2 I argue that gender is individual but also that there are prevalent ingredients, including culture, anatomy, and internal object-relations, that most people draw on to animate this personal gender. In Part 3 I take issue with anthropologists who are cultural determinists about constructions of self and emotions or who do not fully understand the psychodynamics of the emotions and fantasies they describe, but I also take issue with psychoanalysts who do not fully recognize culture in the consulting room. I believe that all these views are partly right. Both childhood psychological experience and cultural determinations are filtered, and in a sense personally created, in and through psychological activity, which is always contingent, historicized, individual, and biographically specific.

Continuing the both-and approach (perhaps even more shakily), I have tried to write a book for both academic scholars and psychoanalysts, each of whom may find some chapters of more relevance to their concerns than others, each of whom may find some chapters rehearsing already familiar arguments. In this context, I have two goals for this book: to articulate my current understanding of psychoanalysis and the psyche, and to respond to those who think that meaning is purely sociocultural. The first goal arises from my newer identity and practice as a psychoanalyst; the second elaborates concerns I have always had in my original intellectual homes in social science and feminism. Both goals generate dialogue with psychoanalysts and academics, and my overarching concerns and theoretical stance are addressed to both audiences. My dialogue with academics centers on my arguments that personal psychodynamic meanings are constitutive of meaning in general as much as are culture, language, or discourse and that personal meaning created by the power of feelings is central to human life. I take issue, then, with many trends in the social sciences and humanities that are antipsychological or that occlude or ignore the psychological, and with social-scientific stances that criticize and reject an interest in individuality. I argue against the view that subjectivity is shaped, determined, or constituted by language and culture, or that feelings, identities, and selves are culturally constructed. Subjectivity is equally shaped and constituted from inner life, and the inner world is not a direct reflection or a result of that which is given and exterior. I also imply that, like psychoanalysts, psychoanalytic academics— including literary scholars, psychohistorians, psychobiographers, anthropologists, and others—need to question their reliance on traditional psychoanalytic developmental theories which use the past to explain the present or which assume universalized psychosexual trajectories of development and meaning. For academic scholars as for psychoanalysts, a focus on the transferential-projective-introjective here and now of psychic meaning and the clinical encounter renders psychoanalysis more accurately than do accounts that tend to present psychoanalysis as a pure theory almost removed from any on-the-ground empirical referent. (I am indebted in this matter to George Klein [1973], who most succinctly articulated the differences between psychoanalysis as a clinical theory and metapsychology.)

My dialogue with psychoanalysts revolves around considerations of problems of clinical individuality and general theory, of universalizing tendencies, of the relations of past and present, and of the occlusion and ignoring of culture, both as cultural assumptions underpin psychoanalytic assumptions and as culture is partially constitutive of psychic meaning. I hope that this book will help to move psychoanalytic thinking beyond too simple oppositions between "psychic reality" and "external reality" and to complicate and deepen psychoanalytic understanding of what is called external reality. Both "psychic" and "external" reality are complex and created: neither is exclusively presented or determined; each helps to constitute and create the other. I also suggest to psychoanalysts, especially through my extended treatment of psychological anthropology, that psychoanalytic theory, epistemology, and methodology all link psychoanalysis closely to cognate social sciences. I imply that there are good grounds for considering psychoanalysis one of the social sciences—those sciences in which people study people, often with methodologies that involve interaction between practitioner and person studied. These grounds are at least as strong as those leading to its putative location in medicine, neurobiology, natural science, philosophy, or "art."

The Power of Feelings addresses concerns and questions that have been enduring preoccupations for me, concerns and questions that must certainly have unconscious childhood roots but that were consciously (if partially) articulated shortly after I began college. These preoccupations can be formulated in terms of the relations between inner and outer, individual and social, psyche and culture, that place where the psychological meets the cultural or the self meets the world. I trace (pre)conscious awareness of these interests to my reading of Erik Erikson's *Childhood and Society*, Ruth Benedict's *Patterns of Culture*, and Oscar Lewis's *Children of Sanchez*, an intellectual screen memory that I situate in the summer after my freshman year in college. Each of these books focuses on such relations; each tries to wend its way between internal and external; Erikson and Lewis give us vivid portraits of individuals in their cultural-psychological space and time. For me these books seem to have been evocative objects

(Bollas, 1992) or personal symbols (Obeyesekere, 1981) that resonated with and helped me to elaborate some enduring unconscious preoccupations. As Bollas would put it, they provided "a syntax for [my] self-experience" (1992, 38). Fortunately for me (perhaps), these unconscious preoccupations have not been "resolved"; they continue to endow my professional life with personal meaning. Unfortunately, as with many unconscious preoccupations, there is a repetitive and driven quality to my obsession. This generates a worrying quality to my considerations here, as I directly address questions about cultural and personal meaning that I consciously left many years ago: Can you have a cultural psychology that is not culturally determinist and that can account for the force of personal psychological experience and motivation? Can you have a personal psychology that includes culture? Can you have both culture and psychology, or do you have to choose between them?

My first substantive foray into these concerns was as an undergraduate anthropologist with a focus on psychological anthropology. When I was in graduate school in sociology and for many years afterwards, feminism was the arena in which I considered psyche and culture, though my continuing interest as a feminist in psychoanalysis, parent-child relations, and psychological development was also consonant with concerns that I brought from culture and personality. But social science and feminist theory themselves only briefly or at certain moments recognize the psyche as important. They always take cultural, social, and political determinisms more for granted, even if it is the psyche that is determined. My own evolving work also reflected these prejudices and attitudes, a listing toward the outer rather than the inner. Psychological anthropology and psychoanalytic sociology enabled me to theorize more fully the force of personal experience and the power of personal motivation, but I temporarily rejected psychological in favor of structural anthropology, and my early feminist writings have a distinctly social-determinist flavor.

(This did not prevent many feminist sociologists and other feminist theorists from criticizing and dismissing my interests in the individual and the psyche-from-within.)

Yet my move as a feminist and a sociologist following publication of *The Reproduction of Mothering* (1978) and other related writings was not toward extending my investigations into the links between gender and society or toward embracing poststructuralism and other culturalist theories. Rather, it was toward becoming a clinical psychoanalyst—finding out as intensely and deeply as I could about the psyche itself. I responded to what I have elsewhere (1989) called a passion for psychoanalysis, and for a number of years, I focused my attention exclusively on the psychoanalytic world and on clinical understanding, on the inner more than the outer. This book represents another swing or shift of the pendulum, back toward outer from inner. More precisely, I attempt to situate myself right on the cusp, where both exist together and neither can be thought or experienced without the other. I read psychoanalysis as precisely the theory that describes in detail how the individual mediates and creates inner and outer at the same time.

The Power of Feelings includes, in addition to this introduction, three parts and a conclusion. Part 1 sets the stage by putting forth a reading of psychoanalysis as a theory of personal meaning—of the power of feelings—expressed and created in the clinical encounter. Chapter 1 elaborates on what I take to be the key concepts of psychoanalysis, the creation of personal meaning through transference, projection, introjection, and fantasy; in Chapter 2 I consider some implications of this account for our thinking about psychoanalytic assumptions concerning development and the determinations of psychic life in the present. Part 2 brings this reading to bear on questions of gender. Chapter 3 argues, in the context of contemporary feminism, for the inextricable personal and emotional contributions to constructions of gender and for the importance of aspects of individual subjectivity and self-creation that come from within. Chapter 4 shifts the focus to psychoanalysis and points psychoanalysts to the inextricable cultural contributions to gender meaning and the clinical individuality of gender.

Part 3 widens the concerns taken up in Part 2, to take on considerations of culture and psyche more broadly. Chapter 5 evaluates the anthropology of self and feeling in ways consonant with my evaluation of contemporary feminism. I find a too exclusive cultural determinism in this work and a failure to recognize the ways in which selves and emotions are created from within through the nonreducible psychodynamic processes that psychoanalysis describes. Chapter 6 reads some of contemporary psychoanalytic anthropology as making significant progress toward theorizing and describing the psyche-culture nexus ethnographically and transferentially, thus creating a perspective that holds both psyche and culture in view, neither reducible to the other, both operating together as one intertwined process. Chapter 7, turning the psyche-culture lens back on psychoanalysis, advocates a more integrated consideration in psychoanalytic theory and clinical understanding of the constitutive role of culture in the psyche and points to some clinicians who, like some psychoanalytic anthropologists, take a step toward this goal.

Finally, in Part 4, Chapter 8 returns to themes broached in Part 1, but this time with the explicit goal of recognizing psychoanalysis as a grand theory of the human mind and human fulfillment. This endeavor responds to a not unreasonable diffidence among psychoanalysts about making sweeping claims. It also reacts to a psychoanalytic preoccupation with technique and process, and to those historical strands and trends that lead as much as possible toward seeing psychoanalysis as a natural science with objective claims rather than as an art, a philosophical anthropology, a theory of ethics, mind, morality, or meaning. It responds to contemporary academic skepticism about grand theory in general and to academic dismissal of theories of subjectivity in particular that do not focus on split subjectivity, partiality, fragmentation, alienation, and cultural and discursive constructions of the self. Psychoanalytic visions of subjectivity, by contrast, take their place within centuries of thinking about the meaning of life, the nature of the self, and the quality of good relations with others.

PART 1 PSYCHOANALYSIS

1 Creating Personal Meaning: Transference, Projection, Introjection, Fantasy

In some form or other transference operates
throughout life and influences all human relations.

MELANIE KLEIN

"THE ORIGINS OF TRANSFERENCE"

There is neither such a thing as reality nor a real
relationship, without transference.

HANS LOEWALD

"ON THE THERAPEUTIC ACTION OF

PSYCHOANALYSIS"

PSYCHOANALYSIS IS A THEORY ABOUT HOW WE CREATE PER-
sonal meaning, our unconscious psychic reality, through what I am
calling the power of feelings. "Feelings" here encompass feeling-
based stories or proto-stories—unconscious fantasies—that constitute
our unconscious inner life and motivate our attempts to change that
inner life to reduce anxiety and other uncomfortable or frightening
affects or to put such uncomfortable affects outside the self. Several
psychoanalytic terms, descriptions of emotionally laden psychodynamic processes that themselves overlap or can be translated one
into the other, most clearly describe for us this creation of personal

meaning. They include transference and, incorporated in it, projection and introjection, all of which express and create unconscious fantasy. The capacities that enable us to create personal meaning—capacities for transference, projection, introjection, and unconscious fantasy—are innate human capacities that develop and unfold virtually from birth, in a context of interaction with others. Psychoanalytic understandings of these capacities and processes come from the clinical encounter, with its centering on the psychic reality expressed in transference, and from clinical observation of and inference about psychological development in childhood. In this chapter I consider transference in the clinical encounter.

Transference is the hypothesis and demonstration that our inner world of psychic reality helps to create, shape, and give meaning to the intersubjective, social, and cultural worlds we inhabit. It is the original psychoanalytic vehicle documenting for us the power of feelings. Psychoanalytic investigation suggests that people are motivated or driven, in order to gain a sense of a meaningful life and manage threatening conscious and unconscious affects and beliefs, to create or interpret external experiences in ways that resonate with internal experiences, preoccupations, fantasies, and senses of self-other relationships. In transference, we personally endow, animate, and tint, emotionally and through fantasy, the cultural, linguistic, interpersonal, cognitive, and embodied world we experience. Stephen Mitchell likens transference to a prism: "The patient's subjective world is organized like a prism whose facets refract and disperse entering illumination into customary and familiar wavelengths" (1993, 212). Christopher Bollas calls transference "the private language of the self" (1987, 61): "Our external world evokes unconscious elements of the self as object relation, and . . . our experience of reality is therefore influenced by those unconscious associations elicited by environmental conditions" (1987, 48).

In transference, we use experiences and feelings from the past to give partial meaning to the present as well as to shape the present, as we act and interpret present experience in light of this internal past.

At the same time, it can also be said that through transference our current unconscious feelings and fantasies—contemporary psychic reality, whatever its temporal origins—give partial meaning to and shape conscious feeling and experience. What is "transferred" will be seen differently depending on the particular metapsychology the psychoanalyst holds, but the processes that compose transference are similar.

Projection (sometimes called externalization) and introjection (sometimes called internalization), as these express unconscious fantasy, are the major modes of transference. In projection and projective identification, we put feelings, beliefs, or parts of our self into an other, whether another person with whom we are interacting, an internal object or part-object that has already been created through projective-introjective exchanges, or an idea, symbol, or any other meaning or entity. In introjection and introjective identification, aspects or functions of a person or object are taken into the self and come to constitute and differentiate an internal world and reshape the ego.[1] All projection and introjection express unconscious fantasy, an affect-laden image or account, often nonlinguistic, nonverbal, and simply sensed, of what the nature of the object is, what the object's intentions are, how the self can or should react or is liable to be affected by the object, what the effect of the self-object interchange might be on both, and so forth.

Freud discovered transference in the analytic encounter. He found "new editions and facsimiles of the impulses and phantasies which are aroused and made conscious during the progress of the analysis; . . . they replace some earlier person by the person of the physician. . . . A whole series of psychological experiences are revived, not as belonging to the past, but as applying to the person of the physician at the present moment" (1905a, 116). He thus described how patients, when they enter analysis, "transfer" onto the analyst a variety of desires, fears, expectations, and fantasies that they originally felt toward important figures in their early life—mother, father, siblings, nurses. Freud described patients falling in love with their analyst, and he also considered the negative therapeutic reaction, but it was later analysts like Klein who stressed the perhaps greater significance of envy and hatred toward the analyst. A man in analysis feels exactly as he did when he was a child: he experiences me as imposing my needs on him as his mother did. This is an objective reality: by a stroke of really bad luck, he has managed to end up with a woman analyst who is just like his mother.[2] It is for each analyst or patient anew a remarkable discovery that within minutes or hours after being in the analyst's office, a person has strong feelings and beliefs about the analyst and about therapy or analysis, and she finds herself not only describing familiar anxieties and patterns of behavior but bringing them in and feeling them in her interactions with the analyst.

Since Freud, our understanding of transference has broadened and changed. Contemporary psychoanalysts describe transference not so much as bringing feelings about the person of the parent to the person of the analyst but in the context of the psychoanalytic situation as a whole (see, e.g., Joseph, 1985; Klein, 1952; Loewald, 1960, 1986). Transference expresses and creates the unconscious fantasy and emotional meanings of whatever the analysand says or does and whatever goes on between analyst and analysand. We are no longer talking only about "new editions" of old relationships, "mother-transferences" or "father-transferences," but about how the analysand expresses inner psychic reality in whatever she does, whether in talk about feelings, during some happening at work, a party, in the family, or in silence. Whereas in the old view the interpretation of transference was more a translation project focused on the content of what was said, usually in relation to persons the analysand was once involved with—a vehicle for repeating or remembering what happened before and outside—now the goal is to understand and bring to consciousness in a more global way the analysand's unconscious being and mind (and the recreating and changing of her being and mind) in the analytic encounter. In this view, the patient continually creates psychologically her experience of the intersubjective external world, her internal world and self, and the way these relate one to the other. These are the expressions of psychic reality that we observe in the clinical encounter.

Three characteristics of psychic life are particularly crucial when we begin our account of psychic life from transference, projection, and introjection. First, we are immediately in a relational world—both internally object-relational and interpersonally intersubjective. Transference expresses unconscious fantasy and feeling, but it projectively endows or introjectively shapes an (internal or external) object and is created within an interpersonal (analyst-analysand, self-other) matrix. These concepts imply the presence of an other to the self who transfers, so that there are not necessarily two actual people but, minimally, a two-person, or self-other, psyche. (I discuss the consonance between a clinical approach to psychoanalysis and an object-relations metapsychology in Chodorow, 1986.) The concepts also imply that feelings are always located in a self-other field, even if this field is entirely intrapsychic, if it is composed entirely of split-off or fragmented part-objects and part-selves, or if absence of the other and aloneness characterize its dominant relational constitution.[3] Transference-countertransference points us toward the mutuality of transference processes and the mutual, or negotiated, construction of emotional meanings of situations and interactions.

Melanie Klein, who founded object-relations theory, draws on her conclusions with regard to infants to describe transference. As she puts it: "The analysis of very young children has taught me that there is no instinctual urge, no anxiety situation, no mental process which does not involve objects, external or internal; in other words, object-relations are at the *centre* of emotional life. Furthermore, love and hatred, phantasies, anxieties, and defences are also operative from the beginning and are *ab initio* indivisibly linked with object-relations. . . . I hold that transference originates in the same processes which in the earliest stages determine object-relations. Therefore we have to go back again and again in analysis to the fluctuations between objects, loved and hated, external and internal (1952, 53)."[4]

Unlike Klein, Loewald begins his discussion of transference with the analytic encounter itself, foreshadowing a perspective that has moved to the forefront of American psychoanalysis. Against a traditional view of the uninvolved, neutral, evenly hovering analyst he poses an inevitably two-person relationship constructed through the feelings and intellect both parties bring to the encounter. In his classic paper "On the Therapeutic Action of Psychoanalysis," he speculates about why this interaction, which takes place on many levels of psychic integration and disintegration for both patient and analyst, has been overlooked: "Apart from the difficulty for the analyst of self-observation while in interaction with his patient, there seems to be a specific reason, stemming from theoretical bias. . . . The theoretical bias is the view of the psychic apparatus as a closed system. Thus the analyst is seen, not as a co-actor on the analytic stage in which the childhood development, culminating in the infantile neurosis, is re-staged and reactivated in the development, crystallization and resolution of the transference neurosis, but as a reflecting mirror, albeit of the unconscious, and characterized by scrupulous neutrality" (1960, 223).

The analytic encounter, in Loewald's view, is characterized by transference and countertransference, the analyst's as well as the patient's emotion and fantasy: "The analyst's emotional investment, acknowledged or not by either party, is a decisive factor in the curative process. . . . If a capacity for transference . . . is a measure of the patient's analyzability, the capacity for countertransference is a measure of the analyst's ability to analyze" (1986, 285–286). Whether countertransference is seen as the analyst's reaction to the patient's transferences, as any feeling or reaction on the part of the analyst to the relationship or to events within it, or as the analyst's transfer of unconscious to conscious or past to present in the analytic encounter and in the creation of the analytic space, the recognition and theorizing of countertransference move us further toward seeing the inevitably object-relational character of transference, the complex and continual creation of interpersonal and intrapsychic meaning, within the analysis and by implication within life. As Loewald puts it, transference and countertransference are "two faces of the same dynamic, rooted in the inextricable intertwinings with others in which individual life originates and remains throughout the life of the individual in numberless elaborations, derivatives, and transformations" (1986, 276).

This perspective implies that, although you can certainly view transference as an expression of an internal drive-defense dynamic in which the analyst is no more than a projective screen, a view that stresses the mutual constitution of the transference-countertransference field and the mutual constitution of selves seems to reflect more accurately what actually happens in the analytic situation. Winnicott also conceptualizes this field in his portrayal of the analytic situation as a potential space in which both partners create, from inner and outer reality, a newly emergent and irreducible reality between them (e.g., Winnicott, 1971; see also Ogden, 1994).

Transference also implies a second characteristic of psychic life. Created through projective and introjective identification that expresses unconscious fantasy, transference is the concept that best enables us to move beyond psychic or cultural determinism and sustain recognition of the continuous, changing nature of psychic process. As many contemporary American analysts have argued, transference-countertransference is contingent and continually emergent, a process created mutually by analyst and patient (see, e.g.,

Hoffman, 1983; Loewald, 1986; Mitchell, 1993; Ogden, 1994; Schafer, 1983, 1992). Both parties draw on conventional cultural and linguistic usages in their interaction, and they have overlapping repertoires of metaphor, cultural images, stories, and sayings that contribute to constructing their conversation. Each has also a lifetime of creating self and other through emotion- and anxiety-laden, fantasy-driven projective and introjective constructions of self and other that also help to shape the emotional quality of their interactions.

But the interaction itself, the conversation itself, the transitional process created in this potential space, this lifetime of fantasy and meaning creation, are themselves emergent in the here and now of intrapsychic process and intersubjective interaction. None of these is fixed once and for all in infancy or childhood, and each moment of the analytic encounter itself creates each new meaning. (See, for example, Ogden's "analytic third," in which a particular meaning is given to an object or process that has been created between analyst and analysand only at that particular time and in that particular context [Ogden, 1994]. This is one area where the contemporary Kleinian–contemporary American synthesis breaks down, not only in my own attempts at synthesis but also, I think, among other Americans who wish to use Klein—see, e.g., Mitchell, 1993; Schafer, 1997. Contemporary Kleinians are not narrativists and constructionists.)

When we think of child analysis or children's play, it is easy to see that a child uses a particular toy or object for individually specific emotional and symbolic ends, to create a personally relevant fantasy or story. For Klein, the capacity to symbolize personally is essential to psychic health—to creativity and to the imaging of others and feelings about them (1930, 1955). Klein notes that "we have to consider each child's use of symbols in connection with his particular emotions and anxieties and in relation to the whole situation which is presented in the analysis; mere generalized translations of symbols are meaningless" (1955, 137). It is for this reason that Klein kept a separate drawer of toys for each child—as she puts it, "the equivalent of the adult's associations, . . . only known to the analyst and to himself" (1955, 126). Similarly, the meaning of a cultural object and the language and beliefs of adults are never self-evident. By focusing on projection, introjection, and fantasy in the creation of psychic reality, we move from determined universals to the emergent particularity of the individual and of the individual psychoanalytic encounter between two people.

Finally, and perhaps most important, analysts remind us that transference is universal; what Freud discovered in the analytic encounter goes well beyond the specialized analytic relationship. Unconscious fantasies expressed in transference processes of projective and introjective identification are the way we give meaning to our lives and experiences in general. The capacity for transference (in this sense subsuming countertransference) is thus one of the great abilities and defining capacities of the human mind. As Bird puts it, following Klein and Loewald (see chapter epigraphs), transference is "a universal mental function which may be the basis of all human relationships . . . one of the mind's main agencies for giving birth to new ideas and new life to old ones" (1972, 267). We begin by investigating the analytic encounter—what goes on between analysand and analyst— but we rapidly realize that transferences are found *whenever* feelings, fantasies, and emotional meaning are given to people and situations. Transference, projection, introjection, and fantasy are those continually active processes through which, in any immediate moment, we have the ability to bestow multiple emotional and cognitive meanings on perception or experience. These processes are an active and ongoing fact of life, and even within an analysis, they derive not only from early relations, situations, and people; they may also come from or be expressed in a person's current situation or in any important relationship or experience. They may be fostered by the analyst's behavior itself (Hoffman, 1983; Loewald, 1986).

Klein tells us that through projection, "the picture of the external world . . . is coloured by internal factors. By introjection this picture of the external world affects the internal one" (1963, 312). Robert Caper describes the radical implication of such a claim. From a psychoanalytic perspective, projection and introjection, expressing and mediating fantasy, act to enliven and make personally meaningful a world that is otherwise intrinsically meaningless: "Klein believed that it is the balanced interplay of projection and introjection that produces, from the beginning of life, the dreamlike melding of internal and external reality that Freud discovered over and over to be the modus operandi of the unconscious. She could now also add that the same process is responsible for animating experience and making it psychologically meaningful. . . . By investing the external world with emotions, positive and negative, projective identification animates it for the subject. This endowment enables one to find emotional meaning in the external world, permitting a subjective rather than a mechanical experience of it" (1988, 165, 232).

Loewald makes a similar point about how transference creates subjective meaningfulness and even subjective reality. He acknowledges that there may be some distinctions to be drawn between the "real relationship" of analyst and analysand and the "transference relationship" based on putative transference distortions, but he goes on to claim: "There is neither such a thing as reality nor a real relationship, without transference. Any 'real relationship' involves transfer of unconscious images to present-day objects. In fact, present-day objects are objects, and thus real, in the full sense of the word . . . only to the extent to which this transference, in the sense of transformational interplay between unconscious and preconscious, is realized" (1960, 254).

This perspective does not mean that the world is a projection without objective reality as we might observe its existence empirically; it means, rather, that our sense of the meaning of the world must come from within. Transference thus brings external objects to life *psychologically*, not in empirical fact. Psychoanalysis, as Jonathan Lear puts it, concerns itself with how "the world exists for us because we invest it with sexual energy" (1990, 137), how it becomes "an objective world *for us*" (139). Lear argues that psychoanalysis extends the Aristotelian position that emotions are orientations to the world. In particular, psychoanalysis shows that emotions, however they may appear or we may label them, are rational or reaching for rationality. That is, they make sense and justify themselves through their unconscious meaning. As we understand emotions, then, we also understand and can conceptualize our personal investment of the world.[5]

Two important and related claims are being made here. First, transference is ubiquitous, for it is the means by which we give personal psychological meaning to persons or experiences. Second, transference is psychologically necessary: without transference, our inner life, our relations to others, even our experiences of the physical world, would be empty and devitalized. Yet although psychoanalysis began in the clinical encounter, and in spite of the obvious importance of the psychoanalytic discovery and theorizing of transference, it can also be claimed that psychoanalysts resisted looking directly at this encounter. The psychoanalytic situation was a vehicle for investigating what happened before and outside, rather than now and within, the psychoanalytic encounter. The view that we can best understand psychological life, indeed that psychological life most clearly expresses itself, in the here and now of the clinical encounter, is an achievement of theory construction and the development of psychoanalytic thinking. This achievement is a result of theoretical contestation as well as (it would seem) intrapsychic conflict and struggle.

Freud's history is in some ways paradigmatic here. His first goals, described in the *Studies on Hysteria,* and in the cases of Dora (1905a), Little Hans (1909a), the Rat Man (1909b), and the Wolf Man (1918), were symptom removal. In the *Studies* (Breuer and Freud, 1893–1895), removal of symptoms was achieved via a retracing (or "reconstruction") of the occasions in which the symptom occurred, back to an originary event or experience, usually a consciously remembered or recalled event or experience from the patient's recent life. Breuer and Freud discovered transference, and indeed most of psychoanalytic technique, in the *Studies,* but the technique they describe was oriented toward discovering these extraclinical processes and experiences. By the time of the later cases, treated either contemporaneously with or after Freud's "discovery" of infantile sexuality and the Oedipus complex, symptoms and neurosis were understood to result from an unresolved Oedipus complex, libidinal fixations, and repressed infantile libidinal wishes. The goal of treatment was to uncover and elucidate childhood residues covered by resistances and repressions. Understanding them would bring symptom relief.

Only in "Mourning and Melancholia" (1917) does Freud give us an account focused centrally on current psychic reality. Melancholia, he claims, results from the loss of an ambivalently loved and hated, narcissistically cathected object. There is a "regression" here, from narcissistic object choice to narcissism (250), in which the object is internalized and merges with a part of the ego, but this regression takes place within present-day ego dynamics and not in relation to an earlier developmental period. There is also a "disposition to obsessional neurosis" (251), which could, as a stretch, be read as a reflection of earlier development, but Freud does not note it as such. Similarly, the succession to mania is viewed as playing out entirely in the context of present-day energy dynamics. The implication here is that both the causes and the treatment of melancholia lie within current, rather than past, psychic reality, and it is indeed in this essay that Freud most strongly asserts the importance of psychic as opposed to actual reality: "The point must rather be that he is giving a correct description of his psychological situation" (247).

Slightly earlier, Freud presented his "Papers on Technique" (1912; 1915), including those on transference. In these papers, Freud recognizes transference as an impediment, albeit a necessary impediment, to analytic treatment: transferences are an inevitable outcome of development, which typically leaves portions of instinctual life tied to early objects and destined to be replayed in relation to new objects, and transferences in neurotics are particularly intense. Freud claims, on the one hand, that "transference, which seems ordained to be the greatest obstacle to psycho-analysis, becomes its most powerful ally" (1905a, 117). On the other hand, transference is a "creation of the disease [that] must be combated" (116) and "emerges as *the most powerful resistance* to the treatment" (1912, 101). Freud, therefore, was driven to advocate the analysis of transference. He resigns himself to this inevitability, as he resigns himself to analyzing the other resistances that must be removed by analysis. This view of transference as a resistance, and transference analysis as resistance analysis, retains a powerful hold on many analysts (see Gill and Hoffman, 1982).

Both in his discussions of transference and its analysis and in his account of melancholia, then, Freud opened for us the possibility of a view of the psyche created and transformed in the current psychoanalytic encounter and in contemporaneous reality. But the main thrust of his writings is toward the view that current psychic reality results from the psychic reality of the past, particularly the vicissitudes of infantile sexuality, the structuralization of ego and superego, and the organization of defenses against anxiety that arise to manage and control these early anxieties. He vacillated on the importance of transference, both as a psychoanalytic discovery and with regard to its centrality in the treatment. In 1923, for example, he claims that his major discoveries—the "cornerstones" of psychoanalysis—are unconscious mental processes, resistance and repression, sexuality, and the Oedipus complex. These are the "principal subject matter of psychoanalysis, the foundations of the theory. No one who cannot accept them all should count himself as a psycho-analyst" (1923, 247). Three years later, he includes transference, claiming that the "three cornerstones" in the psychoanalytic theory of neurosis are repression, a recognition of the importance of the sexual instincts, and transference (1926b, 267).

Such vacillation continues sporadically within some analytic traditions (and maybe within every analyst). Among American ego psychologists and structural theorists, the goal of analysis is often taken to be "resolving" the transference neurosis, as if after that no further transferences will remain. In this view, transferential distortions and creations will be replaced by an orientation to the "reality" of the analyst and of the analysand's life experiences. Ego psychologists, as Loewald notes, continue to conceptualize transference as a resistance, perhaps the most powerful defensive impediment to insight, rather than, as he puts it, "intrinsic to psychic life in both its interpersonal and endopsychic dimensions" (1986, 276).

Along with analysts like Loewald and others, I argue here that transference and its constituent processes are broader and more important than Freud at first thought. In my view, the discovery of transference constitutes, perhaps, *the root psychoanalytic discovery.* Freud claimed that he did not discover the unconscious. The poets discovered the unconscious, he said, and psychoanalysis simply gave it a name and a theory of operation. Nor did Freud discover infantile sexuality: Sophocles first portrayed the Oedipus complex that Oedipus acted out, even if he did not know the identity of the other players in his personal drama. According to Freud, Diderot certainly recognized the oedipal impulses a man fosters toward his known mother and father. Freud, however, both discovered and named transference, describing how the unconscious which the poets evoke comes to affect our lives. Moreover, one can also make the case that the evidence for all the other "cornerstones" of psychoanalysis comes from transference: from transference, we infer the existence of unconscious mental processes, including resistance, repression, and the expression of infantile sexuality in adulthood.[6]

If Freud was troubled by transference, he nonetheless came to conclude that it was necessary to analytic progress, even if it was only later analysts who came to see transference as a fundamentally important feature of psychic life. Freud also discovered countertransference, but it took decades for most analysts even to acknowledge its pervasiveness, and decades more before investigating and using the analyst's countertransference came to seem essential to the analytic process. Even today, many analysts continue to see countertransference much as Freud saw transference—that is, as an impediment to analysis and as symbolic of the analyst's problems.[7]

Transference, then, is not just an obstacle to clear thinking or a resistance. By invoking the concept of transference, psychoanalytic theorists argue that emotion is always intertwined with cognition, perception, language, interaction, and the experience of social, physical, and cultural reality, at least in those areas of our lives that matter to us. Loewald, as usual, puts it best: "Far from being . . . 'the enduring monument of man's profound rebellion against reality and his stubborn persistence in the ways of immaturity,' transference is the 'dynamism' by which the instinctual life of man, the id, becomes ego and by which reality becomes integrated and maturity is achieved" (1960, 250).

Although transference is pervasive in human life and defines it, it is in the clinical encounter that we can investigate most fully the minute by minute creation of personal emotional meaning in relation to the self and others. The clinical setting makes the relations among intrapsychic meanings, senses of self, and fantasies especially clear, because it limits (or tries to limit) action to talk and reflection, and it subjects to scrutiny the smallest perceptions, movements, feelings, and turns of phrase. We can perhaps see the creation of such emotional meaning best in mundane examples even more than in the grand passions and crises. A few instances can be illustrative; certainly, many such instances arise daily in any clinician's practice. Because the analytic encounter centers on observing what daily interactions and the analytic relationship can tell us about the patient's unconscious inner life, the meanings of such exchanges about everyday matters are more available than they otherwise might ordinarily be. But that such exchanges have meaning, both within the analytic encounter and without, can be observed by anyone in everyday life. Furthermore, analytic experience documents how, because of the emotional and fantasy meanings with which they are imbued, everyday matters are often at the same time grand passions.

First, let us consider an academic researcher and writer who spends an enormous amount of psychic energy acting helpless and getting people to do things for him in what turns out to be a fairly aggressive, manipulative way. He expresses his wishes loudly and forcefully, but he does not want to recognize how often he does so. Writing the acknowledgments for his now completed book is extremely time-consuming and difficult, because it forces him to make clear what he has previously obscured from himself, especially how many people he has made demands on and what fundamental needs friends have fulfilled for him: they have provided him with meals for days and weeks at a time, and when he does not have an invitation, he subsists on fast food and take-out meals. When he gets an advance copy of his book, he has a small gathering to thank all his friends for their help, and he displays the book. It contains no acknowledgments, and he realizes that he never submitted them to his publisher. He has somehow stashed them away in a lower desk drawer.

In a second mundane event, another analysand has moved a few weeks previously. I mention to her that I do not have her new address or phone number. She ponders giving me her new address and, as she does so, realizes that she resents what she perceives as an imbalance in our relationship: "You know my address and I don't know yours. You know about my character and I don't know about yours." According to her, this is an unfair imbalance, and one that reproduces the unfair imbalances that have existed throughout her life. She has felt invaded and penetrated by me, as I try to figure out what is going on with her: I know too much about her, can inquire and comment, and she does not feel that she can do the same about me. She does and does not want me to know her address: "I don't want you to know. I want you to know without effort on my part. Why should you know? Knowing my phone number [which she has not given me] should be enough." She actively resents my attempts to address her thoughts and to elicit information about her new address and phone number, indeed, she resents, as she puts it, the requirement of any interactive effort on her part. Why can't she just write the address on a piece of paper and hand it to me as she leaves the office? Immediately, however, she decides that writing it down is giving in to something. This thought in its turn generates an even stronger sense of resentment.

Here we see a struggle in someone who feels inordinately deprived in her life, who believes deeply, both consciously and, in more complex ways, unconsciously, that, as a result of previous deprivation, she should have to make no efforts or sacrifices and no one should expect things of her. She also feels depleted as a result of the deprivation, and resentful of those whom she sees as more favored, like me: "You don't need to know that I live on a noisy corner, without a garden, things you probably have." Through self-criticism she anticipates and wards off the implicit criticism that she expects from me and believes I have already expressed, by bringing up in the first place that I do not know her new address or phone number. She is, as she readily acknowledges, well aware that my lack of knowledge could cause some difficulty—if, for instance, I had to cancel a session or reach her for any reason, and she berates herself, in a consciously poor-me stance, for making comparisons between herself and me and for "leaning on externals like an apartment or clothing" as a substitute for her "weak ego." I direct our attention back to her belief that I live in a quiet place with a garden, while she doesn't. "Yeah. You come home to a family, a husband, children; I come home to an empty apartment." She is consciously filled with envy, because in her fantasy I have so much and am not deprived. Therefore, in her view, she should have to do nothing for me, including give me her new address and phone number.

A third patient reacts when I ask her to change hours and begin one day's session slightly later. My request elicits an instantaneous reaction that she should say yes—as it turns out, in order not to think about what my request might mean. As we explore her thoughts, we find that to her my request means that I need space to see someone else, but she wishes to maintain the belief that she is my only patient and that nothing goes on in my life outside my relationship with her. She claims that her belief is absurd: she has seen my name on the door; she has seen other patients entering and leaving; she knows of particular other people I treat. But she is losing something whenever I see another patient, and if she says No to my request, I will not be able to see this other person whom I wish to see. She faces a dilemma: she can be mean and refuse, and then I will be all hers, or she can be nice and say Yes, but then she has to share me. In addition, my request to move her hour indicates that I do not care about her other commitments.

She switches again and is tempted to say, "Do what you want; it doesn't matter." Sensing that she will eventually say Yes, she wonders why she should think about *anything* that occurs to her in relation to my request. If she does not think, she can avoid the anger, resentment, and powerlessness she feels because I can get her to do things for me that she cannot get me to do for her. In fact, over the course of our work together, I have changed hours several times to accommodate her, but this datum is at the moment completely unavailable to her. She also felt momentarily powerful when I asked her about the change, as she imagined herself saying No. But if she has power, she will be mean and destructive; really, her meanness will be out of control. Her dilemma is over whether to be nice and powerless, protecting herself and me from her anger but losing me to others, or whether to be powerful, mean, and destructive, thereby keeping me for herself (if she doesn't destroy me) but possibly eliciting my anger and emotional withdrawal.

All these examples document the expression and creation of emotional and fantasy meaning within the analytic encounter, and they show how emotional meanings are given by analysands to interchanges and experiences that occur outside the analytic encounter as well. Such examples in all likelihood have some roots in childhood or the past, both in the continuous conscious and unconscious self-stories told by these analysands—about not getting taken care of, having a deprived childhood, feeling less important to someone than that person is to them—and in the modes of operation and fantasy interchanges that such thoughts elicit. Analysts find in their patients (and in themselves) endless "renditions" of early infantile stances. Some of these seem much more direct and immediate than others, as, for instance, when you sense that your very voice, regardless of what you say, seems to soothe, hold, or contain what a moment ago the analysand felt to be an overwhelming, intolerable, needful rage and fear, or when the mere whisper of a thought of dependence on the analyst leads a patient to fall silent, invent a quarrel, or miss several sessions on end.

But in the clinical setting, transferences shift moment by moment and across the span of the analysis: "The swift changes— sometimes even within one session—between father and mother, between omnipotently kind objects and dangerous persecutors, between internal and external figures" (Klein, 1952, 54). These transferences may build on infantile memories, fantasies, and stances, but they also seem to build on yesterday's experiences and fantasies, both with regard to the analyst and in the world. The depth psychology expressed in transference—a psychology of unconscious, affect-laden fantasies that picture self-object relations and their threatening contents and consequences, of projective and introjective exchanges—is continually created and transformed. It is fed by infantile sources but also by many sources in daily life—by the moment-to-moment animating of the world and investing it with subjective meaning, by the meanings that emerge in interchanges between two (or more) people, each involved in creating meaning from within and through their encounter.

We are accustomed nowadays to analytic awareness that intersubjective and intrapsychic meanings are ambiguous and paradoxical, as well as to a clinical emphasis on partial interpretations and the multiple consonances of narrative. Such a view of meaning focuses us on ongoing psychological agency and activity—fantasies and self-other constructions that are fluid, ever-changing processes rather than expressions of libidinal fixations or enactment of structures of ego or self. Accordingly, we analysts are more likely to pay careful attention to the unconscious fantasies and affects—the subjectivity, rather than the developmentally created objective structures—that transferences express. As I have noted, some writers question the ease with which analytic theory once distinguished between the transference relationship and the real relationship, as if transference were created through distortions carried over from the past, whereas reality reflected an accurate perception of an objective actuality and the analyst's actual behavior (Hoffman, 1983, Loewald, 1960). In the broader view of transference-countertransference, all experience is created by and imbued with the subjective, even as it also works with and reacts to that with which it is presented.

A rethinking of the analyst's role and influence goes along with this expanded view of transference. We pay increasing attention to the analyst's countertransference: the personally meaningful, idiosyncratic, inherently ambiguous participation, experience, and conduct that indicate what is going on in the patient and in the analyst and from which the patient also creates interpretations—and shapes herself and the analytic relation. Analysts now see themselves as one of two people with ever-present and ever-influential psyches but different roles, training, theoretical knowledge, and clinical experience, who interact and influence each other in the process of building a relationship and engaging in analysis.

The psychology expressed in transference, then, is emergent and not determined. Even if we guess at the general patterns of transference in a particular case, we can neither predict its specific expressions nor reduce it to a result of the past. This creates a tension, I believe, for analysts and those who use analytic theory, both because for most of us indeterminacy is less comfortable than determinacy, explanation, and cause and because psychoanalysis in particular has operated with a causal, explanatory theory. That theory, or theories, is one or another account of childhood and its determining effects on the psyche throughout life. A reading of psychoanalysis that begins with transference leads to a revised view of the relation of early childhood experience to psychic reality and to a reconsideration of the relation of past and present in psychoanalytic explanation.

2 The Anxieties of Uncertainty: Reflections on the Role of the Past in Psychoanalytic Thinking

When in doubt, play trump: call on childhood.

STUDS TERKEL

IN *NEW YORK TIMES* INTERVIEW

WITH MEL GUSSOW

IN PSYCHOANALYSIS AS ELSEWHERE, STRUCTURAL THINKING IS on the wane. In our contemporary view of transference, the analytic encounter is mutually constructed and contingent rather than intrapsychically orchestrated by one person. This clinical emphasis on the contingency and ambiguity of emergent personal meaning makes things messier and more indeterminate than accounts that tie clinical observation or interpretation to putative developmental determinants. Traditionally, amidst ever-shifting clinical communications, we could rely on one or another theory of the childhood past and its determinative effects on the psyche throughout life, but our contemporary focus on the here and now has moved us away from such theories.

This chapter addresses the tangled, alternating, perhaps irresolvable relations between past and present in psychoanalytic thinking. I suggest that analytic work necessarily entails uncertainty, that uncertainty generates anxiety (in both analyst and patient), and that this anxiety produces a defensive search for greater certainty. One of the certainties we have fixed on is a conception of the past as an objective truth preceding and causing the present analytic encounter. In this view, the past is a fixed point or foundation to be discovered rather than a conception to be created. Such a view protects both analyst and patient from acknowledging that life, as a process, calls developmental certainties into question.[1] I do not argue here for giving up developmental theories but for shifting our conceptualizations of childhood. A move away from the causal theories of stage and structure bequeathed to us by Freud and others and toward processual accounts of childhood that document the contingency and individuality at work in the creation of personal meaning brings us closer to the contemporary realm of analytic interpretation.

The relation in analytic thinking between interpretation in the present and the privileged interpretive authority of the past has always been tangled and problematic. We can trace these two seemingly irreconcilable stories to Freud. The Freud of *Studies on Hysteria* (Breuer and Freud, 1893–1895), *The Interpretation of Dreams* (1900–1901), *The Psychopathology of Everyday Life* (1901), *Jokes and Their Relation to the Unconscious* (1905b), and "Mourning and Melancholia" (1917) focused on the meaning of symptoms and understood and interpreted meaning very much in the psychologically created present. The Freud of the *Three Essays on Sexuality* (1905c), the case studies, and the structural theory argued that childhood sexuality and the Oedipus complex were the nodal determinative roots of neurosis and character. Although I argue in the previous chapter that all of the central psychoanalytic tenets can be inferred from the single concept of transference, it could also be argued that all the central terms of psychoanalysis ultimately have their referent in childhood sexuality: "the unconscious" is composed of repressed archaic sexual wishes; repression and resistance organize themselves around—and through—early development and its vicissitudes and are permanently structured by the resolution of the Oedipus complex.[2]

Freud's view of transference enabled him to link these two approaches together—that is, to link the analytic present to the past of childhood. For Freud, transferences are an inevitable outcome of development, which leaves portions of instinctual life tied to early objects and destined to be replayed in relation to new objects. As I have pointed out, in Freud's view of transference, "a whole series of psychological experiences are revived, not as belonging to the past, but as applying to the person of the physician at the present moment" (1905a, 116). The "transference neurosis" directly replays the "infantile neurosis."

Genetic reconstruction—if not of actual events, then of childhood fantasies—also tied present to past for Freud and his followers. The method of historical reconstruction first appears in the *Studies on Hysteria,* but it is exemplified in all of Freud's major case studies, in which reconstructed moments of childhood sexuality and reactions to them are seen as shaping adult neurosis. Symptoms and neurosis, according to this view, result from an unresolved Oedipus complex, libidinal fixations, and repressed infantile libidinal wishes; the goal of treatment is, through the analysis of transference, to uncover and bring to consciousness these childhood residues covered by resistances and repressions.

Freud's views here reflect one conception of the past, but they contain in germ an alternative conception. When he speaks of "a whole series of psychological experiences," Freud is viewing the childhood past as an element in current subjectivity. Fantasies, screen memories, actual memories, current emotional meanings, and projections onto past experience can all be unconscious, but they are nonetheless experienced phenomenologically and can be recognized during an analysis. Such an approach differs from a conceptualization, whether in the early psychosexual stage theory or the later oedipal-structural theory, of the childhood past as a series of universal developmental stages.

Thus, there is a difference between what we might call (borrowing from Fast, 1984) the subjective and the objective past, or the experiential and the nonexperiential past. The subjective past is characterized by a person's unconscious and conscious senses, memories, or interpretations of her past; the objective past is described by developmental theories. The objective past is in the eye of the scientific observer-analyst who assesses or measures current functioning and its causes, but it is not necessarily potentially subjective or experiential for the patient. This dichotomy precedes the question of the privileged relation of these pasts, themselves not the same, to the experienced, constructed, or observed present.

The dichotomy originating in Freud's work between the created present and the determinative past has become sharper recently because of two potentially contradictory developments. One development was that with the growth of ego psychology, structural theory, and some versions of object-relations theory, causal thinking increased. What had originally been seen as an individual subjective past to be uncovered or genetically reconstructed—that is, the actually experienced, personally unique oedipal fantasies and wishes—became transformed and reified into general models of development. These models were applied to individuals, whose communications were heeded to the extent that they confirmed general theory. First, the Oedipus complex moved from being considered an individual subjective fantasy construction to being viewed as a universal developmental process and structure. Next, ever more highly elaborated theories about developmental lines appeared, as did theories about development of interrelated structures or systems and theories about stages in object relations or development of self and about the deficits and flaws in experiences of self and object that result from faulty mother-child relations.[3]

Ironically, but perhaps not surprisingly, as these more objectivist structural theories evolved, genetic reconstruction of subjective memories and experiences decreased. Developmental considerations were thus transferred to the analyst's theories about causes and away from the patient's unconscious fantasies and meanings. Analysts assessed structural deficits, flaws, and lack of oedipal-level functioning, and diagnosis moved away from the subjective analytic encounter. Neurosis (treatable by analysis) was regarded as reflecting unresolved sexual and ego issues at the structural "oedipal" level, whereas ("unanalyzable") severe character pathology and borderline and narcissistic disorders were caused by structural problems left from various "preoedipal" stages. New theories also took on this dual focus. The rapprochement crisis, for example, was taken to be not only an empirically prevalent anxiety in toddlers about separateness from and connection to their mothers but also a subphase that resolved or failed to resolve emotional constancy of self and object. Assessment of pathology and analyzability now becomes immensely more complex, as the analyst, depending on theoretical predilection, discovers truncated developmental lines, nonresolution of the rapprochement subphase, defective mirroring that calls for restitution, anxiety and fear that have led to regression from an oedipal constellation to an anal-sadistic one, depressive position functioning that has not been consistently achieved, impingements in early infancy that have prevented a true self or an innate idiom from developing, and so forth.

I do not question the validity or intrinsic interest of developmental investigations and theories in themselves, nor do I judge the relevance of such investigations for child treatment. I am not talking about the psychobiological margins: we now know that severe trauma, in childhood and after, can alter aspects of the nervous and memory systems, and that children do not develop if they are not held and interacted with in some regular way. We have greater understanding of the cognitive-subjective unfolding of selfhood (I-ness or we-ness), of gender identity, ego structures, and capacities for thinking, of perception and language use, and of the generalized capacities for relating and for developing a sense of self that may be shaped and fixed in the first year. These are research findings that analysts may have in mind, but they are generally not part of the content of analytic dialogue.

I am talking, rather, about what we deal with directly in the clinical encounter—what is expressed verbally and nonverbally and observed about unconscious and conscious fantasies and emotions. In this dialogue created between us analysts and our patients, although it is often the developmentalists who have offered the essential and irreplaceable insights into psychic functioning that are necessary to any clinical work and assessment, it is not clear that fixtures of psychopathology (lack of ego functions, concrete thinking, fragmented selfhood, paranoid-schizoid functioning, and so forth) must be conceived in developmental terms. My point is that in these cases, when analysts draw on developmental thinking, the subjective, interpretable part of the past takes second place to the objective scientific observer's assessment and causal account. All these explanations draw on the notion that adult psychopathology results from and can be correlated with early childhood trauma, conflict, fixation, or experience. Such a move distances psychoanalytic notions of the past from the concept of transference, which remains firmly rooted in the analysand's subjectivity. As Poland puts it: "Dazzled by the past, in analysis we have at times lost our bearings in the present, as if we could reach for the past without putting our full weight on the present" (1992, 186).

In a second current development, described in the previous chapter, the concept of transference, as a description of how the subjective unconscious comes to affect our lives, gained a life of its own, apart from and beyond re-editions of childhood. It became clear that transference expresses a psyche created and transformed in the current psychoanalytic encounter and contemporaneous reality, that the analytic encounter and the transference and countertransference were shaped by the patient and the analyst, not only in relation to their pasts, but also in relation to each other in the present. Even when we know or become aware of someone's general patterns of reaction and construction, or when we have hypotheses about the objective structural sequelae of their development, we cannot predict the specifics of how or when these will be expressed. Psychobiological structures and capacities make such processes and the psychic content they produce possible, but the content itself is constructed at the moment. Meanings may build partially on infantile memories, fantasies, and stances, but they also seem to build on yesterday's and today's experiences and fantasies, both with the analyst and in the world.

Thus, a dichotomy grew: on the one side conceptions of development moved in the direction of fixed developmental concepts, causality and objectivism; on the other, we increasingly came to understand the analytic process in subjectivist and intersubjectivist ways, not as determined by the there and then but as contingent, ambiguous, and emergent in the here and now. Our concept of transference expanded from the hypothesis and demonstration that we use experiences and feelings from the past to give meaning to and shape the present to the claim that unconscious feelings and fantasies shape, constitute, and give partial meaning to conscious feeling and experience.

An interpretive approach to the psyche that focuses on the contingent, emergent here and now of the analytic encounter is in potential contradiction, epistemologically and empirically, with the view that psychological expressions and processes in this encounter represent unresolved conflicts and structures from the given, fixed, there-and-then past. At the same time, several considerations lead most analysts to an extraclinical appeal to childhood. First, the complexity, contingency, ambiguity, and indeterminacy of continually changing transferences and countertransferences make those of us who are analysts uneasy, both psychologically and epistemologically. The relations between the subjective and the objective past and between the past and the present, and the unpacking of the present on its own terms, all pose a challenge.

Second, current transferences continue to seem imbued with the subjective past. Though our empirical observations in these matters are of course shaped partially by our theories and pretheoretical assumptions, it is nonetheless the case that connecting present suffering and mental life to past mental life still feels intuitively right to many of us. We continue to be faced with transferential meanings—emotionally tinged projections and introjections and conscious and unconscious fantasies—that seem to be not only situated, evoked, and emergent but also stable, repeated, and determined. As we focus our interpretive attention on the here and now of the psychoanalytic encounter, we also find ourselves trying to explain these repeated and predictable patterns of interaction and expression. Especially if these patterns seem tenacious and resistant to transformation, it is hard not to think that what the patient expresses comes from the there and then of childhood and the past. In hearing about a patient's difficulty in some sphere, we as analysts are likely either to be reminded of a specific childhood pattern or experience she has discussed or of a general developmental theory that illuminates this difficulty. We observe in ourselves and our patients stable representations being enacted or expressed and stable functioning that seems predictable both to us and to the patients (as well as the felt destabilizations that bring people to analysis). We see a pattern of relatively fixed or rigid functioning that may be repeatedly evoked in our patients by external experiences and experiences with us. For analysts, it seems impossible to imagine that there is no stability or predictability to a person's behavior, interactions, or psychological life. If this were the case, neither the self nor the other would have personality or selfhood.

Third, some of the most poignant and powerful psychoanalytic accounts and concepts, those which feel emotionally deepest or most real, focus on early life. Winnicott (1951; 1960) describes the precariousness of the infant's actual subjective existence or "coming-into-being," as, if things go well, she builds up an increasingly rich and complex transitional space between self and mother, and he also describes the "fear of breakdown" in which anxiety about existence dominates psychic life. Schachtel (1947) describes how infantile perceptual and emotional experiences simply do not get named, so that there are no schemata for storing them in memory or recognizing them, leading to affective impoverishment and a sense of emptiness and futility. Klein, Mahler, Erikson, and others describe infantile anxieties about maintaining relational ties and inner stability, agonizing attempts to be independent and attached at the same time, developing a sense of basic trust, managing destructiveness, greed, and hatred so that one doesn't destroy one's love objects or oneself. Very generally, we are persuaded that when one is powerless as a child, and when the infantile, rudimentary, potential self is all there is, because self and psyche are forming for the first time, certain experiences are likely to be particularly important and profound.

Finally, our pretheoretical, taken-for-granted cultural and professional narratives foster a turn to childhood.[4] As analysts, we believe that having a coherent sense of one's life as a whole is a necessary psychological universal. Further, both our cultural and our professional narratives tend to create this coherence (or to assume that it is created) by giving temporal continuity to the self. We assume a life cycle coherently unfolding from past to present and into the future and our accounts fuse assumptions about wholeness and continuity with biographical terms like "case history" and "personal narrative." In spite of our richly elaborated theoretical and clinical sense of unconscious mental processes, we do not, finally, seem to have a way to imagine human life outside a life cycle linking past and present, childhood and adulthood. It makes intuitive sense to us to interpret a life cycle as biologically driven, regularly progressing, and having a beginning, unfolding, and end. But temporality is not the only way to conceptualize a coherent life (see Personal Narratives Group, 1989), nor the Western life-cycle story the only possible way to provide such temporal coherence (for instance, Hindus and Buddhists explain and conceptualize a life story in a way that includes previous and future lives).

That all these considerations lead contemporary psychoanalytic writers across the theoretical spectrum to strive to adopt a both-and position expresses the contemporary analytic discomfort with the privileged role of childhood in the genesis of adult neurosis and character and the psychoanalytic interchange but also expresses notions of the past as determinative. Analysts still want to hold both that the clinical encounter is important in its own right and that it expresses and actually is a vehicle for finding out about extraclinical and past experiences. These writers claim that when they refer to the role of the past in the transference, they are referring to an inner psychic past rather than to an actual environmental, historical, or even fantasized past. They are not concerned with reconstructing what actually happened, including the fantasies constructed in the past about the past, or if they are, it is for particular reasons only—for instance, because *patients themselves* feel a sense of continuity if they can create a life story that links past and present, because a focus on the past shows the analyst's interest in the patient, or because such a focus is a route back to transference interpretations that the patient resists.

Among Kleinians, Betty Joseph, for example, puts forth an account of transference that focuses both on present emergence and on past determination. Transference is "a living relationship in which there is constant movement and change" (1985, 167). In transference, for Joseph, "something is going on all the time but we know that this something is essentially based on the patient's past and the relationship with his internal objects or his beliefs about them and what they were like" (164). For Ruth Malcolm, the transference expresses "the past in the present," so that the analyst's "understanding of the present is the understanding of the patient's past as alive and actual" (1986, 75). Integrating this "alive past" and the "inferred historical past" may also be a goal of analysis, because it gives a patient a sense of her own continuity, but such an integration is not part of what Malcolm considers to be analytic interpretation, and it does not foster or increase ego integration or strength.

Analysts from other traditions similarly fuse past and present. For Roy Schafer, "reconstructions of the infantile past and the transferential present are interdependent" (1983, 196). For purposes of assessing the "relevance of the here-and-now transference interpretation to the reconstruction of early development," the analysand's past and present become virtually identical: "What was is, and what is, was; the narrated present originates in the narrated past and vice versa" (1982, 78). Contemporary British Freudians Anne-Marie Sandler and Joseph Sandler (1984, 1994) create a topography of depth and surface that distinguishes the "past unconscious" from the "present unconscious," thus tying topography to past and present. The "present unconscious" is close to Freud's preconscious, while the "past unconscious" is a structuring agency that shapes the intrapsychic content of deeper, more infantile unconscious wishes and fantasies. Thomas Ogden speaks of the "two forms of history . . . the consciously symbolized past and the unconscious living past" (1989, 193).

Loewald, reminding us that transference occurs most centrally from unconscious to conscious rather than from past to present, notes that "the patient's behavior, while importantly determined by transference displacements from his past, often is triggered by the analyst's behavior or words, so that it represents also countertransference on the part of the patient." He adds, "Countertransferences are influenced, but not wholly determined, by past experiences" (1986, 279). Transference comes equally from past and present: it "is a new rendition, shaped by these [past] origins, by later experiences and growth, and increasingly modified by the libidinally based transactions in the analytic encounter" (1986, 286). Subjective past and present are finally, mutually, determinative and constitutive: "Reliving the past is apt to be influenced by novel present experience. . . . Inasmuch as re-enactment is a form of remembering, memories may change under the impact of present experience. . . . It is thus not only true that the present is influenced by the past, but also that the past—as a living force within the patient—is influenced by the present" (1975, 360).[5]

All these formulations—"the past in the present," "alive past," "past unconscious" and "present unconscious," "what was is, and what is, was," "unconscious living past"—represent an attempt to resolve two apparently contradictory views: on the one hand, that psychic reality is created subjectively and intersubjectively in the here and now; on the other hand, that psychic reality (especially as it interests the analyst and relates to unresolved issues) was created in the there-and-then past. What is important for the analytic conversation, these writers insist, is the patient's creating a subjective past, rather than discovering, as in previous psychoanalytic times, an objective past. The work of interpretation goes to elicit and bring emotional conviction to the "past in the present" or "alive past" without regard to the actual past, or "inferred historical past," that "the past in the present" represents.[6]

These writers strive toward a nondeterministic integration of past and present, but their accounts still tend, as my examples make clear, to retain a metaphoric vagueness that substitutes for convincing argument. This is at least partly because they still retain implicit objectivist and determinist assumptions about the past. None holds that transferences are direct impositions of previous object-imagos onto current relations, but these new accounts finally do not offer a view of development other than that which our traditional theories put forth. Even the privileging of alive over inferred past retains a universalized objectivist quality, for in certain clinical situations, attending to the actual past is vital and relevant.

Theories of development as well as of transference may also reach toward a both-and position. Klein and her followers conceptualize the move from the paranoid-schizoid to the depressive position as a developmental achievement, and they claim that the early phase of splitting, projection, and introjection of part-objects is a developmental phase (see, e.g., Klein, 1935). But they also claim that a position is not a phase or stage and that a person may move back and forth between positions in any particular analytic hour, over the course of an analysis, and throughout life (Segal, 1985; Spillius, 1988; Joseph, 1985; Anderson, 1992). Loewald points to a lifelong oscillation between differentiated, oedipal, secondary process, ego autonomous forms of existence and thought, and "our psychotic core"—merged, preoedipal, primary-process, nonlinguistic forms (1978a, 1979), an oscillation, seemingly, between nontemporally distinct modes of being and between earlier and later developmental modes.

Mahler describes the rapprochement negotiation of self and other as the central crisis of childhood and the main dilemma of human life: "For the more or less normal adult, the experience of being both fully 'in,' and fully separate from the 'world out there' is taken for granted as a given of life. Consciousness of self and absorption without awareness of self are two polarities between which he moves. . . . Like any intrapsychic process, this one reverberates throughout the life cycle" (Mahler, Pine, and Bergman, 1975, 3). Erikson's epigenetic cycle (1950) began as a developmental stage account modeled on time-dependent biological unfolding, but he transformed it into a fabric in which every stage of the life cycle was interwoven with every other stage (perhaps it was at this point of eight-by-eight nuance and multiple mutual determinations that analysts gave up trying to think in Eriksonian terms). Developmental notions (preoedipal precedes oedipal, the paranoid-schizoid precedes the depressive position, and mother-infant merging precedes separation) are embedded in all these formulations, but the formulations also portray what we have thought of as developmental stages—the one stage resolved when the person moves into the next—as modes of operation extending from infancy throughout life, the one never permanently transcended by the other.

Yet even as we argue for transference as an expression of an "alive" or "unconscious" past—to all intents and purposes, a present—it seems difficult not to assume or make explicit the actual past roots of present-day psychic reality. With the exception of some detailed accounts of analytic listening and technique, case descriptions and theoretical discussion frequently describe a past whose contours are delineated by childhood experience read in the light of the specific developmental theory to which the analyst holds. And despite alternate claims, these accounts also imply that this actual past causes or is expressed in the transference.

Such tendencies cross the analytic spectrum. Kleinians describe how fluctuations in early internal object relations and oscillations between internal and external experience mirror and give rise to fluctuations and oscillations in the transference. Contemporary Kleinians describe the analytic interaction in microdetail, but just as Klein's descriptions of transference processes are dwarfed by richly detailed accounts of the infantile psychic life of projection, introjection, splitting, fantasy, love, and hate, so it seems that her contemporary followers make developmental assumptions about the infantile origins of envy, aggressive and fragmenting projective identifications, and attacks on linking and thinking (see, e.g., Britton, 1989; Bion, 1959, 1962; Joseph, 1987).[7] Object relations psychoanalysts claim to talk about "internal" rather than real mother-infant relationships but make assumptions about the psychodynamic and behavioral reality and consequences of a patient's past (see, e.g., Bollas, 1987 and Ogden, 1986).[8] Self psychologists draw on countertransference experiences and experiences of being used as a selfobject to form definitive conclusions about failures in early maternal mirroring and early parentally generated barriers to positive narcissistic development. Ego psychologists and structural theorists observe the operation and failure to operate of different developmental lines or structures (for example, structures of self or superego) in their patients and draw conclusions about whether these patients developed a true infantile neurosis or achieved a true oedipal crisis and resolution.[9]

Among all these, Loewald succeeds perhaps better than most in conveying a sense of the analysand's present that is fully a present. His ghosts do not seem to be ghosts from the past but hauntings in the present—"ghosts of the unconscious." Their "awakening" is not into the present but into consciousness. The "lost connections" are between unconscious and preconscious rather than past and present (1962, 249). Although he offers great insights and formulations about infantile mental development, it does not seem that for Loewald infantile mental life is at issue in an analysis. His insistence on the ongoingness of all positions of ego reality and ego instinct throughout life bolsters this stance.

Caper (1997) echoes Loewald's position and reminds us that this creation of the past takes place in the present because psychic reality always exists in the present: "It is often said that the transference is a repetition of the patient's relationship with objects from the past, experienced with the analyst in the present. . . . This statement is just as true if one puts it the other way around: that the relationships that the patient seems to have had with objects in the past are a 'repetition' of the patient's present relationship with the analyst. . . . This is because both the 'past,' as the patient experiences it in the present (so to speak), and the transference are influenced by the same active present-day dynamic processes" (1997, 21).

Even the strongest narrativists and intersubjectivists seem to hold objectivized as well as subjectivist views of the past in relation to the present. Schafer has extensively elaborated the methodological program to follow a narrative, yet his hermeneutics, finally, require a signified (however potentially polysemic) as well as a signifier. He notes that the analyst uses "specifically psychoanalytic abstracting and organizing concepts" (1982, 78) and that "interpretations are redescriptions or retellings of action along the lines peculiar to psychoanalytic interest" (1983, 255). These "specifically psychoanalytic organizing concepts" and "lines of psychoanalytic interest" include a developmental theory of childhood and its effects. The multiplicity of analytic theories all lead to "life-historical narratives" (1982, 77), in such a way that a "narrative strategy" organizes one narrative (that which the patient is telling you) into another, which "expresses the desired point of view on the past . . . along lines laid down by pre-existing theoretical commitments or life-historical strategies" (1982, 77, 81). The transferential present and the infantile past may be constructed or reconstructed narratively, but Schafer does not question the necessity of centering the analytic narrative on past and present in the first place.

In a related vein, Irwin Hoffman argues that what occurs in the analytic encounter is generated by that encounter itself, but he nonetheless suggests that one of the best ways out of tenacious transference-countertransference enactments is the analyst and patient's "evolving understanding of the patient's history." In a familiar way, Hoffman likens the analysand's interpretation of the analyst's experience to that patient's childhood interpretation of her parents' experience and claims that the patient will come to understand her reactions on the basis of "what has happened in the past" (1983, 419).

Our views, then, are caught between two perspectives. Most contemporary analysts hold that psychoanalytic theory and practice are principally about what goes on in the clinical consulting room. This sui generis experience is related to that which goes on outside and before, but it is not simply an epiphenomenon—a result, reproduction, or expression—of these. In the clinical encounter, people process and create their psyches in ways that take more or less account of early psychic realities and are more or less influenced by them. Childhood does not determine and cannot explain these contingent, intrapsychically and interpersonally emergent clinical processes.

At the same time, it seems that one cannot do psychoanalytic work without some conception of a patient's early experiences and theories about early development and its challenges (at least it is an empirical observation that analysts for the most part do not do psychoanalytic work without such conceptions and theories). Many of us seem unready to give up assumptions about the determining importance of childhood in adult psychic life. To complicate matters further, most conceptions of the psychoanalytic process are themselves intertwined with theories about childhood: particular clinical encounters are conceptualized in terms of the mother-child encounter; of childhood fantasies like an oedipal fear of castration, a search for paternal protection, or a desire to separate the parental sexual couple; of primitive (first year of life) projective and introjective processes and destructive envy of the breast, and so forth. The psychoanalytic process is conceptualized as a developmental process (e.g., Loewald, 1960; Settlage, 1980, 1993). We focus on the "here and now" both because it is the here and now and inherently interesting as such—we are more interested than we were formerly in the emergent present—

and because it is the best route to understanding the "there and then"—we still want to know the past and reshape its effects.

This apparently unresolvable dual reality suggests that another solution to our epistemological and empirical dilemma is to assess accounts of childhood and development according to their compatibility with clinical understanding. It seems to me that such compatibility requires several elements. First, as I elaborate in the previous chapter, a perspective on psychic life in the clinical here and now of transference and countertransference situates us immediately in a mutually constructed relational world in which the emotional meanings of situations and interactions are negotiated. Second, analyst and analysand create transference and countertransference as a contingent, continually emergent process unique to those two particular people. Finally, by definition, the clinical encounter fuses talk with nonlinguistic unconscious psychic realities of emotion and fantasy.

Developmental theories in accord with our clinical understanding, then, need to situate development in an internal and external relational matrix, and, unlike the classical psychosexual model of developmental stages, the structural–ego-psychological model, or some versions of the Kleinian model, they need not tell us what is set down, enacted, and determinative for psychic contents and modes of functioning. Rather, they must describe for us how people function throughout life, and must document the development and operation of processes of creating unconscious fantasy and emotional meaning. Of merely empirical importance is the extent of fixity of the past—the possibility that for many people, special conditions of childhood, childhood in general, or their own particular childhood make these early experiences especially shaping or resonant. In the remainder of this chapter, I point to useful directions such a theory might take and suggest what is wrong with other developmental approaches for the conceptualization of clinical process. Developmental theories useful for clinical thinking seem to be couched in the same phenomenological register as are clinical interaction and transference rather than in terms of the observer's nonexperiential causal or structural models. They do not so much tell us about particular sequential childhood stages that determine later psychic contents, modes of functioning, personality, or pathology. Rather, they document human psychological life as a whole extensively and in great detail. Together, Loewald, Klein, Winnicott, and contemporary infant researchers elaborate an account of childhood consonant with these premises.

Loewald begins from the premise that for the subject there is initially no inner and outer, no ego versus reality, no drives versus ego. All these are created or differentiated out of a global structure at the same time that the ego comes into being (1951, 1960, 1962, 1978a, 1978b).[10] Development consists, then, not just in subjectively creating the affective and cognitive meanings of self (selves) and object(s) whose existence is assumed to be given, but in creating their existence itself. Only after internal and external have been established can projection and introjection occur or can one speak meaningfully of libido or aggression's being directed toward an object or toward the self (1960, 235). Loewald describes those primary processes that create the existence and meaning, one in relation to the other, of self and object, internality and externality, thus: "Primary externalization signifies that *externality is being established;* primary internalization signifies that *internality is being constituted.* On this level, then, we cannot speak of externalization (projection) and internalization as defenses (against inner conflict or external deprivation); we must speak of them as boundary-creating processes and as processes of differentiation of an undifferentiated state. It is true, nevertheless, that defenses against inner conflict and against outer deprivation promote and color such differentiation" (1962, 266). In Loewald's view, then, inner and outer are not qualities given in any direct, empirical sense, for all time. From the outset, they have both emotional and physical-perceptual meanings, and this initial creation sets off a lifelong process in which not only the meaning but also the constitution of inner and outer are negotiated, as new meanings and objects are seen to be either within the person or in the outside world, and as internal self or internal other: "Without further differentiation of the inner world no further differentiation of the object world takes place. . . . Internal and external relationships . . . continue to supplement and influence each other in various ways during adult life; there are more or less continuous shifts and exchanges between internal and external relationships" (1962, 267–268).

Along with internality and externality, drives are also constituted. Loewald thus does not start from the givenness of drives but from the premise that the developing person shapes what come to be her drives, her characteristic experiences and invocations of aggression and libido. The child's emotionally laden interpersonal experiences influence this shaping. Loewald claims: "The primary datum for a genetic, psychoanalytic psychology would be object relations. The relatedness is the psychic matrix out of which intrapsychic instincts and ego, and extrapsychic object, differentiate" (1978b, 216). Drives, then, are not innate energic forces seeking release: "Instincts . . . are to be seen as relational phenomena from the beginning and not as autochthonous forces seeking discharge" (1972, 321–322).[11]

The Kleinian and Fairbairnian (1952) contributions extend Loewald's.[12] Whereas for Loewald inner and outer, ego and object, and ego and drives must be constituted by the baby, for Klein and Fairbairn an infantile ego, object relations, and drives exist from birth.[13] For all three, however, the meanings of these must be created: the infant invests ego and objects with fantasies and affect and in the process creates an inner object world and sets in motion anxiety- and defense-driven processes of splitting, projection, and introjection that continue throughout life. Klein and Fairbairn, then, focus on the character of the relations between inner and outer—the way an inner object world is created through processes that also create and form the basis for later self-orientations and transferences. Throughout development, as throughout life, inner and outer reality are continually reconstituted through projective and introjective fantasies, so that experiences of others are shaped or filtered through fantasies of inner objects and in turn reshape these inner objects: "An inner world is being built up in the child's unconscious mind, corresponding to his actual experiences and the impressions he gains from people and the external world, and yet altered by his own phantasies and impulses" (Klein, 1940, 345). Transferential reshaping is ubiquitous in infantile life: "Altogether, in the young infant's mind every external experience is interwoven with his phantasies and on the other hand every phantasy contains elements of actual experience" (Klein, 1952, 54).

Kleinian (and Fairbairnian) language is sometimes overly concrete and simple, but its very concreteness mirrors the assumption underlying our notion of transference. In her account of the doubling of experience, for example, Klein attempts to characterize and answer the difficult clinical question concerning how fantasies that shape and reshape the inner world exist in the inner realm of fantasy (in the transferential reality) and in the world of actuality, where they have actual effects on our perceptions, experiences, and feelings about external reality: "The 'internal' mother is bound up with the 'external' one, of whom she is a 'double,' though one which at once undergoes alternations in his mind through the very process of internalization; . . . her image is influenced by his phantasies, and by internal stimuli and internal experiences of all kinds. When external situations . . . become internalized—and I hold that they do, from the earliest days onwards—they follow the same pattern: they also become 'doubles' of real situations, and are again altered for the same reasons" (1940, 345–346). As she puts it elsewhere, "It is in phantasy that the infant splits the object and the self, but the effect of this phantasy is a very real one, because it leads to feelings and relations (and later on, thought-processes) being in fact cut off from one another" (1946, 6). It is of course especially in transference in the analytic situation that one can see these "real" effects most extensively, as the analysand engages in splitting, projective fantasies about what the analyst is doing to her, projective identification of feelings into the analyst, and introjective fantasies and identifications that take in and appropriate parts of the analyst. Klein (1935) and Fairbairn (1940) also describe the almost dizzying continual activity involved in the projective and introjective management of inner objects and of hatred, aggression, and envy that characterizes shifts in the transference—the doing and undoing, reversing good and bad, love and hate, and self and other, along with the rapid-fire shifting of affect and drive as the infant feels anger at the breast, feels the breast is angry, fears the angry breast, takes it in, fears the angry self, fears that the angry self will destroy the good breast, tries to get the good breast to soothe the angry self, worries that it has destroyed the breast, tries to restore it, and so on.

Winnicott's developmental account of transitional phenomena and transitional process (1971) contributes further to a here and now consonant developmental theory about the there-and-then past. Winnicott begins from both the fantasy life of the baby and the reality of the two-person mother-baby interaction. As he theorizes this two-person space and its development, he is theorizing a sui generis relational space in which personal meaning requires taking account of the actual presence of the other. Winnicott thus adds a conception of how the object or other itself plays a role to Kleinian and Loewaldian accounts of how projective meanings are created from within and accord personal animation to self, other, and objects. His account helps us to see how meanings in transference-countertransference can both be emergent (created from within by each person) and have regular features (given from without or from before). This developmental account has been elaborated clinically in conceptions, for example, of the potential space of the analytic situation and the "analytic third" (e.g., Ogden, 1986, 1994), the evocative analytic object (e.g., Bollas, 1987), and the inherently ambiguous but generative behavior of the analyst for the patient (Hoffman, 1983). Because they are attuned to emergent psychological activity and to subjective meanings—fantasy, affect, and drive processes that continually create and re-create relations to others and an internal world—these developmental approaches all resonate with descriptions of transference-countertransference. For these theorists, the focus is on *meanings* of ego and object. Even the structural outcomes they describe, having to do with patterns of fantasy, drive, and affective construction of self and other that have become relatively stable, have this phenomenological cast. Such theories can also be read exclusively as accounts of developmental stages, yet no matter whether infants can or cannot engage in the processes that these accounts describe, as some critics of Klein have held, any clinician experiences and observes such processes daily. These developmental theories thus document the emergence in childhood of that very psychic activity that enables and creates transferential processes throughout life, rather than the emergence of a structured unconscious, psyche, or cognitions that determine later transferences.

Rather than portray a fixed developmental schema concerning psychosexual stages, developmental lines, or interrelated systems, these accounts are consonant with the indeterminacy and emergent complexity of transference, the multiplicities of potential meaning, and the ambiguities in interpretive possibility. Winnicott's transitional phenomena and transitional space characterize a world of paradoxical, situated meaning—the object or experience or person objectively perceived and subjectively conceived, negotiated between two people. For Loewald and Klein, contingent fluidity characterizes primary and secondary internalizations and externalizations. These accounts reformulate but do not undermine the psychoanalytic insistence on the importance of early development. They lead to a notion of continual coming into being rather than a correlational replaying in the transference relationship.[14]

Infant researchers also contribute developmental accounts consonant with contemporary views of the clinical encounter. Stern (1985), for example, describes the fluidity and transformational possibilities of affect and perception: infants translate information from one perceptual mode to another and experience qualities of intensity in different affects or perceptions as equivalent: intense anger has something in common with intense joy; intense light is more like forceful than like soothing music; the dynamic components of fading, exploding, and rushing give some equivalency to different affects. Directly expressing the both-and position, Sterns speaks of "clinical-developmental" issues and claims that in contrast to psychosexually linked developmental stages, different aspects of the sense of self develop sequentially over the first two years of life and are also "issues for the life span" (1985, 12).

Attachment theory (Bowlby, 1969, 1973, 1980) and intersubjective theory (Stern, 1985; Trevarthen, 1979, 1980) may also indirectly influence our current refocusing on the analytic relationship and changes in analytic stance, authority, and technique. The carefully theorized research in these fields makes us all more aware of how human experience and selfhood are interpersonally constituted and how intersubjective relationships build particularized histories. Analysts, though they once thought that gratification of drives was the primary human goal, now grant that people seek attachment, response, recognition, and meaning.

Contemporary infant researchers document emotional signaling between infant and caregiver and the way the feeling-tone of this relation goes to form an "affective core of the self" (Stern's term). They show how the child imbues objects with emotional meaning through sharing her perceptions with the mother or caregiver: emotional interchanges are not just about me and you but about "our" experience and communication concerning the world of physical and cultural objects (Emde, 1991, Emde and Sorce, 1983). Self development is also an interpersonal project on the level of unconscious fantasy: infants develop from birth onwards within the sphere of "interfantasy"—within the matrix of the mother's fantasies of the meaning of their exchanges, which in turn are ingredients in (but do not determine) the infant's fantasies (Stern, 1985, 134).

When we claim that personal meaning begins in the infant-caregiver relation, we are also saying that there are from the beginning nonverbal, preverbal, nonlinguistic, or prelinguistic aspects of meaning—aspects of meaning that go unambiguously and emphatically beyond language. Such a view again accords with our clinical experience that language and cognitions are always infused with emotion and unconscious fantasy. Analysts describe how this psychological infusing of perception and experience, created both from within and from the uniqueness of the caretaker-child matrix, arises well before language, so that language itself develops in and gains meaning from this idiosyncratic emotional and fantasy context. Stern puts this forcefully: "It is a basic assumption of this book that some senses of the self do exist long prior to self-awareness and language. . . . Self-reflection and language come to work upon these preverbal existential senses of self and, in so doing, not only reveal their ongoing existence but transform them into new experiences. . . . Some preverbal senses of the self start to form at birth (if not before)" (1985, 6). Bollas, likewise, distinguishes "existential" from "representational" knowing and claims that "we learn the grammar of our being before we grasp the rules of our language" (1987, 36). As any person develops, then, emotional resonance is established for some concepts, situations, experiences, and fantasies, and the capacity to endow experience with emotional meaning is also developed. Cognition is infused with emotion through the projections and introjections that create ego and reality psychologically, and meanings become specified or located for the individual in particular interpersonal or intrapsychic (object-relational) contexts.

Specifically, the meanings of words used by the mother, though drawn from a common language, have for the child the particularized resonance of the relational and affective context in which they are used, so that words have not just consensual linguistic meaning but what Loewald calls "magical-evocational aspects," experienced in the first instance in the maternal context (1978a, 194). As Loewald notes, "Language is typically first conveyed to the child by the parental voice and in an all-pervasive way. . . . In these situations [the mother's] speech and voice are part and parcel of the global mother-child interaction" (180). In these early experiences of language, the primary caretaker speaks with the infant not so much to communicate consensual cultural meanings as to create a global sense of we-ness or being together with the infant: "The words of which her speaking is composed form undifferentiated ingredients of the total situation or event experienced by the infant. . . . he is immersed, embedded in a flow of speech that is part and parcel of a global experience within the mother-child field" (1978a, 185). Loewald notes that this form of experience and use of language express a primary process, rather than secondary process, global character and density. "Words here are . . . indistinguishable ingredients of global states of affairs. The mother's flow of words does not convey meaning to or symbolize 'things' for the infant . . . but the sounds, tone of voice, and rhythm of speech are fused within the apprehended global event" (1978a, 187).

That language is personally and idiosyncratically tinged does not, of course, make language unimportant. Language, as the vehicle for expressing and understanding intrapsychic and intersubjective meaning in analysis, and for communication more generally, enables analyst and patient together to make an agreed-upon story. Language and use of symbol enable the child to incorporate what would otherwise be exclusively global, embodied, disconnected experiences into a cognized subjectivity and selfhood. The sense-making capacities of language articulate and make possible self-making, and the ability to symbolize is crucial to development and psychic health. Symbolizing capacities address and mitigate anxiety by moving beyond the anxiety-producing object or experience through symbolic extensions, transformations, and interest in new objects and experiences (see, e.g., Klein, 1930; Segal, 1957; and Bion, 1961, and elsewhere).

All these accounts describe a childhood mental life that emerges from a relational matrix and creates an unconscious, emotion- and fantasy-imbued internal world and a coloring and animation of the external world through transferential, interfantasy, projective, and introjective processes. They show that transference and countertransference happen not only in daily life but also in the initial processes of perception and meaning creation.[15] Such developmental accounts also enable us to reread childhood, as we read psychoanalytic process, in a less determinist fashion. In them, psychological meaning and subjectivity are not determined in early childhood, though from infancy children create psychological meaning and subjectivity. Because psychological meaning is constitutive of internal and external perceptions and experiences from childhood on, the past is always drawn into the present. But this drawing in is always complex and indeterminate, perhaps not invented anew at each moment but continually constructed, reconstructed, and changed. The past does not cause the present, but the present includes and incorporates the past. Authors of these developmental accounts do not eliminate the importance of childhood, but they regard subjective experience as a continual process to be engaged intersubjectively and interpretively— rather than assuming that childhood causes, determines, or correlates with present functioning.

These accounts, like the transference-countertransference encounter, make emotion-laden fantasy, or fantasy-laden emotion, central to meaning and to self. There may be from birth rudimentary cognitive perceptions of self and other, but experience is also registered affectively; self and other always have affective meaning. There is thus from the beginning a primary-process density connecting language and word with interpersonal, emotional, and fantasy context. The primary-process and emotional saturation of words gradually becomes intertwined with secondary-process articulation. These are also the intertwinings found in the analytic encounter and in other interchanges that are subjectively meaningful to the individual. Intrapsychic and interpersonal goals, of consistency and object attachment, the felt need to reduce anxiety, and bodily experience, all affect how the object world and the self are experienced and perceived, and such attributions—through projections and introjections or transferences—continue to give personal affective meaning throughout life. I have argued that we come to these conclusions in two ways: through our expanding knowledge of infant and child development and most especially through the clinical encounter, which gives the analysand the opportunity to explore, in fine-tuned and extensive detail, how each of his or her reactions and behaviors expresses previously unknown or disclaimed conceptions and feelings about self and others.

The accounts I have described contrast with those in which the empirical fantasy contents of the psyche are presented as primary (psychosexual drive stages, oedipal conflicts, destructiveness, rage and envy of the breast, fears or conflicts revolving around separation and individuation) and with developmental accounts cast in nonexperiential terms—of psychic structures, systems, or developmental lines. Our ostensibly universal development theories, I would suggest, often describe nonuniversal, non-necessary, yet empirically widespread patterns of fantasy, ego, and object-relational psychic contents (the Oedipus complex is a major case in point). These have been misconstrued as universal theories of mental operation that have consequences for universal fantasy as well as for structure. Patterns and tendencies are useful clinical reminders of possible empirical repertoires and orient us, in our listening, in a generalized preconscious way. They are useful in the individual case, or at different times in the analytic process, but they cannot be more than that for a particular patient at a particular moment.

The analyst recognizes patterns and possibilities partly by bearing in mind the varieties of developmental knowledge (many of which, incidentally, are incompatible with one another: it is only when applied in a way specific to case and moment that they can coexist). Similarly, particular childhood traumas seem to affect development (statistically, perhaps, they tend to arrest development), but not always negatively, not for all people, and not in the same predictable way. Speaking of a young patient with organic brain problems (at the extreme end of what we might take for granted as developmentally or constitutionally determinative), Erikson says: "The damage . . . would, of course, constitute only a potential, albeit necessary, condition to convulsion. It could not be considered the cause of the convulsion, for we must assume that quite a number of individuals live with similar cerebral pathology without ever having a convulsion." He goes on: "We know of no 'cause.' Instead we find a convergence . . . which make[s] the catastrophe retrospectively intelligible, retrospectively probable. The plausibility thus gained does not permit us to go back and undo causes. It only permits us to understand a continuum, on which the catastrophe marked a decisive event, an event which now throws its shadow back over the very items which seem to have caused it" (1950, 34, 37–38).

A less determinist, more processual or constructionist, view of child development and the psyche affects and shapes our interpretive understanding. I have suggested that beginning in infancy, and throughout life, we find the same central psychological processes of personal meaning creation—transference, countertransference, affect, fantasy, projection, and introjection—that we find in the clinical encounter. Such a finding serves as a caution to clinicians and to those who apply psychoanalysis to biography, autobiography, history, or personal narratives or testimonies. When we attempt to untangle the relation of past to present, it is important to remember that psychological agency is always in the present, where memory, subjectivity, and personal meaning are not simply reproduced or determined but are revised and shaped.

Such a view still leaves room for accounts of individual development that emphasize fixations, or patterns that are not easily broken. We can think of Balint's "basic fault," of Winnicott's description of the development of a false self in the context of environmental impingement and lack of an adequate holding environment, of Klein's account of the achievement or nonachievement of the depressive position, all of which, in the individual clinical or biographical case, seem to place limits on the possible. An unresolved "infantile neurosis"—conflict patterns, prevalent defenses, and unconscious fantasies organized in childhood—also apparently delimit and shape. But patterning self and object, or ego and reality, as an ongoing process that begins in childhood, is not the same as describing a fixed psychic structure that expresses itself.

In this chapter I argue that we should be wary of clinical explanations positing objectivized universal childhood stages or psychobiological drives that determine or predict later psychological experience and universalist claims about the panhuman content of unconscious fantasies. We should also be wary of developmental theories that promote such interpretation and explanation. Psychological meaning in the clinical encounter is continually emerging and created through fantasy, collaborative and tentative transitional negotiations, and transferences and countertransferences created in the here and now. We can observe, be surprised by, and help ourselves and our patients to create these new meanings more easily if our listening is not filtered and shaped by assumptions that an Oedipus complex, castration fears, fantasies about "the" primal scene, or envy of "the" breast or "the" mother's insides are universally given, universally determined by the conditions of early infancy or a panhuman psychobiology, and universally primary in everyone's psyche. We must sustain an inductive openness to the content of psychic fantasy and look for corroboration not in a universal childhood or psyche but in the particular subjective childhood and the unique evidence of individual transferences.

Analytic focus on transference and countertransference in the here and now entails a rethinking of childhood and of the relations of past and present in psychoanalytic explanation. It decouples analytic interpretation and knowledge from developmental understandings and reconstructions, except insofar as these reconstructions or conceptions of the past play a role in a particular analysand's fantasy and affective life or in the analytic interchange. I suggest that conceptions of childhood that focus on human capacities for personal meaning that unfold virtually from birth rather than on developmental stages, lines, or structure formation point us toward a more promising understanding of psychic functioning throughout life. This understanding may offer us less clinical certainty but more capacity to accept the uncertainties generated by the analytic encounter.

The contention that we create personal meaning from birth on, throughout life, suggests that only in a limited sense can one claim that cultural meaning precedes or creates personal meaning. From earliest infancy, meaning is always tinged with projection, emotion, and fantasy and is not merely linguistic or cognitive. Language has specific interpersonal and object-relational meaning as well as consensual, cultural meaning; it is created from within and between, even as it is also presented from without and given culturally and socially. Intrapsychic fantasy and emotional tonality interact with and give individual animation and interpretation to cultural and linguistic categories. This chapter and the preceding chapter document that neither psychobiological or childhood universals nor culture and language explain the individual psyche and its experience. I have argued that transferential processes describe an area of creation of personal meaning in which the individual negotiates and reforms meaning from within and from without, through internal fantasy and emotional processes and through the immediate intersubjective contexts where transitional phenomena emerge. This clinical documentation of the power of feelings is among the most significant contributions of psychoanalysis.

In the next two parts of this book, I examine two areas in which problematic psychological universalisms and cultural and linguistic determinisms come together and contest with one another. In thinking about gender, many psychoanalysts assume a precultural, biological basis for gender differentiation and sexual orientation, whereas feminist theorists insist on the cultural and political determination of gender identity and feelings about gender. In anthropology, cultural theorists of self and feeling, who for the most part claim that emotions and the sense of self are socially or culturally generated, discount both the personalized, emotional, idiosyncratic contexts in which individual selves are formed and the personal individuality of projection, introjection, and fantasy. By contrast, psychoanalytic anthropologists for the most part assume certain universally given psychosexual stages and contents. I argue, in contrast to both these positions, that feelings and categories of gender and self are created both culturally, in historicized, socially specific contexts, and at the same time biographically, through individually specific projective and introjective fantasy and emotion.

PART 2   GENDER

3 Gender as a Personal and Cultural Construction

Crucially, a person is not a text.

RICCARDO STEINER

"HERMENEUTICS, OR HERMES-MESS?"

THE VIEW OF PSYCHOANALYSIS THAT I HAVE BEEN DEVELOP-
ing, arguing that each of us creates personal emotional meaning
throughout life, has implications for both feminist and psychoanalytic understandings of gendered subjectivity and gender identity.
Individual psychological meaning combines with cultural meaning
to create the experience of meaning in those cultural categories that
are important or resonant for us. In Part 2, I argue that an individual,
personal creation and a projective emotional and fantasy animation
of cultural categories create the meaning of gender and gender identity for any individual. Each person's sense of gender is an individual

creation, and there are thus many masculinities and femininities. Each person's gender identity is also an inextricable intertwining, virtually a fusion, of personal and cultural meaning. That each person creates her own personal-cultural gender implies an extension of the view that gender cannot be seen apart from culture.

Contemporary feminism has made central a cultural and political analysis and critique of gender and sexuality and has been rightly wary of universalizing claims about gender and of accounts that seem to reduce gender to a single defining or characterizing feature. These two criticisms have especially focused on psychological claims of all sorts. In response, much academic feminist theory seems to have moved away from psychology (see Mahoney and Yngvesson, 1992). Contemporary feminists see gender as variable, fragmented, contested, destabilized, and contingently constructed, but the feminist view of gender, influenced by Foucault and other poststructuralist and postmodern thinkers, is almost unvaryingly linguistic, cultural, and discursive. In turn, language, culture, and discourse, composing gender meanings in general, are at base political—generated by power.[1] Feminism recognizes differences, but it defines them politically rather than individually, in terms of political-social identities like race, class, and sexual orientation. In this view, meanings are imposed as cultural categories rather than created in contingent, individual ways. According to this hegemonic feminist viewpoint, cultural order takes precedence over a more nuanced and variable individual personal meaning, and the psyche is entirely linguistic.

In accord with this linguistic and cultural focus, contemporary feminism, when it includes a psychology, tend to draw on Lacanian theory. As I have argued elsewhere (1989), both the Lacanian insistence on the importance of language and the symbolic in the psyche and the argument that development is a move into culture and not just into a noncultural individuality have been important as general correctives and investigative admonitions for psychoanalysts, and

particularly apt in the case of gender. But this Lacanian move, ironically, also polarizes men and women and makes the gender divide
absolute: although subjects can, in the Lacanian view, have different
relations to the symbolic and to the gender categories it represents,
the symbolic realm itself is reserved exclusively and universally for the
phallus and the name of the father; the meaning of the mother,
precultural and nonsymbolic, considered again universalistically, is
limited to the sphere of the imaginary or the semiotic.

Psychoanalytic understandings of the powers of transference,
projection, and introjection run counter to feminist assumptions
about the exclusive cultural or political construction of gender and
gender meanings. In this chapter, I claim that feminism has elimi-
nated the realm of personal emotional meaning or made it subordinate to and determined by language and power. (In Chapter 4, I
point out that psychoanalysis has, inversely, tended to minimize the
intrinsic cultural and political embeddedness of psychological gender
that feminism has documented so well.) I suggest that gender cannot
be seen as entirely culturally, linguistically, or politically constructed.
Whether racial-ethnic, international feminist, linguistic, perfor-
mative, micropolitical, or based on the analysis of discourse, gender theories that do not consider individual personal emotional and
fantasy-related meaning cannot capture fully the meanings that gender has for the subject. They miss an important component of experienced gender meaning and gendered subjectivity.

When I claim that gender is inevitably personal as well as cultural, I mean not only that people create individualized cultural or
linguistic versions of meaning by drawing on the cultural or linguistic
categories at hand. Rather, perception and the creation of meaning
are psychologically constituted. As psychoanalysis documents, people
avail themselves of cultural meanings and images, but they experience them emotionally and through fantasy, as well as in particular interpersonal contexts. Emotional meaning, affective tone, and

unconscious fantasies that arise from within and are not experienced linguistically interact with and give individual animation and nuance to cultural categories, stories, and language (that is, make them subjectively meaningful). Individuals thereby create new meanings according to their own unique biographies and histories of intrapsychic strategies and practices—meanings that extend beyond and run counter to cultural or linguistic categories.

As I noted earlier, neither emotion nor unconscious fantasy is originally linguistic or organized. Initially, unconscious fantasy globally bodies forth aspects of self and other in immediate emotional terms. Articulation of story, characters, and affect in unconscious fantasies can then be more or less highly elaborated, and they can be expressed to some degree in conscious or preconscious fantasy. Unconscious fantasies that are not ostensibly about gender at all may also help psychologically to articulate aspects of gender experience. At the same time, it is certainly the case that aspects of gender identity and unconscious gender fantasy draw on language, cultural stories, and interpersonally transmitted emotional responses, themselves conveyed by people (in the first instance parents and other caretakers) with their own personal-cultural sense of gender.

Gender meanings, as feminism has argued, are certainly indeterminate and contested, but they are indeterminate and contested not only culturally and politically but also as they are shaped and reshaped by an emotional self. Like other processes of psychological creation of meaning, gender identity, gender fantasy, the sense of gender, and the sexual identifications and fantasies that are part of this identity are formed and reformed throughout the life cycle. Senses of self, the tone of individual feelings, and emotionally imbued unconscious fantasies are as constitutive of subjective gender as is language or culture.[2]

My approach aligns itself with other feminist theories that make claims for the potential autonomy and creativity of consciousness.

Alison Jaggar (1989) criticizes epistemologies that privilege cognition, value, and reason and artificially divide them from the emotions that are inextricably embedded in them and fuel them. She claims that women, rather than accepting the false divide between emotion and reason, should pay attention to their "outlaw emotions" that can generate political and epistemological critique. Patricia Hill Collins, in *Black Feminist Thought* (1990), asserts the autonomy and individuality of consciousness, although she certainly does not minimize the centrality of relations of domination. Emphasizing that consciousness is created and not determined, she stresses the importance for feminists of bringing constant attention to bear on both the social-cultural-political realm and the individual creativity of consciousness. She points in particular to two traditional foci of psychoanalytic interest and of psychoanalytic feminist critique—heterosexuality and motherhood—and argues that African-American women's experience of both is created individually as much as imposed through domination: "The same situation can look quite different depending on the consciousness one brings to interpret it. . . . There is always choice, and power to act, no matter how bleak the situation may be" (227, 237).

Similarly, Gloria Anzaldúa (1990) sounds like an intersubjective psychoanalyst as she describes how the masks that Chicanas or Mexicanas are required to wear "drive a wedge between our intersubjective personhood and the *persona* we present to the world" (xv) and how women of color need theories that "will explain how and why we relate to certain people in specific ways, that will reflect what goes on between inner, outer and peripheral 'I' within a person and between the personal 'I' and the collective 'we' of our ethnic communities" (xxv). Like Loewald, Schafer, and others who write of reconstructions of past and present, she argues for "acquiring the tools to change the disabling images and memories, to replace them with self-affirming ones, to recreate our pasts and alter them—for the past can be as malleable as the present" (xxvii).

Personalized autobiographical accounts by feminists, even those which claim that consciousness is culturally or socially determined, also document how subjectivity, standpoint, and identity are on the one hand situated, contextual, and contested and on the other are actively created psychodynamically, rather than given. Out of many possible examples, I focus here on Pratt (1984) and Mernissi (1994). In "Identity: Skin, Blood, Heart," Minnie Bruce Pratt describes a Southern Christian childhood and identity. Each partially positioning memory and experience and each description of cultural, historical, or social location is infused with grief, pain, joy, anger, uncertainty, fear, and other emotions that particularize that location, memory, and experience for her. Visceral personal experience underlies and creates Pratt's identity. In a key passage, she describes her father's taking her to the top of the courthouse clock tower to look down over the town. She cannot see out as her father can, and she finds herself dominant and subordinate—white and a person whose grandfather was a judge in this court, but small and a girl, someone who would never hold the same position as male citizen or adult. Pratt describes how she consciously rejected her father's (symbolic) position by leaving home and giving up the white Southern identity and hegemonic worldview she was born with. But her gender identity is constructed also by the emotional reaction to that exclusion within inclusion, to the personal meaning of this one encounter (and thousands more) that helped to shape her personal sense of whiteness, middle class–ness, and femininity. Pratt's narrative describes passion and pain: the experienced deadening that accompanied her coming out as a lesbian, as she gave up her children when she left her husband; her fear and terror of isolation; the wrenching distance from black and Jewish women whom she wished to be close to and identified with; her shame at her own ancestors' historical role as slaveholders and appropriators of Native American lands. We feel the emotional animation of these identity categories as Pratt describes everyday walks through her black neighborhood in southeast Washington, D.C., and with her we gauge every encounter and reel from those which jar her or go awry.

In her enchanting autobiography *Dreams of Trespass: Memories of a Harem Girlhood*, Fatima Mernissi (1994) likewise conveys the individualized emotional and sensual experience of a specifically gendered culture: the smells and tastes of foods and make-up, the tactile feel of oily jars, fabrics, marble floors, the steam baths, sounds and sights, and how each individual projectively creates and reacts to this culture and his or her gender in specific ways. Mernissi describes the cultural meanings and physical-social organization of different harems, of women in Morocco and in Islamic history, of stories and legends; yet she also makes it clear that the harem, which draws a boundary between male and female, is experienced differently by each of the women and men (or girls and boys) in her account. Each individual has his or her own personality, way of participating, interpretations, ways of escaping emotionally, taking a break, resisting, or retreating, and ways of participating in and appropriating cultural practices.

There are of course commonalities. All members of the household agree that they live in a harem (a household that keeps women and girls inside and controlled, not a polygynous family), and some of the women react more similarly to each other than to others. But in each person's integration of culturally gendered forms and in the individual way of playing with them in emotion and fantasy, the component parts are different. Gender here is not simply internalized. Each little step in gender socialization is ruminated upon by the young Mernissi and her boy cousin, and each value is charged, conflictual, and elaborated on in individual and collective stories and plays. Indeed, the emotional charge constitutes the cultural meanings of gender and keeps them alive for all the participants.

Pratt and Mernissi make it clear that one's multifarious cultural and social positioning always includes psychological history—transference and emotionally infused development. As they also make clear, this psychological history, like any history, is not fixed once and for all in early childhood but continually unfolds and changes, lending emotional animation and personal coloring, through current and past relationships and through fantasy, to all aspects of identity—class, nationality, race or ethnicity, and religion, as well as gender. Mernissi shows how women who hold identical positions in society and are situated in similar ways culturally can yet have very different psychological experiences of gender. Such narratives highlight the contribution of individual, personal animation to gender identity. By contrast, feminist suspicion of psychology or of psychology's tendency to universalize precludes understanding of the role of such personal animation.

To consider our experience of personal meaning in the light of an individual's inner psychic reality of emotion and fantasy, then, is to revise and expand our understanding of cultural and linguistic meaning. Insofar as we are talking about individual subjectivity, cultural meaning does not "precede" individual meaning. From earliest infancy, meaning is emotional as well as cognitive. Creation of personal meaning and the potential for emotionally resonant experience antedates the acquisition of language. Cognitions, such as knowing one's gender and having thoughts or experiences of gender, are infused with emotions, fantasies, and personal tonalities.

With this psychoanalytic argument, I am making a universal claim about human subjectivity and its constituent psychodynamic processes, just as a cultural or poststructuralist theorist might universalize the equally essentialist claim that subjectivity is linguistically or discursively constituted. For those who draw on psychoanalysis, the capacity to endow experience with meaning from nonverbal emotion and unconscious fantasy—to create personal meaning—is an innate human capacity or potentiality that continues throughout life. Subjectivity creates and re-creates, merges and separates, fantasy and reality, inner and outer, unconscious and conscious, felt past and felt present, each element in the pair helping to constitute and give meaning and resonance to the other. Both in the psychoanalytic and in the cultural approach, we hold in abeyance any universal claim about the content of what is thought or felt: the content of that subjectivity or process cannot be universalized.

Clinical examples, by persuasively documenting the way in which emotion and fantasy saturate personal gender, point to the complexity of individual gender. Examples also illuminate how people re-create recognizable cultural meanings, personal experience, and their bodies in ways that charge and construct their individual sense of gender—emotionally, often conflictually, through unconscious and conscious fantasy. The meanings I describe are, finally, articulated in language, but as any analyst or patient knows, this language often only approximates the feeling of inner psychic reality. It is a product of interaction between therapist and patient as they work to create a consensual account of an experience that is initially (and throughout) emotional, partially conscious, fragmentary, and marked by disconnected thoughts. The two struggle, that is, to render experience that is not necessarily conscious or linguistic into language.

I believe we can see, from just a few examples of contemporary middle-class white American women—women who are heterosexual in their behavior and their conscious identity—how individual and idiosyncratic a sense of gendered self is. (I mention behavior and conscious identity because, especially in the clinical setting, where attention is directed toward such matters, once we explore any person's unconscious fantasy life and multiple sexual and other identifications, nobody has a single sexual orientation. On heterosexuality, see Chodorow, 1994; on the multiple aspects of sexual identity, see A. Stein, 1997). These few examples give some sense of the multiplicity and variability of individual constructions of gender and indicate some of the axes of definition and emotional castings that different individuals may bring to their own gender construct. They thus both support and challenge contemporary feminism. They document clearly the instability, multiplicity, layering, contradiction, and contestation in constructions of gender, but they also document that this unstable, multiple, layered, contested contradictoriness affects emotional and intrapsychic as well as cultural, linguistic, or discursive meaning. The women I describe range in the nature of their diagnoses and the levels of their psychic functioning. They do not stand out by virtue of their extraordinariness, beyond the fact that all our individual psyches, fantasies, fears, and conflicts are extraordinary. In some cases, the preoccupations these women express are central to what they and I have worked on throughout treatment; in others, they are constructions that are simply noted in passing. Other issues, in which gender is not so salient, are more central for them.

My initial restriction of case examples to women who share certain attributes of sociocultural position strengthens the case for the individual construction of gender. These patients presumably share a similar cultural and social organization of gender: they were primarily taken care of by mothers; they saw fathers as dominant and attractive in culturally recognizable ways (exciting, seductive, cuddly, or domineering); they were not explicitly taught that women were inferior and men superior; they could be said to have followed the Lacanian path developmentally from the imaginary mother-child semiotic realm to the phallic-symbolic world of the father.

Although I draw on female case examples (see note 2, Chapter 1, on clinical examples in this book), my point that gendered subjectivity is a melding of personally created idiosyncratic meaning and cultural meaning holds for my male patients (and all men) as well. The particular women I discuss come from a variety of European-American backgrounds. My clinical experience, however, as well as my reading of autobiographical, fictional, and ethnographic literature and feminist and gay-lesbian research and theory, all lead me to conclude that the processes I describe—though not, I emphasize again, the content—of emotion, fantasy, and self-construction characterize nonheterosexual subjectivities and American racial-ethnic subjectivities as well. (The account in Moraga, 1986, provides an exemplar of a particularized, emotional, fantasy-imbued construction of a bodily-sexual, gendered, and racial-ethnic subjectivity that is also culturally constituted.) These brief examples are meant only to suggest the personal projective construction of gender: I will not follow the details of change or variation in any one person. I will also not focus on commonalities, although such an approach would be possible. My patients have been conscious of some of the constructions, conflicts, and fantasies I describe for some time; others were previously unconscious and are now recognized; still others did not exist in their current form but were created through our work together.

For one woman, J, male-female difference is central to the meaning of gender, and an emotion, anger, is one key to gender construction. In the first part of her analysis, she strives constantly to cast me in the image of a father with whom she struggles and to get me to engage in such struggle. She wants to experience a dismissive, condemnatory, accusatory anger toward me that she identifies with her father and with other men. Our interaction is experienced in the form of emotional power struggles, struggles that take on undertones of gender. Alternately, they are between man and woman and between man and man.

J is terrified of her own anger and is also fearful of mine. Women's anger, as J tells it, destroys absolutely. There is no surviving it. Mothers can destroy children, and children can destroy mothers. J worries that her own rage destroyed her mother and that she might destroy me. If she does so, I will not be there for her. By contrast, men's anger is sudden, violent, and explosive, but when it is all over, you are still there. If J could be a man, she wouldn't have to fear destroying with anger, and she could still express her considerable rage.

For J, then, invulnerable anger is one of the main meanings of masculinity, and her frighteningly destructive anger is a link with femininity. Gender struggles, victory, and defeat animate images of gender difference, and her fantasy particularizes an adolescent daughter's angry struggle with her father. I emphasize the subjective centrality of adolescence here: when we look at individual constructions and animations of gender, different periods may be more or less salient for different people. Stage theories of different varieties draw our attention to potentially important processes for numbers of people, but they do not adequately predict what will be crucial periods in an individual case.[3]

J also sometimes constructs gender around a different male-female polarity and desire to give herself masculine attributes. Her preoccupations and fantasies here have their origins in latency, a period in which I have found that gender fantasies and feelings become consolidated for many people. The object-relational origins of these sorts of latency-period gender fantasies are likely to be associated with a brother or with (fantasied or perceived) maternal or paternal expectations about a brother in comparison to oneself. In her analysis, we discover a previously unconscious fantasy of being forever young—in fact, a young boy. As friends married and had children, J did not compare herself to them. She realizes that the reason was that she experiences herself as not grown up and not female. Like Peter Pan, she contemptuously dismissed such practices. Having a child would have destroyed the fantasy of being forever young and a boy (heterosexual intercourse also challenges it).

Being a boy has other advantages: you are in a much less vulnerable position than if you are a grown woman or a little girl. "Part of the secret is being a boy: that changes everything. I'm childless and can't decide to settle down with G because I've chosen not to. It makes it okay to be angry and on edge; that's how boys are. Not only is it okay, but you can't be hurt—a sense that part of myself is male, and powerful. That makes it okay, and there's pride in that, part of my strength. I don't have to be afraid because of that. I'm secretly strong." She remembers exuberant images of power, playing king of the mountain and football with the neighborhood boys. She says, "Boys and men are free; they have more room; they take up more physical space. They don't have to care how they look or dress." Such fantasies serve as a defense against J's notion (a notion recognized at different times by different women but often prepubertally) that a woman or girl should grow up and fulfill a powerless, dependent feminine role. Not wanting to grow up, imagining not growing up and time's not moving on, also connect for J with specific cultural images that have resonance psychologically, especially Peter Pan, but also Tom Sawyer. J also recalls childhood fantasy identifications with heroic knights who swashbuckled their way to success, rescuing damsels in distress (which she emphatically was not), and she is intrigued with the boy-dressed-as-a-girl-playing-a-boy parts in plays like *As You Like It* and *Twelfth Night.*

At one time, then, J's fantasy about gender and power concerns the fantasy of male anger and interpersonal aggression; at another, it concerns comparative strength and the ability to defend oneself. Gender difference also expresses itself in her eyes as boys' and men's ability to not care. In all these cases, central to J's gender construction is the sense that femininity is vulnerable in a way that masculinity is not. If she is accosted or threatened sexually or physically, she feels, as a female, that she provoked it because of the badness of female anger (and sexuality). But in the fantasy of being a boy or young man, she has no such feelings.

Coming straight from meetings with her male employer, B often arrives late for her hours of analysis. She herself has set up these work meetings to occur just before her hours, and she finds them very hard to leave. Despite having consciously and intentionally sought out analysis, she experiences her sessions as an obligation and an un-wanted pull away from the excitement of her relationship with her employer. She compares the obligation to the childhood experience in which she found the weekly good-byes to her father, who was divorced from her mother, painful and difficult. During many of her hours with me she is preoccupied with concerns about her employer. By contrast, she pays little notice to me. Sometimes she dismisses her delay with a perfunctory "Sorry I'm late," but usually she just ignores it. I feel like—and she confirms that I am—taken-for-granted back-ground, a maternal nag who can be kept waiting, who wants only to talk about boring, petty issues like lateness, schedules, and phone numbers. Most of the time, B feels strongly that what she needs is a powerful man, a perfect, ideal man who will rescue her and make her feel wonderful, rather than rejecting her as she feels her father did. As she puts it (unwittingly borrowing a cultural trope from Patsy Cline), she "falls to pieces" whenever she thinks of an old boyfriend who has rejected the overtures she has made in an effort to get back together.

In contrast to her idealized images of her father and men, her images of her mother and maternal femininity are almost sordid. Her mother, she feels, was weak, unable to care for herself or her children, unable to find good love relationships, unable to keep a nice house. Here, B compares her father and, alternately, me with her mother. At these moments, I am not a petty nag, a drag, or a doormat, in implicit or explicit contrast to an exciting man. Rather, in contrast to B's pitiful mother, I am seen as good and pure.

The psychological defense B employs in constructing these con-scious and unconscious fantasies of self, other, and gender is that of splitting. All the good parts of the other go to one person—good father/men versus bad mother/women/me; pure me versus impure mother. Splitting also occurs within the self. B has, as she tells it, good secret wishes that have to be kept secret, because then they will come true. She has to protect these good wishes both from the bad parts of herself, parts that she identifies with her mother, and from me, because I am a woman, and women make things difficult for her. She says, "Recently, my main experiences with women, with my mother, my close friends, are difficult. From childhood, a man could make it all better. Women, my mother, can't give me what I need or long for, to feel desirable."

Yet B also feels shame and conflict about her dominant gender fantasies. She idealizes masculine rescue but (occasionally) also idealizes me; she worries, as she puts it, "that all my positive secrets revolve around men." Putting all the good into men and all the bad into women, when she herself is a woman, leaves her identified with her shameful mother. Moreover, she has political objections to her fantasies: they are not the kinds of unconscious fantasies or thoughts that women today wish to discover. They are therefore quite hard to recognize and acknowledge. She says, "I resist that idea—how *could* I think that way?" But she then immediately wonders, "Have I ever admired a woman I worked with?"

B's construction of gender has a unique emotional configuration that differs in emphasis from J's. B does not want to be, and does not fantasize herself as, a man. Rather, she emphatically wants to have a man. Emotionally, cognitively, and in conscious fantasy she emphasizes heterosexual femininity. B's idealization of men revolves around how they can rescue her; for J, men's and boy's seeming self-sufficiency and ability not to care are central. For B, shame and excitement are emotionally central to her gender feelings; for J, anger becomes a defining criterion of gender. In some particulars, these two cases resemble two of three typical patterns of female development described by Freud (1931). B resembles the girl who rejects her mother and women and develops heterosexual femininity. She desires men sexually, to give her something the mother did not and could not give.

J is the girl who eschews femininity and develops a masculine identification (for Freud, identification with the father). Such an identification may or may not include a behavioral lesbian object choice.[4]

For K, the most salient aspects of gender are not primarily organized around the male-female polarity. Unlike J, K is not preoccupied with wanting to have the privileges and attributes of a man; unlike B, she is not preoccupied with wanting to have a man sexually. As Freud's classic theory would have it, K organizes her gender with reference to the body—but not in terms of maleness and femaleness. She organizes bodily gender in terms of the little girl–mother polarity. K feels herself to be an inadequate girl with inadequate little genitals—inadequate not in comparison with males, who possess a penis, but in comparison with grown women with adult genitals and reproductive capacities. Memories of this inadequacy come from both early latency and early and middle adolescence.

The dominant feeling-tone of shame in K's experience of her female body extends to and undermines the comparison in her mother–little girl fantasy, so this fantasy entails its own negation. In K's view, grown women's bodies have their own problems. Pregnancy and menstruation, for example, give women cramps, make them weak, sluggish, and heavy, and remind them that they are tied to uncontrollable bodies. Heterosexual relationships pose a conflictual solution to this shame, one that generates a further quandary. Strong, masculine men can help K appreciate her feminine body and make her feel successfully feminine, but they also by their presence serve as a reminder of her weakness and the general shamefulness and weakness of femininity. If she chooses men whom she perceives as not so masculine, however, so that she is not so reminded of her own weakness, K feels inadequate as a heterosexual feminine woman—and that is shameful in its own way. A further quandary comes from her identifying herself consciously as a feminist. As K puts it, "I hate to think that women are weak."

For K, gender as a male-female polarity and feminine inadequacy vis-à-vis men are not as intensely experienced as the little girl–grown woman dichotomy. When these do enter her fantasy and feelings, they center more on work than on body or sexuality. Being a woman gets tied up with being unable to compete in the work world: "You're too weak, not tough enough to be in that world. Dependent." Work functions, covertly, as a locus for overcoming femininity. K wants to be "king of the hill," "top man on the totem pole," receiving acknowledgment and recognition as a man, from men, or as a nongendered person (implicitly male) from other nongendered people. But this wish becomes tricky in turn, because wanting recognition is a kind of dependence, and hence feminine, and weak.

Because of her fantasy and fear that grown women, tied to their female bodies, are weak and that work success is masculine, for K competent women are something of an oxymoron. She describes a business meeting with a group of women, how impressed she was with their competence: "It wasn't a kill-or-be-killed model of interaction, but I'm not committed to it. I'm stuck in the kill-or-be-killed model. I didn't know how to behave in that setting. I'm more comfortable in the other—what I gloss as men, but it's not only men. I know how to handle myself in situations with lots of direct challenges to ideas. It doesn't make me happy, but it's involving. I feel prevented from fitting into a more flattened landscape, one without hierarchy. If it's not up or down, on the way up or on the way down, struggling against being put down, I'll disappear."

There is no emotional or cognitive space in K's view for being competent, nonhierarchical, and a woman. Her own professional aspirations and ways of thinking and preferring to interact are, in her view, masculine. She doesn't know how to act otherwise, but such aspirations still create conflicts. She experiences, and gets pleasure from experiencing work in the kill-or-be-killed model, but at the same time she does not like it morally or politically. Moreover, the pleasure is conflictual and shameful. And there is always the fear that she will be found out—found to be not a man but a woman—even worse, not a woman but a little girl, an inadequate woman.

C expresses still another construction of gender, another feeling-tone and object of desire. She wants mother, not father; breast, not penis; nurturance, not protective rescue or autonomy. For C, being a woman and being with women elicit thoughts of her mother and feelings of being left out. She experiences a kind of sad neediness, thinking of women's relationships with men. She feels that men have a special ability to bind women to them that women don't have, or that she doesn't have. With women friends, she feels a pervasive sense of wanting more and being angry and sad at not getting it. The problem with being a woman is that, to other women, you are not unique. C imagines that for me, my women patients are all alike. They all get arbitrary, inconsistent attention, whereas my men pa-tients are unique and prized. She feels excluded and hopeless. So she feels jealousy of men because women favor them and of other women, who, she assumes, get the same indifferent attention or lack of attention from mother/women that she does.

I do not believe that the tonality of this "left-out-ness" and jealousy is usefully considered oedipal (or "negative-oedipal": for a girl, wanting mother and wanting to get rid of father) or preoedipal (assuming a two-person relationship). The fantasy is triadic, involv-ing mother and father and images of sexuality, but it fuses breast wishes, greed, neediness, feelings of emptiness, perception of one's interchangeability with other women in the eyes of the mother/ woman (men's desires are not relevant here), and a sense that feeding and filling are what women offer to men. In this construction of gender, male-female differences are emotionally intertwined with and take the form of sibling concerns. Feelings of empty, needy sadness range across C's life and are central to her personal animations and evocations of gender. Clearly, a Kleinian viewpoint, according to which the breast rather than the penis is central to gender difference and construction of gender is organized around the projected and introjected goodness/plenitude and badness/destructiveness of the breast and self, makes much more sense of C's psychology in general and her sense of gender in particular than a classically Freudian understanding does.[5]

All the gender identifications and fantasies I describe are both cultural and personal. A social or cultural critic could claim (and would be partly right) that you do not need a psychology to explain many of these images, fantasies, and gender constructions. It is well documented that men have more power, are allowed to express anger more freely and take up more space than women, and that women cater to them. It is culturally mandated that women be passive. Women in many cultures and families are expected to give in to and give up to men and not to give to their daughters as they give to their sons and husbands. The views my patients express about these matters come from their particular families and from the culture in general, and we should not minimize this culturally induced inflection of the meanings of masculinity and femininity. It is "realistic" to have these beliefs and thoughts; they are a good analysis of a sexist society. We are less likely to find them gender-reversed either in reconstructions or in transferences. Assessment of the cultural and social setting is also part of my patients' appraisals of and feelings about their situations and psyches.[6]

In these accounts we recognize familiar social as well as cultural patterns—for example, a divorce, an elusive father, and a rejected little girl who thinks everything will be all right if Daddy rescues her.

We could consider her, as she considers herself, a victim of family circumstances and gender inequality. Some observers or critics might ask, as she does, how you can have an image of a rich, vibrant, fertile mother when your mother is another statistic in the feminization of poverty. Similarly, in a culture that valorizes exciting masculinity, it might be expected that girls and women would idealize men and devalue women. They would turn not to stories like *Peter Pan* and *As You Like It* but to *Cinderella, Sleeping Beauty,* and gothic romances, or to Patsy Cline falling to pieces.

Moreover, one theme intersects with all my clinical examples and has been central to the feminist appropriation and critique of psychology. Within the gendered subjectivity that they create, all the women I discuss reflect psychological preoccupation with some aspect of gender inequality. The way in which each person brings masculinity and femininity to life and develops a gender identity imbued with emotion and fantasy, includes personal animation not just of difference itself but of differences in value and power. Often but not always, the male-female contrasts are based on male dominance, privilege, or superiority (see Stein, 1995, however, for a particularly interesting case discussion of a man who emphatically experienced his mother and other women as dominant, privileged, and superior). This prevalent psychological intertwining of sexuality, gender, inequality, and power, all saturated with introjective and projective meaning, demonstrates why it is necessary for psychoanalysts to take both a cultural and a clinical stance.

As these cultural meanings are constructed and reconstructed in personal gender, however, they become entangled with the specifics of individual emotion and fantasy, with aspects of self, and with conscious and unconscious images of gender, fostered by particular families. These personal overtones explain why taking just a cultural stance is not enough either, why an explanation on the basis of cultural values or meanings alone is incomplete. For this reason, we are always walking a fine line when we combine cultural and personal understanding. The existence of gender inequality in both the cultural and social spheres does not explain the range of fantasy interpretations and varieties of emotional shadings with which women confront this inequality. We have only to look at the number of autobiographical and literary accounts by daughters of vibrant, creative mothers who were extremely poor and oppressed to understand that the feminization of poverty alone is not an adequate explanation for a particular woman's sense of powerlessness and neediness.

Furthermore, my patients themselves feel miserable, anxious, and conflicted about their thoughts concerning gender and gender inequality—one woman about her hidden fantasy of being a powerful male and about coveting what she sees as male powers, another about her sad desire for maternal nurturance, another about her scorn for uncompetitive women, another about her desperate need for men, another about her rage at paternal dominance and sadness over her mother, another about her sadness at her father's absence. Their warding off and harboring of these unconscious fantasies have kept them from living as they wish—from having fulfilling relationships and from moving ahead professionally, when such professional achievements interfered with the fantasy of being a boy, with feeling needy and dependent, or with the sense that professional participation threatens to shame them sexually.

A belief that men can be angry, temperamental, or demanding and that women or mothers are powerless is both a social analysis and a powerful motivator of guilt and inhibition, of a need to repair the mother and not to move ahead of her. Guilt and sadness about the mother are particularly prevalent female preoccupations, which are as likely to limit female autonomy, pleasure, and achievement as any cultural mandate. This is so even though unequal gender arrangements and beliefs themselves give rise to conditions in which female autonomy, pleasure, and achievement result in a woman's surpassing her mother. Similarly, shame vis-à-vis men, whether over women's dependence or at being discovered in masculine pursuits, is certainly situated in a cultural context in which such pursuits are coded as masculine in the first place. But this shame is also experienced in itself, inflected with many unconscious fantasies that often stem from a time in development well before such coding could be interpreted. It is a conflict in itself, and it inflects the general sense of self and gender in addition to interacting with specific cultural expectations and meanings.

My examples, then, reflect, indicate, and build on historically situated, cultural, discursive constructions of gender. But none of the women I discuss simply entered the realm of the symbolic or placed herself within a cultural discourse or unequal society or polity. From birth to the present, all have actively constructed their gender with intense individual feelings and fantasies—of anger, envy, guilt, resentment, shame, wistful desire, rageful entitlement, sadness, jealousy, horror, or disgust—and with characteristic defensive patterns—of guilt, denial, splitting, projection, repression. This personal cast and individual emotional tonality pervade any person's sense of gender.

Feminists have developed fine-tuned theories of discursively constructed, cultural, and political gender. They are sensitive to specifics of history, class, rank, race, or ethnicity and cognizant of the contingent, fragmentary, and ambiguous character of enactments and constructions of gender. But these cannot alone reveal to us how gender is constructed—what these culturally situated practices and discourses mean to the particular person who experiences and constructs gender and a gender identity. The capacities and processes for the creation of personal meaning described by psychoanalysis contribute to gendered subjectivity as do cultural categories and the enactment or creation of social or cultural roles. Clinical work demonstrates that all elements of existence—anatomy, cultural meanings, individual family, economic and political conditions, class, race, socialization practices, and the impact of parents' personality—are refracted and constructed through the projections and introjections and the fantasy creations that give them psychological meaning.[7]

4　Theoretical Gender and Clinical Gender

A normal ego . . . is, like normality in general, an
ideal fiction. Every normal person, in fact, is only
normal on the average.

SIGMUND FREUD

"ANALYSIS TERMINABLE AND

INTERMINABLE"

JUST AS PSYCHOANALYSIS IMPLICITLY AND EXPLICITLY CHAL-
lenges widespread assumptions within feminist theory, so feminism
has challenged widespread tendencies within psychoanalytic thinking about gender. In this chapter, I respond to and elaborate on
the feminist challenge as I reflect on some epistemological and methodological problems in psychoanalytic thinking about gender. I suggest, first, that psychoanalytic thinking about gender (and, insepara-
bly within psychoanalysis, sexuality) tends to collapse individuality
and difference into universality and similarity, while in the process
turning clinical observations of the fluctuating personal emotional

meanings of gender into fixed developmental tasks. Second, I claim that psychoanalytic thinking tends to be insufficiently cognizant of both the inextricable cultural aspects of gender psychology and the unreflected-upon cultural assumptions in our theorizing; this second set of problems is partially responsible for the first. I argue that more clinically and less theoretically or developmentally based thinking about psychological gender can respond to feminist criticisms of psychoanalysis and provide a corrective to psychoanalytic theorizing itself—by more fully and accurately describing psychological reality. I offer generalizations about constructions of subjective gender that I believe are also consonant with clinical individuality.

As I noted earlier, academic feminism has argued for a variety of gender identities and has documented the centrality of culture to gender. Analysts, however, learn of these facts in the clinical consulting room, even though they may downplay them in formulating theory. I propose, then, that there is a gap between what we experience and observe transferentially, clinically, and empirically with regard to gender identity, sexual and gender fantasies, and individual women's and men's psyches, on the one hand, and what most theoretical and developmental accounts claim about inevitable or necessary stages of development, "the" psychology of women, "the" role of gender in the transference, and other gender-related developmental or intrapsychic processes and tasks, on the other. In our clinical work, we find over the course of treatment a changing constellation of transferences and countertransferences. On the developmental front, too, each caregiver-child pair forms its own relationship imbued with unconscious fantasy and emotion, and each child brings her own capacities for the creation of intrapsychic meaning to every experience and perception. These transference-countertransference constellations, unconscious parent-child communications, and any person's intrapsychic life include aspects of subjective gender and sexuality, and these are always in turn intertwined with other aspects of self, unconscious fantasy, and affect (see Dimen, 1991). In my view, gender identity and aspects of the psychology of gender develop and are experienced in these personal, transferential meaning-creating contexts. From such a perspective, it is apparent that gender, like selfhood, must be unique to each individual (see also Chodorow, 1994).

Psychoanalytic theory, however, does not stress this individual uniqueness. Rather, gender is seen as less contingent, created, individual, and emergent than other aspects of psychic functioning. Contemporary as well as classical theorists make universal claims about women as opposed to men and imply that they describe the core experience or essence of femininity or masculinity. This observation extends to theories of "primary femininity" (e.g., Kestenberg, 1968, 1980; Mayer, 1985) and investigations of gender identity (Tyson, 1982) as much as to those psychoanalytical models based asymmetrically on phallic castration or "sexual difference" (Birksted-Breen, 1996; Breen, 1993; Mayer, 1995; Roiphe and Galenson, 1981). French theorists, whether Lacanian (Mitchell and Rose, 1982), anti-Lacanian (Irigaray, 1985), or mainstream (Chasseguet-Smirgel, 1985, 1986; McDougall, 1986), also make universal claims about gender identity and its psychobiological essence. Following Freud's emphasis on genital anatomy, libidinal stage theory, and theory of the Oedipus complex more or less explicitly, all these writers discuss seemingly inevitable (or at least desirable) stages of development, developmental tasks, innate femininity and masculinity, "the" psychology of men or women, or what "must" in every analysis be discovered and analyzed. Like much of academic psychology and virtually all of popular psychology, the psychoanalytic literature has tended to overgeneralize, to oppose all men to all women, and to assume that masculinity and femininity and their expressive forms are single rather than multiple.

Many critics of the traditional psychoanalytic point of view pose an alternate universalism. Self-in-relation theorists (Jordan, Kaplan,

Miller, Stiver, and Surrey, 1991), theorists of women's ways of knowing (Belenky, Clinchy, Goldberger, and Tarule, 1986; Goldberger,
Tarule, Clinchy, and Belenky, 1996), and theorists of women's voice
or morality (Gilligan, 1982; Gilligan, Rogers, and Tolman, 1991;
Brown and Gilligan, 1992) also present their conclusions not just as
clinically, observationally, or experimentally based findings but as
universal claims about how women are, and even, by implication,
how they should be.[1]

Even within mainstream writings, there are of course exceptions.
A contribution by Applegarth (1976) discusses the many paths and
patterns of conflict that may lead to work inhibitions in women.
More recently, Tyson (1991) suggests that "there may not be *one* story
of female development, but many stories, many intertwining themes,
and many possible outcomes" (583—a claim she reiterates in Tyson,
1996). Person (1995) describes a variety of women's and men's fantasies and daydreams, and Schuker (1996) argues that there are many
etiologies and sets of dynamics within female homosexuality.

Relational psychoanalysts have criticized the still largely un-
challenged Freudian assumption that, in the case of gender (and
self), genital anatomy and body ego come first. These theorists have
taken issue as well with the pervasive psychoanalytic tendency to
dichotomize and polarize gender.[2] Drawing on feminist postmodernism, they have argued for multiplicity, individuality, variability, and
instability in the psychology of gender (see, e.g., Dimen, 1991; Goldner, 1991; Harris, 1991; Benjamin, 1995, 1996; Mitchell, 1996; Gabbard and Wilkinson, 1996). They have documented clinically and
rethought theoretically the relational, contingent, and shifting constructions of the gendered body and sexuality in individuals and
those generated between analyst and analysand (see, e.g., Wrye and
Welles, 1994; Wrye, 1996; Shapiro, 1996; Knoblauch, 1996; Gerson,
1996; Harris, 1996; Dimen, 1996; Harris et al., 1996). They have thus

moved us well beyond simplistic investigations of single meanings of any aspect of genital anatomy, without losing sight of the importance of bodies and desire to mind and relation.

In the case of psychoanalytic universalizing, there is both a methodological and an epistemological disjunction. Our case method focuses on the unique person emerging in the intersubjective analytic encounter, and our claims to knowledge rest on our clinical findings. Yet our theories in the case of gender and sexuality generalize and universalize with regard to developmental lines and tasks, the assumption that bodily functions initiate developmental phases, and gender-differentiated aspects of character or pathology. Our epistemology has practical effects. Too often, the useful patterns we observe or believe in are held preconsciously, consciously, and unconsciously as normative or statistical expectations or as certainties about essential and universal truths. As such, they serve as blinders to clinical, empirical, and intersubjective seeing and recognizing. Epistemologically and methodologically, there is a conflict between essentializing, universalizing, and overgeneralizing and a clinical case approach; clinically, when we work with individuals, we find diversity, variation, and uniqueness.

Various unreflected-upon practices seem to lead to these outcomes. (On generalization, false universalism, and false difference, see J. R. Martin, 1994. It is important to make clear here that some feminist accusations in this domain probably result from a translation error. What has been assumed to be a generalization or observation of prevalent patterns for a clinician or empirical social scientist becomes, for the humanist who does not have empirical categories or methods, "essentializing" or "universalizing.") We begin with generalizations, acknowledged as such: women tend to feel more comfortable with intimacy and dependence than men; little boys are more physically aggressive than little girls; women tend toward hysteria, men toward obsessiveness; boys act out, girls act in. Such generalizations are based on empirical observation, and they are implicitly statistical claims—claims for prevalence or typicality. Behind all statistical claims, there is variation; statistics assume variance, and claims cast in related terms must do so as well. Therefore, within these claims, it is always also implied that some little girls are more physically aggressive than some boys, that some men are more comfortable with intimacy and dependence than some women, that some men are hysterics and some women obsessive, and so forth.

But in the history of psychoanalysis, variance is often forgotten, as empirical generalizations seem to become first overgeneralizations—allowed to stand beyond their empirical basis—and then universalizations. We come to think that all little boys are physically aggressive and all little girls are not; that all men are uncomfortable with dependence; that all women need relationship. These overgeneralizations and universalizing claims have clinical consequences: clinicians begin to suspect pathology when they find a physically aggressive little girl or a boy who is not physically aggressive; they notice hyperaggressive ambition in a woman patient that they would not notice, or would notice differently, in a man. Exploitative sexual acting out or going from one sexual partner to another is thought to have different psychobiological roots in a man than in a woman, whereas the dynamics might be very similar in both cases. By contrast, two men's behaviorally similar compulsive sexuality may have different dynamic meanings.

Universalizing is different from essentializing but can lead to it—defining the essence of what it is to be masculine or feminine. Historically, psychoanalysts have tended to follow Freud's lead in assuming that anatomy in some way precedes or underlies gender identity or has a privileged weight not accorded to other components of gender or sexuality.[3] For Freud as for Galenson and Roiphe, the essence of feminine psychology is penis envy and its consequences and transformations; the essence of masculinity is castration anxiety and its consequences and transformations. Theorists of primary femininity oppose these perceptions and define femininity in terms of an inevitable developmental bodily based primary cathexis of the female genitals and fears of injury to or castration of these genitals. Rather than follow the psychoanalytic methodological principle that the meaning of the body is never self-evident but always imbued with individual fantasy and conflict, constructed as we construct all aspects of meaning, in the case of femininity we assume that female embodiedness inevitably generates particular meanings and that it is always salient in the construction of gender (for a recent example, see Breen, 1993). In my own clinical experience, however, I have found that genital and reproductive anatomy, the internal debate whether or not to become a mother, and other aspects of gendered and sexual embodiment are extremely central to some women's sense of gender, psyche, and self and experienced as much less essential to the psyche, self, and gender of other women.

Essentialism is not restricted to mainstream psychoanalysts. Self-in-relation theorists imply that the essence of femininity or female psychology is the need for relation. For Winnicott (1971), the essence of femaleness is being; of maleness, doing. What is *essentially* female is penis envy and defenses against it in body imagery and fantasy, ego development, and object relations; or what is *essentially* female is the desire to maintain connection and relation. Within the clinical literature, many other empirical observations of specific people have been overgeneralized, universalized, and then essentialized. Like universalizing, essentializing has consequences when clinicians find, as we all must at one time or another, a female whose psychology is not centrally about connection and relation, or about how she experiences, fantasizes about, and reacts to her genital anatomy.

Psychoanalytic essentializing and universalizing can be explained partially through another feminist insight, first put forth by Karen Horney, Clara Thompson, and other interpersonalists, into the role of culture in our conceptualizations of gender. As I have argued elsewhere (Chodorow 1978, 1989, 1994), we psychoanalysts embed unconscious and preconscious, unthought and unnoticed, pretheoretical cultural assumptions about gender in our theories and thus shape what we see and hear clinically. Schafer (1974) first noted a disjunction between psychodynamic explanation of most aspects of psychic functioning and the issues that seemed to call for explanation and treatment in the case of gender and sexuality. Pretheoretical assumptions that I and others have pointed to include the assumptions that women are naturally maternal or that they are instinctually passive and masochistic; that heterosexuality can be taken for granted but homosexuality needs explaining; that a masculine psychology centered on superiority over women, or based on traumatic fear of castration, does not require clinical analysis; and that masculine aggressivity and violence do not call for special explanations, whereas feminine aggressivity and violence do.

Psychoanalytic accounts of mothers and fathers, whether or not they are directly about gender identity, also reflect assumptions about normal gender that inform our theories and clinical work. I am thinking of theorizing and clinical accounts that pathologize nontraditional parental role patterns (active, managerial, aggressive mothers and passive fathers are more problematic than the reverse), as well as the plethora of assumptions, particularly in the object-relations and self psychology traditions, we have about mothers, the breast, primary maternal preoccupation, and so forth, and the fantasies of mother-blame and psychoanalytic rescue that these assumptions can generate (see Chodorow and Contratto, 1982; Phillips, 1993).

As contemporary commentators note repeatedly, within the history of psychoanalysis Freud's claims have been less subject to theoretical or empirical scrutiny than those of other thinkers. In the case of gender, within psychoanalysis, and everyday culture as well, many unquestioned assumptions about gender rest on supposedly biological reasoning. Freud and Deutsch, for example, explain much of female psychology as an outcome of "women's service to the species" (on Freud's teleology, see Schafer, 1974). As I describe elsewhere (Chodorow, 1994), part of the reason heterosexual object choice does not seem to need explaining in the individual clinical case, as do homosexual object choice and a variety of noncoital perversions, is that heterosexual coitus is needed for species continuity. With the exception of Lacanian theory, which has influenced French psychoanalysis more generally, most post-Freudian branches of psychoanalysis (American ego psychology, object-relations theory, Kleinian psychoanalysis), even as they start from the view that the psyche must be seen in terms that go well beyond the drive theory and the physical body, continue to assume that gender is a matter of sexuality and genitals (as I first noted in Chodorow, 1978).

The recent focusing of attention on the here and now of transference and countertransference, with their focus on the unique, contingent, emergent creation of intersubjective and intrapsychic meaning, does not seem sufficiently to affect understandings of gender. Gender remains a matter of sexuality, genitals, or body parts like the breast—at most, an early genital phase replaces the phallic-oedipal phase as critical, or primary femininity replaces penis envy and the female lack. Cutting-edge, radical, original, contemporary thinkers claim that we are hardwired to organize experience along the lines of gender-inflected universal fantasies like primal scene, castration anxiety, and the Oedipus complex—fantasies that to the cultural or clinical observer are clearly culturally and individually specific, perhaps widespread but certainly not universal. (I focus here on the unquestioned universalisms of psychoanalysis. I could note, by contrast, the universalisms of feminism; for example, the "Notes to Contributors" of the leading feminist journal *Signs* until recently stated that "authors are encouraged to address diversity issues involving race, class, sexual preference, etc."—also indicative of unquestioned universalisms and pretheoretical assumptions about "diversity issues." Currently, *Signs* claims to look for "articles engaging gender, race, culture, class, nation, and/or sexuality.")

Although nonpsychoanalytic thinkers, in the case of gender as elsewhere, may be unwilling to acknowledge the noncultural, nonlinguistic, body-derived, unconscious emotional and fantasy components of subjectivity, it is also the case that psychoanalysts need to recognize fully the inextricable cultural and linguistic contribution to constructions and fantasies of gender. Instead, accounts imply that there is a precultural or noncultural core to femininity and masculinity, usually based in anatomy. Even accounts sensitive to the cultural determinations of gender imply that those determinations are superimposed on a precultural essence, either a genitally determined subjective identity (classically, a reduction of the psychology of women to female sexuality) or some observed universal gender differences in psychic operation that we can "find" if we factor out culture. But the clinical and cultural evidence does not suggest that we can differentiate between something fixed (a basic universal core of psychological gender) and something that varies from individual to individual (for example, fantasies about the body, the emotional tonality of gender, or identifications).

Because of cultural assumptions that inform both psychological gender and theorizing about gender, there also seems to be a tendency among psychoanalysts, as among psychologists, to study the psychology of women by searching for differences in what defines or characterizes men as opposed to women and to pay less attention to or occlude within-gender variation and between-gender similarities (a point made by Maccoby and Jacklin, 1984, and Bem, 1993, regarding academic psychology). The unquestioned assumption is that we will find the observable and clinical regularities of gender difference that we expect. Indeed, my impression is that if we compare those clinical observations which become universalized and those which do not, we find that clinical observations about non-gender-related phenomena are often left to stand as interesting in themselves. By contrast, writers on gender-related phenomena tend to use clinical vignettes to confirm generalizations and universalizations (often rooted in female genital anatomy) about necessary aspects of female psychology or development.

It is not only the case, moreover, that psychoanalytic theories of gender rest on unacknowledged cultural assumptions. It is also the case that everyone's sense of gender and sexuality has cultural as well as personal resonance and meaning. As feminism documents, because gender has cognitive components, we cannot think of gender entirely apart from language and culture. From our earliest years, culture enters the gendered psyche, as nonverbal communications to a child about her gender or about the gender of the person who is communicating help form a basis for the emotional resonance of cultural categories. From the time a child is spoken to, read to, or put in front of the television set, myths, fairy tales, and stories contribute to unconscious as well as conscious fantasy about gender. Investigations of life histories, biography, autobiography, and fiction also make especially clear how available cultural images, understandings, gender scripts, and narratives shape any individual's unconscious self-understanding and any individual self-story, and how great are the historical and cultural variations in gendered meanings (see, e.g., Person, 1995; Heilbrun, 1988).

Feminist understandings are thus essential in that they argue against psychoanalytic and everyday cultural assumptions that gender is self-evident, that particular personality characteristics universally differentiate the sexes, that biology determines gendered self, or that the organization of gender is historically or cross-culturally unvarying. These understandings imply that psychological gender may not be more fundamental than other psychologically constructed aspects of identity and show how gender and these other aspects of identity may become intertwined with, inflected by, or representative of one another.

In trying to understand the hold of pretheoretical cultural assumptions about gender, we can also factor in the anxieties of uncertainty. In order to tolerate clinical unpredictability and the radically uncommonsensical and anxiety-provoking understandings underpinning psychoanalysis—that projective and introjective fantasies are ever-changing, that motives are unconscious, that humans interpret and construct the world and our lives in terms of unconscious, emotionally laden wishes, fears, and fantasies, that anxiety generates major aspects of human functioning (including the analyst's own)—we as analysts also defensively rely on some completely mundane and familiar assumptions. Gender and sexuality, I suggest, historically serve this role. A first challenge for psychoanalysts, then, must be to assume that gender and sexuality are as interesting and new as everything else we observe clinically and theorize about—to tolerate the uncertainty that comes from questioning some of our earliest and most entrenched personal and cultural assumptions.[4]

We are not left, however, entirely in a morass of epistemological uncertainty, in which gender disappears entirely into individuality and we can no longer think of it as a category of analysis, identity, or subjectivity. In the remainder of this chapter, I turn to a number of concepts and formulations that can help us meet the clinical and feminist challenges while retaining gender centrally in view. To begin, I have found particularly useful Fast's distinction (1984, 77) between objective (I prefer her alternate term, "observed") and subjective gender. Objective gender refers to observed differences in features of psychic or mental life or aspects of personality, character, or behavior that tend to differentiate or characterize the sexes—for example, statistical differences in prevalent diagnoses or character traits. We might find in women's or men's life histories or development, or, as some current research suggests, in neurobiology or in hormone levels, trends that begin to account for these commonalities. Claims about women's self-in-relation, greater ease with dependency or intimacy, weaker superego, or ego fusion and empathy in the service of mothering, in contrast to men's, are parts of observed gender that may or may not be linked to an identity or sense of oneself as female. Depending on how central to many women's psyches we saw these to be, we might consider them part of a (still implicitly statistical) psychology of women. By contrast, subjective gender refers to personal constructions of masculinity and femininity—elements consciously or unconsciously linked to the sense of self as gendered. These personal constructions might include, for example, fantasies about one's gender, sexual fantasies consciously or unconsciously connected with sense of gender as it relates to body image, core gender identity, or gender identifications.

It is an empirical question whether an aspect of someone's identity, fantasy, self-construction, body-ego, or character is subjectively gendered. We observe, for example, that girls and boys tend to develop an attachment to and involvement with their mother, in the case where the mother is their primary caretaker. As observers, we know that the mother is a woman and that her breasts come with her biological sex, but at first her gender or biological sex is not subjectively relevant to her children's conceptions of mother, mothering, or breasts. If aggressivity is, as some think, hardwired in the male brain or in male hormonal patterns, then it is not necessarily part of subjective masculine gender, though there will certainly be a gender-related statistical difference in aggressivity. By contrast, if little boys consciously or unconsciously think or fantasize that big strong men, other boys, their father, or their idealized absent father acts aggressively as part of masculinity, that is part of subjective masculine gender. A *Jane Eyre* or *Rebecca* fantasy of submissive involvement with an aggressive man who turns gentle is part of many women's subjective gender, and we can observe that it is more prevalent in women than in men. But in accordance with traditional thinking, we are likely to conclude that a fantasy that is more prevalent, or even exclusively found, among women, even if among only a segment of the female population, characterizes "the" psychology of women or female sexuality.

Freud made claims about both subjective and observed gender. His account of how girls and boys develop, respectively, penis envy or castration anxiety describes subjective gender—specifically, gendered subjectivity organized around the body. By contrast, his claims about gender differences in superego formation or narcissism are in the arena of observed gender: a woman's faulty superego is not an aspect of her subjective sense of her femaleness (though it may be a *result* of her subjective gender—that is, of her not fearing castration). Klein obviously makes observed gender crucial to her theory when she asserts that fantasies about the breast are central to psychological life, but these fantasies (paranoid-schizoid splitting, depressive reparation, and so on) are cast mainly in nongendered terms. In her writings there are only scattered references to subjective gender in boys and girls—for instance, when she claims that idealization of the penis and the father in both sexes is a way to escape the fear and overwhelmingness of the maternal breast, or when she describes the oedipal child's imaging of bodily gender differences in the fantasy of the father's penis and the mother's babies inside the mother. The extent to which the contemporary Kleinian focus on the exclusionary parental intercourse of the primal scene (both as a sexual act and as a conceptualization of linking and thinking) requires assumptions about a gender-differentiated heterosexual couple or normative heterosexuality will also affect conceptions of subjective gender in Kleinian theory.

The distinction between subjective and observed gender enables us to sort out the relation between individual uniqueness on the one hand and commonality, generalization, or universality on the other.

On the basis of clinical observation, developmental research, or findings about human biopsychology, for example, we might make the (to all intents and purposes) universal observation that everyone constructs a gendered and sexual subjectivity. However, each person subjectively constructs this gender and sexuality in unique ways. Neither anatomy nor core gender identity has automatic effects, and, as Freud first noted, there is no single way in which the psychology of women proceeds. (In fact, Freud theorized both one normal femininity and three typical female developmental patterns, as well describing a number of unique and complex individual cases; since Freud, tensions have arisen within psychoanalysis between universalizing and essentialist claims about theoretical woman—women in developmental theory—and particularized observations about clinical women in all their difference, context, individuality, and specificity [see Chodorow, 1994]).

We have here both universalizing—everyone constructs her or his own gendered subjectivity—and clinical individualizing—the particular construction, the particular unconscious and conscious fantasies will vary. There is, then, no single femininity or masculinity, feminine or masculine identity, or way of constructing a sense of male or female self, but everyone will do so. (Bem, 1993, however, reports the research finding that the centrality of gender to the overall sense of self varies: some people's sense of gender is highly significant, central to their overall schema of self, and invested with meaning and emotion; for others, gender is less invested with significance. This was my own reluctant conclusion, reported in Chodorow, 1989b, as I tried to get second-generation women analysts to claim that gender was as important to their sense of self and psychoanalytic identity as it was to mine.)

Here, as elsewhere, my goal is to maintain this both-and stance, and not to leave us with only individuality and difference. The concept of pattern provides a useful bridge between generalizing and

individuality (see Frye, 1990). Clinically, there is a difference between on the one hand assuming that we are talking about how "the"
girl or "the" boy will or must develop, what constitutes the essence of
masculinity or femininity, or what are the universally necessary tasks
to achieve these, and on the other hand keeping a wide variety of
patterns of development and psychology in the back of one's mind.
The latter approach is much truer to how we work clinically. We keep
all sorts of potentially contradictory theories and generalizations (not
just those about gender and sexuality) in mind, recognizing them as
patterns as we come across them in a particular moment. But if we
have fixed developmental schemas, preconceived ideas about the
meanings of particular fantasies or dreams, or assumptions about
what in the wide spectrum of the analyst's action will be relevant to
the patient, we cannot truly listen or hear.

In my experience, some women express "penis envy" (already, in
the literature, a concept that covers many fantasies, wishes, and beliefs) during some of the time when they are talking about their body,
sexuality, or gender. Penis envy may or may not be central to their
sense of gender or to their feelings and fantasies about their body or
sexuality, and gender and sexuality may or may not be central to their
construction of self or to the conflicts and fantasies that emerge in our
work together. Some women construct a sense of pleasure, identity,
or bodily integrity primarily from an image of and fantasies about
their female genital anatomy. Some men experience women as ter-
rifying engulfers; others are more likely to fear humiliation or castration by other men. Some women are afraid that achievement will
leave them alone and lonely; others believe that it gives them a
welcome sense of autonomy and pleasure. But in each of these cases,
the same qualifiers and caveats that I suggest about penis envy apply.
Knowing how Jessica Benjamin, Sigmund Freud, Melanie Klein,
Karen Horney, Judith Kestenberg, Elizabeth L. Mayer, Phyllis Tyson,
and other writers have described these and other dynamics situates

them and makes them recognizable as patterns. Complementarily, when we find something that we have never read about or experienced with another patient, that is also interesting. We may tentatively begin to elaborate from it another pattern. This kind of clinical stance and theory differ, however, from claims that all girls or all boys must traverse certain experiences or fantasy organizations in order to achieve femininity or masculinity.

Such a formulation complements, rather than criticizes or dismisses, generalizations about gender psychology. We can probably generalize usefully about aspects of many women's and men's subjective senses of gender, about prevalent variations in subjective senses of gender, and about observed aspects of gender personality that may or may not be related to a person's subjective sense of gender. We can also generalize usefully about gender within particular cultural, racial-ethnic, and class groups and during different historical periods. In all such generalizations, however, we need to be careful that our claims do not go beyond our data base or that we specify the basis of our more generalizing speculations. As I have noted, generalization, certainly about features of personality or psychology, is implicitly statistical and rarely universal. Overgeneralizing or universalizing is never accurate, and, especially in a field so easily subsumed into unreflected-upon cultural assumptions, caution is warranted. In the arena of observed gender, we need to guard against overgeneralizing from our observations, selectively searching out gender differences, and ignoring observations of commonality between and within the sexes. We need also to guard against allowing the various patterns of observed gender difference to stand as the essential psychology of women or men.

We can see how the concept of pattern enables us to draw on ostensibly contradictory or mutually exclusive theories in the course of clinical work and theorizing. At one time, we preconsciously rely on object-relations theories, focusing in our minds on how the transference-countertransference expresses parent-child patterns of interaction, fantasies mutually created in potential space, particular patterns of affective communication, attunement, and identifications, not just as these patterns and fantasies directly express unconscious gender, but as they involve parents and primary others whose initially nongendered status has come subsequently to include their gender. At another time, like Kleinians, we notice in our patients gender-inflected projective and introjective constructions of greedy, loving, paranoid, hate-filled, envious, and other fantasies about parental bodies. At still another, we find ourselves paying attention, as would a classical analyst, to unconscious understandings about genital and reproductive anatomy, often based on infantile fantasies of desire and harm, on what one has and what one is missing, or on defenses against these fantasies. Finally, we become French theorists as we note how linguistic and cultural meanings of gender and sexual difference have been transmitted and created unconsciously and consciously and have been intrapsychically appropriated and transformed.

A brief look at my own earlier work (Chodorow, 1978) can elucidate the concept of pattern. This work was a generalizing argument. I attend especially to observed gender (I generalize about gender differences in constructions of self and internal self-object constellations) and perhaps less to subjective gender (the sense of femininity or masculinity, though I do focus on the unconscious internal world and sense of self that underlie many women's sense of self as maternal). I attend to commonalities that seem, from my research and observation, to characterize the mother-daughter and mother-son relationships and to prevalent patterns in female and male constructions of self and gender. I summarize a number of individual processes of self-construction and reconstruction, abstracting particular aspects of complex subjectivities, unique and individual selves. My summary is a developmental generalization but also a rethinking of preoedipal and oedipal development in boys and girls and pre-oedipal and oedipal configurations and preoccupations in men and women. I argue that there are noticeable gender differences in the preoedipal relationship—that is, supposedly before the differentiation of gender. My initial questions concern the psychological effects on daughters (sons had been better studied by previous investigators) of being cared for primarily by mothers (women). Today, I might rephrase this as what it means psychologically to be mothered by women. I describe how developing girls and boys construct their unconscious inner self-object world, their unconscious sense of self-boundaries (of connection to or difference from others), and their sense of gender. I also suggest that typically mothers, unconsciously as well as consciously, experience sons and daughters differently, because of their similarity or otherness in gender. As infant researchers have shown, the mother's unconscious fantasies and feelings are often communicated to the child, but the child herself creates the meaning of these communications, perhaps in typical ways.

My discovery was that these psychological processes contribute to the reproduction of women's mothering (both the capacities and the desires to mother) and other aspects of the ideology and organization of gender (for example, heterosexual asymmetries, ideologies of male superiority, devaluation of women, objectification and blame of mothers). It is, I claim, an account that describes some generalizable, empirically predictable or understandable features of personal gender and self-construction in a particular familial arrangement. This is not the same thing as claiming that gender ideologies are directly internalized or that society and culture precede individual psychological creativity. Indeed, although it can be read as an account of the social determinants or construction of the psyche, *The Reproduction of Mothering* can also be read as an account of how psyches produce social and cultural forms. In either direction, I describe empirically discovered, not theoretically deduced, connections.

Thus I do not seek to define as absolute cultural or psychological essences either femininity as opposed to masculinity or feminine gender identity as opposed to masculine gender identity. Nor do I imply that the object-relational constellations and preoccupations, psychic structure, processes, fantasies, and identifications that I describe differentiate all men from all women (I am careful to state that they do not). I generalize, I believe usefully, about the ways that many women and men operate psychologically and experience and define their selves. My goal is to explain prevalent observed gender differences in psychological life and personality without relying on biology, without centering on genital difference, and without assuming that women are failed men.

Such generalizations are useful to the extent that they speak to any particular individual's experience, help clinicians, or serve as guides for interpreting literature and biographies. *The Reproduction of Mothering* seems to have served all these purposes. According to such pragmatic criteria, my previous work seems to have captured for many women fundamental facets of experience and self, and to this extent it seems to hold truth value, to describe aspects of at least some women's and men's psychologies. To the extent that my claims do not fit individuals or particular groups of people (we have to assume we are considering here such individuals' unconscious emotion-imbued fantasies and processes, not merely what they consciously think they know about themselves), they can be further specified to explain why, or modified through the addition of other psychological or social-cultural considerations or factors.[5]

I am trying to have it both ways, but I also believe that this both-and stance is, finally, the only empirically and epistemologically legitimate way to have it. We do not want to pigeonhole people (whether our patients, our friends, the subjects of our academic investigations, or ourselves) as I believe we do if we think that all women and men follow particular developmental lines and have to deal with particular anatomically based tasks to reach femininity or masculinity, or if we assume that there are normal women and men, with normative roles and normal sexual orientation, so that only deviations from these norms need explaining. But we do want to understand them.

I am taking the position here that nothing is noncontingent in female psychology, that subjective gender is always composed of multiple elements and stories that are themselves not fixed once and for all. This individual view of gender accords with contemporary clinical thinking, in which we pay attention to situationally created transferential meanings and unconscious projective fantasies in the here and now, to an unfolding psyche that is not fixed when a person enters therapy or analysis, and to the individual analyst-analysand relationship. It also accords with contemporary feminism. Clinical experience likewise documents the personal emotional and fantasy construction of individual gender and the individualized projective animations of cultural gender meanings. As the cases in the previous chapter show, people create their sense of gender by emotionally and conflictually charging recognizable cultural meanings, their personal experience, and their bodies with unconscious fantasy. Gender meanings as we observe them are finally articulated in language, but this language only approximates an inner psychic reality that is emotional, partially conscious, fragmentary, and expressed in disconnected thoughts.

Yet, without thinking that all women differ from all men in certain ways or that all women must traverse the same path to end up at the same necessary femininity, we can nonetheless point toward aspects of intrapsychic experience that with some regularity seem to go into constructions of gendered subjectivity. Clinical experience documents both the multiplicity and the variability of individual constructions of gender and indicates some of the axes of definition and emotional tonality that different individuals may bring to their own gender construct. The examples I have described demonstrate many contributions to the sense of personal gender—feelings and fantasies about parents and their relationship to the child, feelings and fantasies about sexual anatomy and desire, consciously held beliefs, beliefs about beliefs that should be held, overall emotional tonalities, and personal animations of gender.

A uniquely constituted inner object world of unconscious fantasies—emotionally charged projective and introjective stories or protostories about aspects of self, mother, father, and other primary figures, observation of them, comparison of them with one another and with other women and men—forms a primary ingredient in anyone's personal, subjective gender. To elaborate on my earlier example, *The Reproduction of Mothering* focused on the mother-daughter relationship and argued for its importance in the female psyche. I noted patterns in mothers' unconscious experience of sons and daughters that helped to create differently constructed inner object worlds and differently formed self-boundaries in men and women.

But it is also the case that the mother-daughter relationship, although almost always important in the female (daughter's *and* mother's) psyche, will be projectively and introjectively animated in individual, particularized ways. Unconscious fantasy constructions and symbolizations of self and mother (or daughter) are not all alike. For individual women, or at different times in a life cycle or over the course of an analysis, the mother can symbolize nurturance or its rejection, an angry or welcoming breast, intimacy or fear of intimacy, guilt at independence or resentment at dependence, passivity or activity, aggression or submission, attraction to or fear of female genitality or anatomy, and many other issues. (We probably will also find prevalent individual and cultural animations of self and mother within different cultural groups.)[6] These unconscious and conscious fantasies can be linked with projective animations of cultural gender in many ways, through images of wifehood or motherhood, through fantasies about giving and the breast, and through images of domination and submission or purity and impurity. These are *some* aspects of the intrapsychic relationship that tend to be psychologically symbolized, accorded emotional and fantasy meaning, and incorporated into the sense of gender. I list them at some length to emphasize both prevalent patterns and the fact that we cannot predict with certainty when it comes to understanding anyone's inner object world and constructions of self in that world.

I do not think that "oedipal" or "preoedipal" does justice either to the overwhelming power of and individual variation within different daughters' guilts, rages, feelings of loyalty and disloyalty, wishes to protect and repair, or sexual desires for their mother or father, or to their relationships to the parents and the way these relationships affect their sense of gendered self. Several of my patients, for instance, fear that if they make their own choices or act on their own desires, they will destroy their mother. But in each patient this fantasy is embedded in and related to an otherwise individually constructed psyche. Both the fantasy and the dominant feelings it evokes, whether of anxiety, anger, guilt, sadness, loss, or fear of falling apart, vary. This variability contrasts with psychoanalytic tendencies to reduce the mother to one particular symbolization—for example, "the" holding environment, or "the" breast, or "the" symbol of castration. It is not universally the case that the mother's lack is necessarily contrasted with the father's phallus, or her baby-gestating capacities with *his* lack. Variation applies also to the place of the father in intrapsychic gender, and to other people who have played a significant role in a person's life (I am thinking of patients who grew up with several primary female caretakers and of others who had many siblings).

The gender meanings of family members go well beyond explicit or implicit gender messages. They derive from the totality of the mutual creation of inner and outer worlds and the defensive and creative splitting that go into development and selfhood. Affects significantly imbue the relationship to a parent and the gender imagery created in relation to him or her. If a mother seems depressed or ineffectual, this tonality lends partial meaning to femininity and to conscious and unconscious senses of and fantasies about womanliness (in any or all of its many aspects—sexuality, maternal identifications, sense of self, competence, power, powerlessness, and so forth). If a father is experienced as domineering, or exciting but absent, gender meanings also develop accordingly.

The senses of femininity or masculinity do not come directly from the parent who is female or male, respectively. Daughters and sons can also experience their father's "femininity" or their mother's "masculinity," and this experiencing itself can take many forms—for example, the affective communication of unconscious parental cross-identifications or unconscious parental cross-labeling of or fantasies about the child. The senses of gender might involve a conscious or preconscious sense that some parental behavior crosses traditional gender lines—say, that of a Marine sergeant mother, a cross-dressing father, a father who helps with child care, or two lesbian mothers. Children may also infer that others (teachers, neighbors, grandparents, clinicians) believe that a particular parent's personality or behavior crosses gender.

Any gender-related category (man, woman, mother, father, sister, brother, femininity, masculinity) gains meaning not just from language but from personally experienced emotion and fantasy in relation to a person connected to that label. Children first observe gender-specific behaviors, sexed anatomy, and genital difference in daily routines, before they understand gender categorizations (de Marneffe, 1997). Each observation or experience, as well as the settings in which language develops, is itself accorded fantasy meaning and has emotional resonance. Integrating and coordinating all of these perceptions lead to primary gender categorizations. Gender and genital concepts are thus affected by the unconscious and conscious gender interpretations and identities of parents and caretakers and the child's interpretation and understanding of them. Any linguistic categorizations pertaining to those concepts will carry personal emotional meanings that vary widely, according to the individual.

The internal gendered world is not fixed once and for all in early development. Gender transferences and fantasies and the emotional tonalities that accompany them in the clinical encounter demonstrate the life cycle, day-to-day and even moment-to-moment shifting of gender and its varying salience and complexity, as different elements in the gendered sense of self become important and as gender itself assumes more or less salience in a current period of transference. At one moment in a session, an early experience of incest may be most prominent; at another, attachment to the mother; at another, idealization of the father. In work with one woman, now the controlling, intrusive mother may be central to the creation of gender, now the dominant father, now the excited little girl, now the one humiliated by her excitement. In treatment of a man, now the swaggering little boy expresses himself, now the fearful one, now the boy excited by his triumphant possession of his mother, now the boy afraid of engulfment or longing for his father. A single identification or relationship, a particular sexual imaging, may bear a variety of relational themes and fantasized, evoked, or memorialized experiences.

From infancy throughout life, psychoanalysis suggests, bodily experience, arousal, and changes, including and especially sexual-genital-reproductive experiences, are likely to be felt with intensity— are likely, in a sense, to demand psychological meaning and to involve strong affects (of exhilaration, anxiety, anger and destructiveness, fear of disintegration, calm, well-being, or envy) that need to be managed. These dynamic interpretations and transformations of bodily experience and anatomy form another component of personal gender. Fantasies and feelings about sexual-genital body parts and experiences are also likely to be culturally elaborated, and part of that elaboration usually involves gender.

Gendered subjectivity for most people thus includes feelings and fantasies about sexual anatomy and desire, but I have found that we cannot predict what their meaning will be. Further, the centrality and content of such feelings in any person's overall construction of gender and sexuality will vary. Again, we have universals, patterns, and individuality: all people make psychological meaning of their bodies and bodily experience, and we can find prevalent patterns within these meanings, yet there is nothing automatic or self-evident about them.

For Freud, subjective gender derived first and foremost from genital anatomy and centered on genital difference. Psychoanalytic theories of gender thus built on Freud's focus on the presence or absence of the penis. Almost immediately, other analysts made clear that the girl's or woman's fantasies of her own inner and outer genitals were extremely significant and not secondary to her fantasies about the penis. Later analysts began to document the importance to many women of menarche, menstruation, and pregnancy (even more recently, of menopause). Kleinians expanded on Freud's work in stressing the psychic significance of the "primal scene"—fantasies of parental intercourse and the mother's pregnancies. Each of these developments remains a part of bodily experience, but each expands and transforms what is significant in bodily experience and enables a more contingent and individualized account of how fantasies and emotions about sexual anatomy, bodily experience, and desire may develop and change. Thus, although it seems hard to find a mother for whom pregnancy and lactation are not psychologically important (not to mention a former child for whom the breast, in its broad Kleinian sense, is not psychologically important), maternal identifications and fantasies vary widely. Among nonmothers I have treated, some feel their lives to center on the issue of possible pregnancy; for others, this question pales before other important issues and conflicts. It may be only with the great rise in rates of breast cancer that we have begun to see how important breasts are to many women's sense of self, sexuality, and gender—to paraphrase (and turn on its head) a distinction made in the case of penis envy, to recognize the difference between wanting the breast libidinally (orally) and wanting it as part of one's own body.

Within these particularized projective and introjective trajectories, gendered anatomical meanings do not necessarily create or oppose masculinity and femininity. In a single woman patient, one day her own breasts, the next day her mother's, are a topic of rage or hope. The following week, pregnancy is on her mind. Two months later, she is preoccupied with thoughts and feelings about her vagina. Next, she dreams about her brother's penis. For any one patient, and for the range of patients, these anatomical preoccupations generate a variety of symbolizations and fantasy constructions and a number of axes of sexual difference. Fantasies, for example, about the anatomically male as opposed to female may at one moment compare father ·and mother; at another, penis and vagina. The comparison might be with regard to presence or absence: penis and no penis, breasts and no breasts. For other patients' imaging of genital anatomy, small and big may be a more crucial difference than male and female. For K, described in the previous chapter, the male-female anatomical difference is irrelevant by comparison with her sense of the intensely shameful disparity between her own little-girl genitals and her mother's large, womanly genitals. I think of another patient for whom her mother's body was a subject of great disgust by comparison with her own pleasurable little-girl body. Big versus little and masculinity versus femininity may fuse, as in a man's sense of being a little boy with a little penis with his big woman analyst with big breasts, or in a woman's sense of being a little girl with a little vagina with a big man analyst with a big penis and hair on his chest. (I have also begun to notice clinically how ethnic, religious, national, and racial characterizations and identities can stand in for gendered anatomy and vice versa.) I take issue here, then, with the continuing tradition in psychoanalysis to assume inevitable meanings for female or male anatomy or to regard the character of female or male sexuality as self-evident.

This does not mean that body feelings are entirely without pattern. Patterns may emerge partially from anatomy itself (it may require less unconscious work to fantasize nursing if one has breasts, or complex insides if one has a vaginal opening, but this has not stopped some men from having nursing or bodily receptive fantasies, and has not led all women to have them). In all cases, moreover, bodily and sexual fantasies are certainly affected by parental treatment and unconscious parental messages. Culture also influences the construal of bodily processes; E. Martin (1987), for example, shows that American women have different conceptions and experiences of menstruation depending on whether they are middle-class or working-class, and many American women writers from racial or ethnic minorities describe the profound effect that the beauty standards of a white culture have on even little girls' sense of feminine body. In cautioning Western analysts about cultural assumptions and ideals concerning bodily gender, the Indian psychoanalyst Sudhir Kakar (1995) contrasts Western classical statues of muscular, lean gods and men with Hindu and Buddhist images of rounded masculine gods with incipient breasts.

Because, among the different factors of self, object, and body that I have described, each person makes some factors more significant than others, we can conceptualize for each individual a prevalent animation of personal-cultural gender. In any analysis, discovering (and creating) this personal animation of gender—the dominant axes and feeling tones around which a patient organizes her subjective gender—will be important. We will also find, as I suggest above, that for some people, their femininity or masculinity, however it is created, will be a central area of conflict and will be central to transference-countertransference; for others it will be less significant. For some women (we can think back to the case examples in Chapter 3), being female contrasts with being male, whether a man or a boy, a father or a brother. For others, it evokes a desperate, driven hunger for men. In this latter case, the male-female contrast is still there, but the woman wants to have a man rather than to be one. For some, the idea of femininity is predominantly associated with the mother who weeps or the mother who is yearned for; for others the contrast is between being an adult woman and being a little girl. In none of these cases does gender have one and only one meaning: different gender meanings can be animated at different times. But as an analysis progresses, gender will organize itself into fantasies and themes that are more dominant and more subordinate.

Prevalent animations of gender involve particular affective constellations—emotions that may not be consciously or unconsciously construed as gendered but that nonetheless give characteristic emotional tonality to the sense of gender. Feelings about anatomy and bodily adequacy, about self, or about parents, may be more or less directly linked with this emotional tonality. Global affects like anxiety or depression may invest a woman's sense of gender (Mayer, 1995, makes this point), and I have also found that more defined emotions seem to affect different women's prevalent animations of gender. Envy or anger, for example, may charge fantasies about mother and self or about father and self. One patient focuses on an anger at her mother and a preference for her father that, while they may have helped her achieve professional success, weakened and destroyed her mother. Another envies and resents her mother's flirtatiousness: her mother even flirts with this woman's boyfriends, making the woman herself feel dumpy, inadequate, and furious. For a third, anger, and her father's anger in particular, describe gender; neither shame, guilt, nor sexual anatomy seems salient.

In my experience, shame seems central to many women's feelings and fantasies about mother, self, and gender, and shame and disgust often color women's sense of bodily self. For K, shame about her inadequate female body compared with that of her mother affects gendered subjectivity; for B, shame about her mother's rundown house, inability to hold down a job, and unattractive boyfriends figures much more prominently than guilt toward her mother, and female sexuality, especially maternal sexuality, is disgusting and shameful in its desperation. B does not fantasize, as some other women do, that she can protect her mother, and she does not express a perception of her mother's entrapment (whether this entrapment is a plight of her own psychological making or a product of a sexist culture). She expresses only repudiation and horror.

A woman's prevalent animation of gender may be characterized by guilt—guilt for leaving home, for being professionally successful, for surviving mother or father, or for having harmed them. I have noted a particularly intense form of guilt in some women who have grown up in classically patriarchal families, expressed in a behavior I have come to call "weeping for the mother." I borrow the term "classic patriarchy" from Kandiyoti (1988), who uses it to describe societies like those of North Africa, the Muslim Middle East, China, and India, which have explicitly, father-dominant kinship systems with strong ideological values and religious undergirding, usually accompanied by forms of exclusion and restriction of females such as purdah or veiling. If we refer in particular to a culturally and religiously transmitted belief that marriage as an institution should be totally controlled by the husband and to the explicit teaching and modeling of female subservience, I might include in the classification of classic patriarchies Mediterranean peasant societies and

Latino cultures as well. From the psychodynamic point of view of the daughter, this situation contrasts with the families of my European-American patients, who do not accord central importance in their descriptions of their families to an explicitly differential valuation of men and women or an observation of maternal subservience.[7]

N cannot stop crying when she thinks of her mother. Her mother was always sad and seemingly helpless, dependent on a patriarchal, angry husband who ordered her around. She images her mother at home alone, dutifully cooking meals, waiting for her husband, crying. N's physical pleasures and independent activities, like walking at night, seeing movies on her own, cooking treats and desserts just for herself, and having lovers, always remind her that her mother could not go out alone, had to cook regular meals, had no lovers before or after her marriage, and probably has had at best a marginally satisfying sex life with her husband. N feels sad and helpless that she cannot help her sad and helpless mother.

N's conscious construction of gender includes a strong feminism and anger at male privilege and societal sexism. She understands her feminism to be a result of her having grown up in an ideologically male-dominant family that explicitly valued her brothers over her and her sisters. She wanted a feminist analyst who recognized male dominance in society and culture and would see that they had caused N's problems. This shared belief was meant to be exempt from psychological exploration. More particularly, N expected that a feminist analyst would not blame N's mother for being passive and subservient but would understand this mother's inescapable helplessness in the face of a marital role and relationship she hated. A feminist would not pathologize N's mother's weeping.

But weeping for her mother and feeling sad and guilty about her interfere with N's own freedom. Accordingly, N also found herself worrying: having chosen an analyst who, in her view, would be sympathetic to her mother could mean that this analyst might not fully accept N's own wants and needs. "I go back and forth," she says. "Children have intense needs, but it isn't my mother's fault." She is caught in a dilemma: How can she stop feeling guilty and sad toward her mother, free herself from her mother, and have her own life, while at the same time not blame but understand her mother? But through maternal teaching and modeling, this mother was, after all, also the agent of so much of N's sense of female inferiority.

S, from a similar family and a different classically patriarchal culture, feels sad over her mother's entrapment in a marriage with a dominating husband who controls everything. Like N, S tempers her feelings of sadness somewhat by feeling strong anger at her mother's situation. Unlike N, she also mitigates her feelings of sadness and anger by identifying, albeit at the cost of conflict and guilt, with the men in her family who dominate. Her substantial achievements are part of this flight to masculine identifications, but she hopes at the same time that her accomplishments will rebound to her mother and give her mother as well as herself strength. She weeps for herself as well as for her mother, recognizing her own dependence on and search for confirmation from men.

P, another daughter from a classically patriarchal family, cries as her mother cried, is miserable as her mother was miserable. She does not know why her mother cried or why she herself has to. P's mother and grandmother told sad, sad stories of their lives. P's grandmother was sent away to school at an early age; her life, she told her grand-daughter, was very sad. According to P, this sadness was passed on to her daughter, and this daughter, P's mother, wept at everything—for her own mother and for her father, who had died when P, the grand-daughter, was three. Thirty years later, P cannot stop crying about her grandmother's life and her grandfather's death. P's mother wanted her daughter to listen to the mother's sad feelings all the time. In turn, P wants her husband and me to listen to her sad feelings all the time.

By contrast, as P sees it, her father was always cheerful, the life of the party. She eventually acknowledges what she has denied, that if things didn't go the way he wanted, her father became controlling and furious. Also, he did not want to hear about personal problems or anything that was amiss. She also reluctantly acknowledges that her mother was always busy, managing a house, household help, and several children, and taking care of her own mother. But these acknowledgments are easily reburied as P returns to the image of her exciting father planning excursions, playing with her in the water, and giving his energy to the family, in contrast to her mother, always crying about her unhappy life and the unhappy life of her mother.

Since Freud, there have been within psychoanalysis tensions between claims about women as they were universalized and essentialized in the developmental theory and the varied clinical observations about women in all their difference, individuality, and specificity. Similarly, contemporary feminism generalizes about inequality and power but points to the differences among women as well as to the contradictory, multiple, and contextualized particularities of any one person's gendered and sexual subjectivity. The fluidity and changeability of emotionally charged transferences in clinical experience make clear the unique character of any person's gendered subjectivity. There is no generic femininity or masculinity derived from an unproblematic cognitive fact of gender or gender-role identity, from a genitally derived concept established either in the second year or in the oedipal period, or from a psychological enactment of prevailing political or cultural gender concepts.

By staying with the clinical, we discover that any particular woman's or man's gender is a continuously invoked project in which self, identity, body images, sexual fantasy and desire, fantasies about parents, cultural stories, and conflicts about intimacy, dependency, and nurturance are constructed. To characterize fully any person's

gendered psyche, we need to give an individual developmental, transferential, and cultural account. We discover that cultural meanings of
gender are experienced in personally particularized ways, projectively
accorded with emotional meanings and unconscious fantasy associations, and transferentially recreated and changed, and we discover
that each person's gender also comprises the individual emotional
tonalities that accompany particular conflictual, defensive, and re-
parative fantasies. All aspects of a particular person's psychological
make-up join together to animate his or her gendered subjectivity
with unique feeling.

I suggest that there is not *a* psychology of gender but many
psychologies of gender. Both the incontrovertible observation that
our patients (and we) inevitably think about, feel, and fantasize gender and our observations of repeated patterns of gender construction
need to be uncoupled from our assumption that we always know
what this thinking, feeling, and fantasy or its underlying basis will be.
We want to hold on to the clinical and theoretical truth that gender
remains a useful category for psychological thinking while also holding on to the clinically observed personal uniqueness of the individual. Continual attentiveness to the psychoanalytic tendencies to overgeneralize, universalize, and essentialize in the areas of gender and
sexuality and to allow preconsciously held cultural assumptions to
infuse theory, along with continual attention to clinical individuality,
will help achieve these goals.

Neither an exclusively psychological account nor an exclusively
political or cultural account fully characterizes individual gender. A
clinical perspective documenting the individual emotion and fantasy
in constructions of personal gender provides evidence against psychoanalytic and everyday cultural assumptions that gender is self-
evident, that certain personality traits universally differentiate the
sexes, that biology determines gendered self, that the organization of

gender is unvarying historically or cross-culturally, or even that gender is somehow more fundamental than other aspects of social location or identity. It provides also evidence against feminist assumptions that gender and gendered subjectivity are exclusively historical, cultural, or political concepts and processes. A feminist perspective is essential in arguing against the assumptions that the psychic reality of gender is unaffected by cultural meaning or normative social organization or that genders are monolithic or invariable. Each person's sense of gender fuses personal meanings created psychodynamically and idiosyncratically from within and cultural meanings presented from without.

PART 3　CULTURE

5 Selves and Emotions as Personal and Cultural Constructions

> Through "interpretation," cultural meanings are transformed. And through "embodiment," collective symbols acquire the power, tension, relevance, and sense emerging from our individuated histories. . . . Histories of experience, and so of affect, are essential to all thought.
>
> MICHELLE Z. ROSALDO
> "TOWARD AN ANTHROPOLOGY OF SELF AND FEELING"

> Cultural descriptions should seek out force as well as thickness.
>
> RENATO ROSALDO
> "GRIEF AND A HEADHUNTER'S RAGE"

IN THIS BOOK I CLAIM THAT PSYCHOANALYSIS IS FIRST AND foremost an account and a theory of personal meaning. I explore the implications of such a view for psychoanalysis and for those who think about cultural meaning. Social and cultural thinkers from a variety of fields have tended to assume that cultural meanings are the primary determiners or shapers of experience and the self. Some take a more constructionist approach and claim that people create meaning by drawing on available webs of cultural meaning, but even these theorists seem to assume that whatever meanings are invented or created in this way come entirely from a common cultural corpus or stock. If they imply or describe motivation, it is in relation to a seemingly conscious strategic rationality or institutionally embedded practice.[1] I have been arguing, using gendered subjectivity as an example, that gendered meanings are personal psychodynamic creations and not only cultural constructions or impositions. My argument, I suggest, applies to cultural meaning in general. The demonstration that we create personal emotional meaning from birth throughout life challenges and potentially affects all culturally determinist or exclusively cultural accounts. In Part 3, I continue to investigate the relations between personal meaning and cultural meaning, of which in Part 2 gender provides one special example. I argue that cultural meanings that matter to us are created and experienced psychodynamically as well as linguistically or in terms of a cultural or discursive lexicon.

I develop my argument through a reading of some debates and developments within anthropology—that social science whose project has been the study of cultural meaning. In this chapter, I consider representative accounts of a culturally determinist anthropology of self and feeling (I use this phrase following Rosaldo, 1984). I argue that fully to understand cultural meaning in general, and cultural selves and feelings in particular, anthropologists need to theorize and investigate personal meaning. In the next chapter, I examine what I find to be particularly useful psychoanalytic anthropological efforts to address meaning and the creation of selves and subjectivity. Part 3 concludes with afterthoughts on culture in the consulting room, in which I consider the bearing anthropological insights might have on the clinical situation.

I have several reasons for selecting anthropology as the site for a consideration of personal and cultural meaning, and there are also several reasons that I should have been hesitant about taking on such a project. The latter reduce basically to the fact that anthropology, although it was an early intellectual love and practice, is not my professional field. When I provide, therefore, an introductory overview of the developments that led to the anthropology of self and feeling, I am well aware that it expresses my own sense-making endeavor as I sought to understand this complex field. My goal here is to provide a necessary context for people not already versed in the field of psychological anthropology and to draw attention to a range of ideas and authors who should be read by all those interested in cultural and intrapsychic meaning. Similarly, when I choose in this chapter particular exemplary texts in the anthropology of self and feeling, or put forth in the next chapter an account of psychoanalytic anthropology, I do so not in an attempt to be comprehensive but with the particular argument of this book in mind. I do not intend to provide an exhaustive review either of the anthropology of self and feeling or of psychoanalytic anthropology—that project has been admirably carried out (see, e.g., Bock, 1994; Ingham, 1996; LeVine, 1982, 1996; Paul, 1989; and Suarez-Orozco, Spindler, and Spindler, 1994).

Having issued these caveats, I turn to the reasons for ignoring them. To begin with, from early in the development of the field there has been anthropological interest in the relations of culture and psyche, an interest that links the substantive concerns of anthropology with those of psychoanalysis. Anthropology is thus not only that social science whose central project has been the study of cultural meaning, including in recent years the cultural meanings of selves and feelings; it is also the only social science in which there has been a continuous (though certainly nonhegemonic) tradition of psychoanalytically inspired inquiry. Psychoanalytic anthropology has developed more extensively than any other field, including psychoanalysis, a fine-tuned account of the complex intertwining of personal and cultural meaning, while also remaining cognizant of the complexity of both the intrapsychic and the cultural. Throughout the history of anthropology a great many studies—ethnographic biographies, cultural autobiographies, fictive cultural autobiographies, life histories, testimonies, books about myths and dreams in a particular culture, and reflexive ethnographies—have described passion, feeling, internal conflict, uncertainty and interpersonal struggle, personal interpretations of cultural fantasies, stories, and life history accounts, and the personal costs of cultural patterns and expectations—all documenting if not theorizing about individual psychodynamic personhood in different cultures.

An extended consideration of why anthropology has been more continuously concerned with the psyche than other social sciences and why it is now the only contemporary social science with a flourishing psychoanalytic subfield falls beyond the scope of my inquiry here, but my guess is that two elements are central. First, the immutable personhood and subjectivity of members of other cultures must always help to shape and disrupt any investigation an anthropologist may attempt, however routinized (including the disruptions of taken-for-granted interactive and cultural expectations faced by the cross-cultural ethnographer, known colloquially as culture shock). Although most anthropologists take a cultural approach to meaning and experience, many aspects of fieldwork cry out for introspective, psychodynamic investigation of both the other and the self, and many nonpsychoanalytic anthropologists express an interest in the personhood of their cultural subjects. Second, as I have noted, meaning is extensively theorized about and central to the anthropological project, whereas it is on the fringe of the other social sciences.

These features also characterize some of the qualitative sociology traditions. I believe that sociologists may have been protected from the insistence and disruptiveness of personal individuality because researchers have a language and culture in common with interviewees and ethnographic subjects, because sociology places perhaps greater reliance on macroexplanatory concepts, and because a field that focuses first and foremost on social structures and institutions does not immediately demand that attention be paid to personal subjectivity in the way that the study of culture does. It is nonetheless within the tradition of qualitative sociology that the sociology of emotions (Hochschild, 1983) arose and that attention is paid to disruptions of the taken-for-granted (Garfinkel, 1967).[2] By contrast, most of sociology insists that individuality is not relevant and is in fact opposed to the sociological approach.

The few applied psychoanalytic studies carried out in the past in sociology (they do not exist in the present) tended by contrast to be deductive and generalized investigations that related macrosocial dynamics and structures (capitalism, modern society, society in general) to personality or values (Slater, 1968, is an exception here). Personality here was for the most part either deduced from the macrostructure in question or induced from a generalized, nonclinical reading of psychoanalysis. Alternatively, psychoanalytically informed social science developed through operationalizing and quantifying psychoanalytic and other psychological variables (such as national character studies).

There are numerous other reasons to consider anthropology among the social sciences in an investigation of personal and cultural meaning. As several commentators have noted (see especially Herdt, 1981; Kracke, 1987a, 1992; Kracke and Herdt, 1987; Obeyesekere, 1991), the methods of observation, methodologies, and epistemologies of psychoanalysis and anthropology are remarkably similar. On the most mundane level, members of both fields see them, like other social sciences, as empirical or data based. Their primary data source—what is observed and interpreted—consists of people like the observer. Although theoretical debate is of course important, practitioners in both fields recognize the persistent need for an appeal to the evidence or for a generating of further evidence. In this way, both fields differ from interpretive fields in the humanities (although some anthropologists currently believe that cultural meanings and cultures can be analyzed as texts and some Lacanian psychoanalysts think the psyche can be as well).

Both anthropological ethnography and psychoanalysis begin from and are unavoidably centered in the intersubjective encounter between people, as the ethnographer and treating analyst respectively try to understand and elicit the native's point of view or the analysand's unconscious thoughts, wishes, feelings, and inner world. They are thus accounts given in one relationship (that of the respective professional communities) of interactions and accounts developed in another (the ethnographic or analytic encounter). Indeed, in both fields training is based on intensive practical immersion, and professional claims to legitimacy are judged on the basis of this experience, in the one case ethnographic, and in the other clinical. (The fields also differ in the treatment of this immersion: analysts in training take the role of both analysand and analyst and meet regularly with a supervisor. A premium is put on the ability to recognize and analyze one's personal and professional difficulties in doing the work. The initial immersion for ethnographers, by contrast, has much more the character of a challenging rite of passage to be faced alone and with fortitude.) There is no psychoanalysis or anthropology apart from this interpersonal encounter, an encounter that draws unavoidably on the investigator's powers of empathy as well as observation. Both fields have come increasingly to emphasize the central participatory role and influence of the practitioner, who is no longer seen as a detached scientific observer. They now recognize that what comes to be understood about the subject (culture or psyche) is a product created within a particular encounter or set of encounters. In this encounter, both fields have increasingly emphasized the real emotional effects on the investigator: anthropologists who are not psychologically inclined write of culture shock; those who are psychologically attuned, of anxiety, fear, and anger discovered through self-observation, introspection, and observation of transferences that emerge in relation to informants or to the culture as a whole; psychoanalysts speak of the widened field of countertransference and the role of the analyst's subjectivity as well as objectivity in the analytic encounter. Because of their intersubjective empirical base, these fields also differ from the philosophy of mind—another field of inquiry currently seen as a cognate to psychoanalysis.

Modes of explanation and debates about these modes also run parallel in the two disciplines. In thinking about the data of experience and inquiry, interpretation is central: what is said is not taken at face value but is thought to signify organized patterns of thought and practice that may be near to experience but are not necessarily immediately available to the subject. Beyond this, similar debates go on in both fields about whether interpretation is enough. In recent years, the prevailing position in anthropology has been pro-interpretation, whether seen as thick description, hermeneutics, or symbolic analysis, although a minority view continues to argue that anthropology is an objective explanatory science. In psychoanalysis, the emphasis is reversed: claims persist that psychoanalysis is a form of hermeneutic inquiry, but a countervailing claim that psychoanalysis is a natural or medical science (or a special science—"our" science) based on testing and falsification of hypotheses predominates. These arguments have their parallel in debates about the practitioner's role as observer, participant observer, or engaged intersubjective actor.

Finally, both fields reflect an epistemological tension between clinical or ethnographic individuality and generalization. In my chapters on childhood and on gender, I examine the contradictions between psychoanalytic case methodology and the universalizing and overgeneralizing found in psychoanalytic theory. Anthropology, too, focuses on the particular cultural case and has a methodology that depends on the rich elaboration of clinical cases, that of ethnography. But, I will suggest that, even as anthropologists argue vigorously for cultural relativism and against universalization, generalization, or the imposition of Western cultural understandings on other cultures, they often introduce other universalisms—unquestioned cultural determinism or poststructuralist assumptions about the ubiquity of power and resistance, for example. Like clinical psychoanalysts, ethnographers describe particular individuals by building their accounts on conversations with "key informants," and the discourse they describe is particular, in that it is historically and interpersonally situated. Yet in generalizing about the motivations for and meanings of cultural practices, they often pass over either individuals who do not fit their generalizations, or exceptions and variations within these processes, in favor of a description of a culture (however contradictory and multifaceted) as a whole. Individuality, personal idiosyncrasy, quirkiness, and difference drop out (or, in recent times, are translated into cultural multilayering, shifting, and fragmentation).

Along with these similarities, psychoanalysis and anthropology can both benefit from consideration of the contributions of the other field. Like other social scientists who make assumptions, in their theories and findings, about human nature and human motivation, anthropologists need to address individual experience and agency, and one major component of that experience and agency is psychodynamic. Theories whose approaches to agency and practice assume only conscious, rational, strategic goals and reasoning do not adequately comprehend individual motivation. Unlike their colleagues, psychoanalytic anthropologists certainly recognize the life of the unconscious, but, like some psychoanalysts (as I describe especially in Chapters 2 and 4), some psychoanalytic anthropologists do not pay enough attention in their ethnographic work to individuality, and others tend, in my view, to argue too strongly for universalized bioevolutionary and bioinstinct-based theories about the psychic contents of fantasy or psychic structure.

On their side, psychoanalysts have been unable to develop an adequate or rich enough understanding of "external" or "outer" reality, in opposition to "psychic" reality (for an early claim to this effect, see Parsons, 1952, 23). This residual concept, seen as the sensuous physical world, parents, parental prohibitions and restrictions, or globally as society or culture, is nonetheless central to most psychoanalytic approaches. As I have suggested in previous chapters, an impoverished view of external reality is responsible for the widespread and an unwitting tendency in psychoanalytic writings and practice to build culturally and socially specific norms into universal necessity or to think that anything cultural or social is built on something more basic and universal.

The psychoanalytic question about how culture gets inside the head was asked first by Freud, who described the prescriptive and proscriptive expression of culture in his early accounts of the censor and later theorized this censor in his concept of the superego. Freud also, as is well known, addressed the relation of the psychic and the sociocultural (especially "culture" as a whole—civilization, group phenomena, or religion) in a number of works, including *Totem and Taboo, Group Psychology and the Analysis of the Ego, The Future of an Illusion, Civilization and Its Discontents,* and *Moses and Monotheism.* Freud's cultural writings of the late 1920s and 1930s, along with the psychoanalytic Marxism of Reich and the Frankfurt Institute and the contemporaneous cultural-school psychoanalysis of Horney, Fromm, and others, meshed closely during the same period with a vibrant psychoanalytically influenced culture and personality anthropology practiced by Margaret Mead, Ruth Benedict, Gregory Bateson, and others and the anthropologies of psychoanalysts like Géza Róheim and Abram Kardiner. These anthropologists, and anthropology in general, shared with psychoanalysis interests in personality, child development, family relationships, incest taboos, sexual behavior, religion, the nature of culture, symbols and meanings, and enculturation. Anthropologists have always been interested in the psyche in the field (thinking, mind, personhood, the self), though this has not necessarily entailed an interest in the psyches of individuals; for example, anthropologists in both strands of investigation I will discuss often interest themselves in collective representations that express or constitute patterns of thought or feeling. This interest has been exemplified in two largely autonomous and even antagonistic traditions within anthropological inquiry, traditions brought together in the anthropology of self and feeling. The first tradition focuses in the broadest sense on forms and content of thought or knowledge (how natives think and what they think about), the other on psychodynamics (originally, cultural personality).[3]

The first strand of anthropological thinking about the psyche or mind includes the work of founding fathers like Durkheim and Mauss, which undergirds the structural anthropologies of Lévi-Strauss, Leach, Douglas, and others, on the one hand, and the more Weberian symbolic anthropologies of Geertz and Turner, on the other. This strand (or these strands) of inquiry has an equivocal relation to psychoanalysis. On the one hand, it is explicitly cultural and explicitly antipsychoanalytic and antipsychological, rejecting application of Freud's clinical approach and concepts of personality to people in other cultures. On the other, like psychoanalysis, it makes universal claims about the structure of the mind, and it borrows heavily and often explicitly from Freud's interpretive method.

Thus, for example, just as Freud describes compromise formations as resolving contradictions and tensions within the psyche, Lévi-Strauss, Douglas, Leach, and other structural anthropologists pay special attention to contradictions and tensions among cultural elements and argue that cultural manifestations like rituals, myths, stories, and taboos attempt to resolve these contradictions.[4] In another example, Clifford Geertz, who takes a counterstance to "Western" psychological conceptions of the nature of the person, likens thick description and its forms of validation to "clinical inference" and "the clinical style of theoretical formulation" found in medicine and depth psychology (1973, 26). His best-known book is called, apparently with reference to Freud, *The Interpretation of Cultures.* Finally, Victor Turner's *Forest of Symbols* (1967) describes how emotions about bodies and bodily fluids—blood and milk, especially— provide the energy expressed in ritual and in ritual symbols, how emotion-laden initiation rites are a crucial means of connecting the individual with social practices. His concepts of liminality and anti-structure also seem to have psychological correlates. In "Encounter with Freud: The Making of a Comparative Symbologist" (1978), Turner reports that his rereading of Freud's *Interpretation of Dreams* enabled him to move beyond surface analyses of social structures and verbal behavior in Ndembu society to a recognition and understanding of nonverbal symbols. He discovered the multivocality or mul-tireferentiality of symbols, "sociocultural sublimation" (particular ritual processes and symbols express and condense typical affects, containing and transforming body imagery that has psychological meaning to the Ndembu collectivity), and conflict between cultural meanings of ritual symbolizations and the emotionally tinged mean-ings (what he calls conscious and unconscious cultural behavior) conveyed by related ritual behaviors. Turner's symbolic anthropology is thus extensively psychodynamic.

The second strand of investigation of the psyche in the field, especially prevalent in the United States, begins with a self-identified anthropology of culture and personality that is tied directly or in-directly to psychoanalysis. Within this literature, Benedict (1934) argues that cultures can be characterized as having a particular per-sonality which can be more or less healthy. Benedict bases her inves-tigations on an analysis of cultural practices and beliefs, and she characterizes individual cultures in global psychological terms. Al-though she focuses on cultural personality, however, it is unclear whether she is interested in the personalities of individuals within the culture. (Because of this contradiction, and because of her firm cultural determinism and holism, Benedict can also be seen as a forerunner of an American cultural anthropology that is explicitly nonpsychological.) The neo-Freudian psychoanalyst Kardiner (1939) also draws on accounts of cultural beliefs and practices, both to infer common aspects of individual psychology and to make the claim that through certain projective institutions—art, religion, myths, and so forth—societies express their basic cultural personality, itself a product of socialization under particular subsistence conditions. Thus, unlike Benedict, Kardiner, as a psychoanalyst, is directly interested in psychology itself.

Traditional anthropologists of culture and personality develop these ideas in related ways, with greater or lesser attention in specific instances to the personalities of members of the culture or to the personality of the culture itself. Mead (1928, 1935) and Bateson (1936) describe typical cultural personalities inferred from and expressing cultural preoccupations and modes (what Bateson, 1936, called ethos), and Benedict, Mead, Kardiner, and others also wrote about national character. (Stocking, 1986, provides a useful overview of culture and personality anthropology and contemporaneous neo-Freudian psychoanalysis.) As psychological anthropologists (a self-identification taken on by some in the culture and personality tradition) became influenced by more scientized notions and also wished to have direct personality data on individuals in other cultures, they turned to the use of standardized psychological testing (e.g., DuBois, 1944, Hallowell, 1955) or systematic observation of naturally occurring behavior, especially patterns of child rearing and children's behavior (e.g., Whiting, 1963; Whiting and Whiting, 1975). Others extended their investigations to how particular cultural practices serve psychological functions and resolve psychological problems. Clyde Kluckhohn (1944), for example, documented how a cultural belief system like witchcraft solved personal conflicts within a society by projecting them outward and into the complex of witchcraft ideas; John Whiting, Richard Kluckhohn, and Albert Anthony (1958) examined how male initiation rites resolved psychodynamic conflicts in masculine identity and socialization in cultures with particular family patterns; the sociologist Philip Slater (1968) developed a related argument to Whiting's for the case of Greek mythology and Greek family structure.

Although studies in psychological anthropology continued throughout the 1960s, the field lost influence and stature. Nonpsychological symbolic and structural anthropologists continued to be interested in the native's mind, but they saw this mind as cognitive, rational, strategy oriented, and culturally molded. They tended to dismiss or ignore the concerns of psychological anthropology and were especially critical of psychoanalysis and its anthropological applications. Their critique rested (and continues to rest) on a number of specific charges. They argue that psychoanalysis universalizes Western developmental stages and their fantasy content and assumes the existence of a universal family structure. Psychoanalysis is psychologically deterministic, reducing cultural and social forms to outcomes of childhood developmental crises or personality conflicts. Finally, cultural applications of psychoanalysis minimize cultural diversity and misrepresent culturally embedded meanings by decontextualizing them and applying to them universalized interpretive schemas. These critics insist by contrast on the sui generis, nonreducible nature of social and cultural forms and processes and the autonomy of cultural meanings. Thus, they criticize psychological and psychoanalytic anthropology for reducing cultural variety and conceptions of the psyche to exclusively Western terms and for ignoring indigenous psychological concepts and cultural context. They dismiss psychological testing, as well as cross-cultural comparisons that attempted to relate particular child-training practices statistically to particular cultural outcomes, not only for their Western origin and bias but also for what is seen as a simplistic scientism in a field that increasingly defines itself exclusively as an interpretive social science. They criticize the method of behavior observation not only for abstracting and categorizing culturally embedded practices but also for bypassing the meanings and subjectivity of those being studied.

As I see it, these divergent approaches to the psyche or mind in the field were forced to take account of each other's existence sometime in the 1970s and 1980s. Mutual recognition was spurred by a number of theoretical developments and led to the emergence of an anthropology of self and feeling. The theoretical developments I have in mind constitute, broadly, the movement that encompasses poststructuralism and deconstructionism and in particular the social-institutional and cultural poststructuralism of Foucault. Poststructuralism follows traditional structuralism in its assumptions about the autonomy of the cultural and the importance of language, even as it also argues, against an anthropological tradition of cultural holism, that cultures are complex, contingent, and historically evolving, and that they have no seamless wholeness. Poststructuralism argues for the multiple contradictions, rather than functional interrelations, among cultural elements and stresses the polysemy and multiple layering of cultural meanings. Poststructuralism's insistence on the power relations inherent in all cultural elements and practices also made it attractive to anthropologists politicized by the movements and theories of the 1960s. At the same time, poststructuralism makes central to its critique of structuralism structuralism's lack of a subject, thereby opening the way to consideration of the person or subject but taking the view, following Foucault, that the subject is discursively constructed or, following Bourdieu, moving to adopt a practice-theoretical perspective that focuses on a culturally meaningful, situationally embedded, strategic rationality. Practice and discourse also came together, as some anthropologists drew upon linguistic pragmatics. Finally, deconstructionism and poststructuralism provided the foundation for considering cultures as texts.

In the rest of this chapter, I examine three works that exemplify the anthropology of self and feeling—one text, by Geertz, that perhaps first secured its existence and two others, by Michelle Z. Rosaldo and Catherine Lutz, that could be said to have established the field. I conclude by considering a text by Renato Rosaldo that destabilized and disrupted this field from within. Although other anthropologists have studied self and emotion, I am considering here a self-defined and named field that is explicitly culturally determinist and anti-psychological. I chose these authors and texts neither because they are full of flaws or are the most up to date nor because no one before has made critiques similar to mine, but because they are in some sense classics and because they argue especially well, in some cases brilliantly, for a privileging of cultural and linguistic meaning in matters concerning the psyche.[5] I have chosen them also because, as I note above, the authors are social scientists and as such give us empirical evidence and not just assertion or argument. My ability to develop my critique, then, is due partly to what I have elsewhere (Chodorow, 1993) called the leakiness of case studies. Unlike research based on abstracted variables or theoretical arguments alone, the narrative and analytic complexity of good case accounts of all sorts (ethnographic, clinical, life historical, based on qualitative interviews, and so on) enables the reader to find that which the writer does not necessarily wish to foreground.

Finally, these texts are useful because, although my intent in this chapter is to describe the problems with an exclusively culturalist and linguistic view of the psyche, to the extent that these writers (and others whom they represent and influence) establish irrevocably (even if they let the part stand for the whole) that there is a cultural-linguistic contribution to self-construction and to the experience of emotions, they provide further evidence for the inextricable fusion of cultural and personal meaning. Thus, they offer an arena for extending my conclusions about cultural and linguistic constructions of gender and, as feminist and psychoanalytic theories of gender both contrast with and complement one another, they also contrast with and complement the psychoanalytic anthropology that I discuss in the next chapter.

The text that I believe helped to secure permission for cultural-symbolic anthropologists to develop an anthropology of self and feeling was Geertz's " 'From the Native's Point of View': On the Nature of Anthropological Understanding" (1974). In this paper, Geertz, considered perhaps the leading cultural theorist in anthropology, directly addressed the psychological—specifically, native concepts of the person. The essay was part of Geertz's interpretive anthropological project (Geertz, 1973) rather than a contribution to poststructural thinking or linguistic pragmatics, yet it would subsequently accord with both poststructuralist assumptions that culture or discourse creates subjectivity and the methods of linguistic pragmatics.[6] " 'From the Native's Point of View' " prefigured both the approach and the blind spots found in the anthropology of self and feeling.

In this essay, Geertz shows that peoples of different cultures have different concepts of self and personhood. He argues that Westerners have misconstrued their own particular and "rather peculiar" conception of the person as a privatized, psychological individual— "a bounded, unique, more or less integrated motivational and cognitive universe, a dynamic center of awareness, emotion, judgment, and action organized into a distinctive whole and set contrastively against other such wholes" (126)—as a universal empirical truth. He provides evidence by describing personhood in three cultures that he knows well. In Morocco, he claims, persons receive "identities" from the particularities of their tribe, village, location, and ethnicity, and personhood is relative to context: any particular interaction shapes itself around the most immediate identity criteria differentiating interactants. This "mosaic" of interaction enables people from different religions, ethnicities, and backgrounds to know how to relate to one another. Balinese personhood, to take another example, rests on cultural demands for a stylized surface public persona. Finally, in Java inner evenness is a central personal goal, and the self operates along the axes of inner-outer and refined-vulgar.

Geertz claims that in these non-Western cultural meaning systems, conceptions and experiences of personhood do not include or rest on privatized, personal, psychodynamic elements or a bounded individual. At the same time, he brackets and dismisses such aspects of self and personhood when he comes across them, implying that they are culturally—that is, with regard to "how the people who live there define themselves" (125)—and therefore personally irrelevant. In Bali, for example, a "public performance" might not work: "the personality—as we would call it but the Balinese, of course, not believing in such a thing, would not—of the individual will break through to dissolve his standardized public identity." In such an instance, "the immediacy of the moment is felt with excruciating intensity, and men become suddenly and unwillingly creatural" and embarrassed, exposing "the disruptive threat implicit in the immediacy and spontaneity even the most passionate ceremoniousness cannot fully eradicate from face-to-face encounters" (130).

Regarding Morocco, Geertz claims to describe a concept of selfhood that "marks public identity contextually and relativistically," but he also notes that these contextual and relative criteria of public identity come from the "private and settled arenas of life [tribal, territorial, linguistic, religious, familial] and have a deep and permanent resonance there" (133). But although Geertz does not concern himself with these "private and settled areas" or the nature of this "deep and permanent resonance," his attempt to abstract public, cultural notions and his claim that these notions are a final truth about cultural personhood run continually up against what we might call the return of the repressed—the particularistic, individual, idiosyncratic, and intrapsychic that his cultural analysis wishes to eliminate. Although he notes their empirical on-the-ground existence, then, neither immediate disruptive moments in Bali nor deep and permanently resonant private identities in Morocco figure in Geertz's account of cultural meaning. The social pattern in Morocco, he asserts, "produces a situation where people interact with one another in terms of categories whose meaning is almost purely position, location in the general mosaic, leaving the substantive content of the categories, what they mean subjectively as experienced forms of life, aside as something properly concealed in apartments, temples, and tents." Personal meaning becomes residual, as the substantive Moroccan categories are so general that anything goes: "It leaves the rest, that is, almost everything, to be filled in by the process of interaction itself" (133).

It would seem, however, that this substantive subjective experience is concealed less in the dwellings than in Geertz's methodology and epistemology, which by fiat remove personal meaning and elements described by "Western" notions of a psychodynamic self. (Moreover, as I have indicated earlier, Mernissi certainly provides ample documentation of the personal psychodynamic subjectivity found within these dwellings and their extensions—the schools, bathhouses, and farm-harems.) Geertz himself is aware that the meanings he claims as the entirety of cultural personhood do not tell the whole story. He remarks, for example, on the Balinese ability to create generic person-types that "obscure the mere materialities—biological, psychological, historical—of individual existence in favor of standardized status qualities" (1974, 129). But he is wary of the goal of grasping the native's point of view by an often self-deluding leap of transcultural empathy. We can ask, however, whether this point of view is reliably captured by an account of public, consensual meanings concerning aspects of selfhood enacted primarily in public life, a view in which "excruciating intensity" in the immediacy of the moment, ineradicable "disruptive threats" to ceremoniousness, the "substantive," "the process of interaction," "mere materialities of individual existence," and "deep and permanent resonance" are left unexplored and unilluminated theoretically. Without theoretical acknowledgment, "the rest," as he calls it, can be observed only unsystematically, as formless outbursts. We are left with the extraordinary notion that selfhood is whatever pattern of meaning the anthropologist can elicit and analyze from publicly recognized symbolic forms.

Geertz further sustains his dismissal of the intrapsychic experience of the bounded individual by a lack of attention to any particular person's experience of cultural categories or of investigation of how different people in a culture might experience cultural meanings in different ways. His "actor-oriented" account (as he calls it in Geertz, 1973, 14), oddly, thus tells us nothing about how any particular actor experiences her situated, "substantive" identity at a given time, even in the public arena. In Morocco, for example, what is the emotional meaning, or any other personal, particularized, meaning, of, say, having a public identity as a Jew when you cannot seek justice because of this particular personhood, or of being a Berber in a community that favors non-Berber Arabs (examples found in Geertz, 1973)? Are your emotional experiences of discrimination and injustice in these contextual and relativistic contexts in no way part of the meanings of Jewish or Berber personhood, or are they subsumable under a public, collective symbolic meaning?

There is no question, as Geertz and his predecessors and followers make clear, that different cultures have different concepts of selfhood or personhood that, as they are enacted as social process, social organization, and personal interaction, affect them, and unquestionably it is worthwhile to demonstrate how culturally bound our own views are. As different cultures name particular emotions, those cultures shape and give meaning to experience and make particular experiences more likely than others. What is needed in the investigation of these cultural meanings, however, is not a formal "vacant sketch" (1974, 133) of coordinates, style, and other cultural constructs but the ability to understand, *from the native's point of view*, how any particular enactment of a cultural form fuses such a sketch with the immediate, disruptive, resonant, intense, and substantive, which Geertz also describes. I do not argue (as Geertz himself almost implies) that "underneath" these cultural conceptions is something more "real," a real selfhood. Cultural meaning and personal meaning are opposed only in the minds of the ethnographer (or psychoanalyst). In the psyche they are inextricable and go toward making up subjective meaning.

I do not agree with Geertz that one cannot use one's own capacities for psychological self-observation and other capacities similar to those of the trained psychoanalyst to understand the native's point of view. I also believe that Geertz, in his critique of empathy as an investigative tool, has confounded two things. In his attempt to get away from the anthropological claim to understand the native's subjectivity or inner life through empathy and other personal psychodynamic qualities, he has finally come to the position that the native's inner life does not exist, for the anthropologist or perhaps for the native either. In devoting exclusive attention to patterns of meaning expressed in symbols, theorists will get at only what they start out looking for: representations of selfhood as a cultural conception. Such attention does not achieve what Geertz sets out to do—that is, to express (Geertz draws upon a psychoanalytic distinction here) "experience-near" native subjectivity in the "experience distant" frame of the ethnographer from another culture. Instead, he substitutes for the totality of the native's experiences of self, including those which are personal, emotional, individualized, situationally disruptive, intense, and contradictory, a perspective in which meaning is exclusively cultural.[7]

" 'From the Native's Point of View,' " with its focus on native conceptions of self and personhood, gave other cultural anthropologists permission to return, albeit with some trepidation and conflict, to the question of the relation between culture and psychology. Their project became the anthropology of self and feeling. It moved self-consciously away from the tendency in anthropology to reject all psychological anthropology—from structural-functional analyses that looked at objective social structures and practices and paid less attention to meaning, and from cultural, cognitivist, or symbolic analyses of cultures that paid intimate attention to meaning but did not customarily interest themselves in a range of seemingly "personal" experiences that were seen to be irrelevant to "culture." Anthropologists of self and feeling argued that an analysis of culture without an analysis of emotion, person, and self is incomplete. Emotions are themselves aspects of culture, and selves differ with the culture and organization of particular societies. In order to interpret actions or practices, then, one needs an understanding of patterns of feeling and self-definition in a culture as well as of its notions of strategy, rationality, self-interest, or practical reason.

A part of interpretive or symbolic anthropology, or anthropology informed by practice theory, the anthropology of self and feeling examines emotions and senses of self not only as culturally constructed but as discursive phenomena. Anthropologists of self and feeling claim that there is no psychological life (or none of interest to a cultural scholar) beyond publicly consensual, linguistically labeled cultural categories that describe that life; anthropologists who are influenced by poststructuralism add that cultural meanings always have power relations embedded in them. They investigate how the web of cultural meanings of emotion and self interrelates with, gives further meaning to, and gains meaning from other cultural webs of meaning (or, depending on theoretical stance, meaning-imbued practices). Because it makes strong arguments about cultural meaning and at the same time empirically studies areas of traditional psychoanalytic interest, the anthropology of self and feeling is a particularly apt arena in which to continue to investigate problems with exclusively culturalist theories of meaning. This anthropology can stand for culturally determinist accounts of subjectivity in general and exhibits limitations similar to those found in feminist cultural determinism and poststructuralism.[8]

At the same time, I am aware that such an investigation could end up, like ethnic warfare, as an elaboration of the narcissism of minor differences (see Freud, 1930, 114). Unlike most other anthropologists, the anthropologists of self and feeling at least think that selves and emotions are important topics of investigation. By directing a critique of culturalist theories of meaning toward these thinkers, I ignore a much wider group (virtually an entire field, along with other contemporary exclusively culturalist and social determinist theories in other social sciences and humanities) with whom my differences are much greater.

Two key ethnographies and writers, in spite of some differences between them, can be taken as exemplary: Michelle Z. Rosaldo's *Knowledge and Passion: Ilongot Notions of Self and Social Life* (1980; see also Rosaldo, 1983, 1984), and Lutz's *Unnatural Emotions: Everyday Sentiments on a Micronesian Atoll and Their Challenge to Western Theory* (1988; see also Lutz and Abu-Lughod, 1990). Rosaldo is repeatedly cited as the scholar most responsible for creating (and naming, 1984) the anthropology of self and feeling and for establishing the ethnographic linguistic pragmatics approach. She is also recognized as being its most brilliant practitioner. Rosaldo set the terms and indeed the goals of the cultural constructionist meanings-and-discourse approach with her rich and complex analysis of language in ordinary life and context, of "knowledge and passion," among the Ilongot (1980).[9] In a project designed to understand Ilongot men's headhunting, Rosaldo reads headhunting as a "text" about the adult male self that "provides . . . an image of collective 'passion' and vitality" (231) and helps ensure the reproduction of the group's powers in the face of the decline of its elder members. The headhunting text can be understood in relation to texts about the Ilongot male life cycle and the organization of marriage and to "Ilongot talk of persons" (224).

Readers who know my history will know that any discussion of Rosaldo, who died tragically and young, is intensely personal, for me along with a large group of other anthropologists and feminist scholars.[10] Shelly was one of my closest friends and certainly my most clear-eyed critic. Because the present work argues for the importance of subjectivity and the transferential influences on meaning and thinking, it is important to point out this personal involvement—my ongoing work of mourning, perhaps—as I continue a conversation and debate that began in our undergraduate days and took specific form in a study group in which we read many of the works (Dodds, 1951; Hallowell, 1955; Schafer, 1976; Doi, 1973) that furthered each of our understandings of selves, feelings, and culture but led us in very different directions before her death. Although I had loved her book, I had not fully appreciated Shelly's role in founding the anthropology of self and feeling until I began the research for these chapters in the early 1990s. I was (and am) ambivalent about putting forth a critique of Shelly's work, but her own relentless honesty about intellectual matters would make my avoiding disagreement specious and inauthentic. Moreover, as I note below, she was much too complex and intelligent a thinker to put forward any account that was simply wrong: especially in her last writings, she provides to my mind some of the best formulations of matters of culture, self, and feeling, as well as some of those with which I most strongly disagree.

Rosaldo is followed by Lutz (1988; see also Lutz and Abu-Lughod,

1990), who studied emotional meanings on Ifaluk, a Micronesian atoll, focusing especially on forms of anger, feelings of danger and fear, and a complex of compassion, love, and sadness. More than Rosaldo, Lutz analyzes exclusively "emotion words" (1988, 6), concepts of emotion, and talk about the emotions among the Ifaluk. Her first task is to explore Ifaluk language of emotion in its web of cultural meaning and thereby to contribute to an understanding of Ifaluk. But she also uses her analysis to problematize Western usages, thus relativizing both Ifaluk and the West, and demonstrates the preconceptions and ethnocentric assumptions about emotions and selves that go into any analysis colored by Western assumptions.

These studies describe the cultural discourse of emotion that gives meaning and shape to everyday experience. They argue that discourse becomes understandable only through being embedded in practice and in other realms of cultural meaning. As she puts it, Lutz wishes to "demonstrate that the use of emotion concepts, as elements of local ideological practice, involves negotiation over the meaning of events, over rights and morality, over control of resources—in short, involves struggles over the entire range of issues that concern human groups" (5). Emotion words are not only "coalescences of complex ethnotheoretical ideas" that evoke particular scenarios; they are also "actions or ideological practices . . . [used to] theorize about events, to moralize about or to judge them, and to advance one's interests" (10). People, that is, do things with words, and they therefore do things with emotion words. Lutz is describing conversations about moral practice, in which emotions are as public, rational, cognitive, and understandable as any other cultural practices.

According to the anthropology of self and feeling, the realm of emotions and self is not qualitatively different from other aspects of experience. People talk about emotions and act in light of the emotions they describe, just as they describe and participate in politics and rituals. Such an approach puts emotion and self firmly within the practice-theoretical purview of negotiation, struggle, and strategy, but it does so by stripping these of any particular status or function that might make them unique. Lutz claims that emotions can be seen as "naming, justifying, and persuading. . . . a social rather than an individual achievement—an emergent product of social life. . . . Emotional meaning is fundamentally structured by particular cultural systems and particular social and material environments. The claim is made that emotional experience is not precultural but *preeminently* cultural" (5). For Abu-Lughod and Lutz (1990), it is a victory to "de-essentialize" emotions. They "begin with the assumption that [emotion] is a sociocultural construct" and then explore how "emotion gets its meaning and force from its location and performance in the public realm of discourse" (7). For them emotion is exclusively a "discursive practice" and an "idiom for communication," not even necessarily about feelings (10, 11). It is found in traditional loci for discourse—conversation, poetics, rhetoric, and argument. Emotional discourse consists of "pragmatic acts and communicative performances" with an audience for the "emotional performance" (11, 10).

Abu-Lughod and Lutz never provide evidence for their view, however, and there is slippage in their methodology. They describe soliciting articles for their anthology that work "to pry emotion loose from psychobiology" (1990, 12), but they then draw on these articles—chosen in the first place to prove the connection between emotional discourse and hierarchy, religion, norms, or social life and to document the historicization and contextualization of such discourse—as evidence that feelings have no internality and that there are no universal aspects of affect. In effect, they begin with their concluding assumptions, look selectively at emotional discourse only as it is socially embedded, and then use what they find as evidence that there is no psychology. After ruling out psychology as well as psychobiology a priori, they fuse (and reject) claims that emotions are natural, irrational, or internal.

In a link not only to symbolic anthropology and ordinary-language philosophy but also to poststructuralism, Rosaldo and especially Lutz take an emphatic stand against referential interpretations of language—against the notion that linguistic meanings refer *to something* as opposed to deriving their sense from their relation to other meanings. Lutz criticizes "the referential and reified view of language" which implies that anger, fear, and happiness are things or labels for "concretized psychophysical states or objectivized internal 'event-things' " (9). For her, emotions are solely "concepts used to do certain kinds of things in the world." Emotional experience, then, is exclusively constituted by the language that describes it.

This approach builds upon the incontrovertible claim that language helps to shape subjectivity, but it is more absolutist. Poststructuralism, some language theories, and symbolic anthropology argue that there can be nothing between the pole of pure meaning, related only to other meanings, and the pole of pure reference, in which meanings are exclusively tied to real things. Emotion here then becomes entirely a matter of discourse and discursive practices. Rosaldo says, "Affects, then, are no less cultural and no more private than beliefs" (1984, 141), and as Lutz turns the study of emotions into a study of linguistic pragmatics derived from society and culture, she dismisses the very experiences—"private, psychological, hidden, interior, and ineffable" (1988, 42)—that make emotional experience unique.

Lutz (1988) contrasts her own understandings with those of psychoanalytic anthropologist Melford Spiro, who preceded her on Ifaluk (194–195). Spiro, she suggests, invokes a hydraulic model in arguing that the Ifaluk belief in frightening spirits results from repressed aggression: intracommunity violence would be too threatening in a tiny atoll community, so it is projected onto the spirits. For Lutz, by contrast, the belief in frightening spirits becomes an issue of a "moral discourse concerned with defining . . . the problem of violence" by using metaphors of "conversation and social project or construction . . . , pragmatically embedded in . . . social practices" (195). But what are we to make of the "intense horror or panic" (Lutz, 1988, 213) felt by Ifaluk at the threat of aggression? Lutz has been to Ifaluk and I have not, but I think Lutz means what the rest of us mean by horror and panic: an inner feeling of intense fear that may or may not be culturally labeled and culturally evoked or invoked. If not, why not just have a conversation rather than believe in frightening spirits? Emotions are states, complexes of physically palpable, feeling-imbued, unconscious fantasy meanings, as well as practices. Emotional experiences and feelings may certainly have communicative intent on occasion, and certain of these experiences may be more likely in particular cultural, social, or interpersonal settings (see Levy, 1973, 1984), but to reduce emotion to situated communication recalls the very Western rationalistic bias that Lutz criticizes. She points to the mind-centered rationalist, antiemotional bent of Western culture as a part of our discursive practice and as a reason for the relative anthropological neglect of emotions; yet her own account implies that emotions are pragmatic, linguistic, and verbal, always spoken, and themselves rationally or practically expressed. One could even wonder—if emotions are just another form of discourse—Why bother to study them? That emotions and elements of self, whether culturally prevalent, personally characteristic, or emergent in a particular historical or biographical moment, give particular *kinds* of meaning to experience cannot be captured through an exclusively linguistic approach.

Rosaldo's ethnography (1980), even as it purports to study Ilongot concepts of persons and emotions, shows a complex picture of actual emotional life as well as cultural meanings. As she describes it, among the Ilongot a bachelor's situation drives him to feel an emotion, *liget,* and to want a wife, an adult spirit, and equality with other adult men. But in order to understand this situation, we need a motivational theory of how people, including Ilongot bachelors, operate, an account of how something makes them desire something else. A feeling is triggered by the bachelor's situation, and that feeling must be an individual, if culturally recognized, experience. Rosaldo describes this motivation in rich detail in her account of the working out of "anger" and "shame." She argues, however, that Ilongot anger is not the same kind of inner drive that Westerners (as believers in a psychoanalytic folk psychology) believe anger to consist in, and that the shame motivating the Ilongot headhunter is entirely without psychodynamic (that is, unconscious as well as conscious) aspects. As a result, Rosaldo concludes that the emotions she is describing are entirely culturally specific; they are not expressions or manifestations of universal psychodynamic capacities and possibilities.

Rosaldo's claim is that Ilongot notions describe completely how shame works for them and what the threats of anger are. If these do not contain a conception of an inner world of unconscious processes or beliefs, then such processes or beliefs cannot be motivating for them. As she puts it, "our inner truths are things for shame to mask, whereas for Ilongots, 'shame' speaks more of reserve than of disguise" (1983, 143), and "headhunting . . . is in large part an angry answer to the distressing 'shame' of childhood. . . . anger for Ilongots is dangerous largely insofar as it is apt to lead to violent acts; it does not acquire added force through being hidden" (144–145). Ilongot youths, it seems, are so "heavy"—sullen, distracted, clouded, and shamed—that they need to sever a head to lighten up, but no element in their inner life need be invoked to account for this.

But although Rosaldo provides a fascinating and persuasive account of headhunting as a cultural practice and an explanation of what makes an individual Ilongot youth take a head, she does not seem to offer a psychological explanation of a different order from one we might give (on this see also Spiro, 1984, 1987). Her vivid description of the distracted, sullen, disorganized, heavy-hearted, erratically behaving bachelors who need to perform a single (albeit culturally recognized and named) act to consolidate a reasonable, relatively conflict-free self (a self recognized both by the man and by his community) seems to provide striking evidence for the importance of what might be seen as "universal" psychodynamic goals: a search or wish for the resolution of inner conflict and the achievement of a sense of cohesion and meaning in the face of disorganization and overwhelming affect. The Ilongot emotions of "anger" and "shame" that Rosaldo describes feel to the Western reader like anger and shame. Moreover, *Knowledge and Passion* itself is completely saturated with actual, palpable passion. No reader could fail to observe that Rosaldo is talking about powerful feelings—strongly felt emotions that drive and shape Ilongot behavior, even if they are of interest to Rosaldo herself only as they are culturally labeled.

I am again talking about the leakiness of case studies; the powerful sense of emotional tonality, of actual feelings and conflicts within particular individuals, is created in spite of Rosaldo's claims for discourse. The rich sense of emotional life Rosaldo conveys stands also to my mind in ironic contrast to some ethnographies that focus on psychodynamic experience as a separate reality—in addition to describing culturally prevalent and named emotions and emotion-laden experiences (e.g., Levy, 1973; Hollan and Wellenkamp, 1994)—but do so with more observational detachment than Rosaldo.[11]

Anthropologists and students of culture may invoke disciplinary purview to explain an exclusive focus on the cultural. Rosaldo claims, "What an anthropologist should do is point to ways in which, where psychological issues are concerned, the public and symbolic stuff of culture makes a difference" (1984, 143; see also 1983, 136). She moves substantially beyond Geertz in this endeavor, as she insists, against Geertz's exclusive focus on public personhood, on the importance of the private and of powerful feelings. Like Geertz's, however, her account is ambivalent about whether she has chosen a particular domain of inquiry—"what an anthropologist should do"—or is describing a complete truth. Having noted that anthropologists should investigate how "the public and symbolic stuff of culture" make a difference, Rosaldo acknowledges the psychological as a potentially separate reality: "what processes account for such involvement of the self—what sorts of histories, capacities, desires, frustrations, plans— may belong to the psychologist's domain" (1984, 143).

But Rosaldo takes away what she has just given.[12] Even as she acknowledges the existence of a "psychologist's domain" that may not be part of the anthropological purview, she also claims feelings exclusively for the cultural investigator, in telling us that "feelings are not substances to be discovered in our blood but social practices organized by stories" (1984, 143). Because she thinks she must make a choice, Rosaldo continually acknowledges individuality but takes it back. She says, on the one hand, "Neither, from the 'interpretive' point of view, does it make sense to claim that individuals—with their different histories, different bodies, and different ways of being more or less emotionally involved—are cultural systems cast in miniature." On the other, she claims that individuality finally derives meaning only from cultural symbols and public cultural discourse: "Nor is it necessary to assume that affect is inherently more individual than belief or that individuality is something other than the apprehension, by a person over time, of public symbols and ideas" (141). In the end, then, people compose their individuality entirely in public, cultural terms, and their histories, bodies, and emotional involvement fold back into culture. The very acknowledgment of personal dynamic meaning that might shape our conceptions of the world and our selves is removed, as the "public and symbolic stuff of culture" not only makes a difference but comes to create the entirety of emotion and self.

Rosaldo thus goes back and forth, as she infuses her culturally determinist position with recognition that the reality of affect is also determining. She argues forcefully for a linguistic-pragmatic approach to feelings, but she grapples as well with what she perceives as the intensity of emotions and the ways that emotions are not simply thoughts. What differentiates affect from thought, she concludes, "is fundamentally a sense of the engagement of the actor's self." Emotions "are embodied thoughts, thoughts s[t]eeped with the apprehension that 'I am involved' . . . the difference between a mere hearing of a child's cry and a hearing *felt*—as when one realizes that . . . the child is one's own. . . . Emotions are about the ways in which the social world is one in which *we* are involved" (1984, 143). But our emotional responses, in turn, reflect culture and are shaped by conceptions of the social world that are themselves cultural: "Thought is always culturally patterned and infused with feelings, which themselves reflect a culturally ordered past . . . just as thought does not exist in isolation from affective life, so affect is culturally ordered and does not exist apart from thought" (137). Thus, Rosaldo, perhaps unintentionally, reaches toward (or, because she will not shy away from contradiction, finds herself holding) a both-and position: "Ilongots are, in short, both like and unlike us" (143).

Like Rosaldo, Abu-Lughod and Lutz (1990) acknowledge that emotions might involve the whole embodied person, but they turn to Bourdieu for reassurance that bodily experience (which, they assume, is where emotion, if it is not cultural and discursive, must be located) is itself cultural. Insofar as they are embodied, emotions consist of a set of "body techniques" observed originally by a child reading a "cultural text" off other bodies and spaces. That emotions might be linguistically "framed" as embodied, then, does not threaten the view that they are discursive: they are simply "cultural products . . . reproduced in individuals in the form of embodied experience" (12).

The native's point of view is once again exclusively what the culture shapes or allows, and the actor becomes once again a passive enactor. (The previously quoted sentence fragment contains at least three discursive removals of experiencing agency or internality.) Thus, as these anthropologists introduce notions of practice in order to move away from static structuralist and cultural analyses without actors, they at the same time reintroduce a reductionist cultural determinism to account for psychological experience: "Emotion can be studied as embodied discourse only after its social and cultural—its discursive—character has been fully accepted" (13).

A culturally inappropriate action on Lutz's part early in her stay on Ifaluk challenges Lutz, reminding her of the "anxieties generated by human contact." But neither this experience nor her associations to other fieldworkers' experiences of discomfort (the "emotional 'eruptions' [that] mark progress in their understanding of others" 1988, 46) leads Lutz to question her exclusive emphasis on linguistic pragmatics directly. In the end, although she recognizes that she has been talking about how Ifaluk become "passionately involved in the world" (225), Lutz still does not see this passionate involvement as a qualitatively, empirically specific cluster of experiences rather than just one among many linguistic practices. People are "almost always 'emotional,'" but this means no more than that they process information and understand the world in "certain culturally and personally constructed ways" (225).

Except as they are trapped by blind allegiance to what is virtually an essentialist culturalism, then, Geertz, Rosaldo, and Lutz all acknowledge that there are generically human experiences that can be characterized only within a psychodynamic or intrapsychic rubric. As I have noted, Geertz (1977) argues that the interpretive anthropologist must move delicately between concepts that are close to experience and concepts distant from it and writes of "creatural" moments "felt with excruciating intensity" and the ineradicable "disruptive threats" to ceremoniousness. For Rosaldo, "the unconscious remains with us. Bursts of feeling will continue to be opposed to careful thought" (1984, 137), and "people everywhere (although in different ways) require social ties to form a self . . . people everywhere confront [dilemmas] in their experience of things like childhood socialization, the waywardness of youth, and the incompatibility of violence with cooperative daily living" (1983, 148). Lutz says, "Emotion is used to talk about what is culturally defined and experienced as 'intensely meaningful' " (1988, 8).

But these accounts are unable to conceive theoretically, even as they describe ethnographically, individual psychological processes of personal meaning creation, nor can they acknowledge theoretically that emotion-laden self-experience can be inextricably personal and cultural at the same time. There is no room for a psychological constructionism, for personally as well as culturally based interpretive capacities, for meanings that can be nonverbal as well as verbal, or for a verbal expressiveness that, in its particular, situated enactment, is not entirely culturally determined. These explanations bypass the idiosyncratic, divergent ways in which emotions develop and are experienced that lead to an energy, contestation, difference, and transformation that might themselves frame and provide impetus for political, economic, and social life. Where, we might inquire, does the child gain the capacity, ability, or habit of "reading" cultural bodies in the first place if not in some internal or psychobiological part of its being?

In the view of these theorists, cultural practices and meanings, but not psychological structures, processes, or meaning creation, characterize us as human. These formulations do not logically or empirically preclude the possibility of an individual psychological construction of emotional meaning—a historically specific individual experience to accompany historically specific social experience—but nonetheless they do not acknowledge it. They recognize the historical specificity of the culture but not of the individual. Culture is "an historically transmitted pattern of meanings" (Geertz, 1973, 89), but psychodynamic history is not a feature of individuals.

We end up with an uneasy and overstated sociocultural determinism, according to which people with their complex psychic life of thoughts, feelings, and fantasies are pigeonholed. A "culturalist account of how our feelings work . . . insisting upon the sociocultural bases for experiences once assigned to a subjective and unknowable preserve of psychic privacy" (Rosaldo, 1984, 138) replaces a recognition that there is a subjective (and not necessarily unknowable) preserve of psychic privacy that may simply not be of primary interest to the anthropologist. Although Rosaldo acknowledges that there may be "desire" and an "inner life," she claims that these are "shaped by culturally laden sociality. . . . Personal life takes shape in cultural terms. . . . Meaning is a fact of public life. . . . Cultural patterns— social facts—provide a template for all human action, growth, and understanding" (140). Agency and subjectivity are preserved, in her interpretation, by the assumption that individuals interpret culture and experience and are therefore not entirely reactive; however, they interpret and react entirely to cultural givens and in cultural terms. The self is reduced to a conscious self, and realms of human experience are thereby removed from the ethnographer's potential purview and understanding. Finally, says Rosaldo, "cultural idioms provide the images in terms of which our subjectivities are formed, and furthermore, these idioms themselves are socially ordered and constrained. Society . . . shapes the self through the medium of cultural terms, which shape the understandings of reflective actors. . . . Culture [is] the very stuff of which our subjectivities are created" (150–151). Lutz echoes her view: "Emotion experience . . . is more aptly viewed as the outcome of social relations"; "the political, economic, social, and ecological conditions of life for particular people provide the impetus and framing for the emotional consciousness that develops among them" (1988, 209, 215).

Indeed, it seems as if the anthropologists of self and feeling, and culturalist thinkers more generally, fall into particular folk assumptions even as they argue against others. They assume, that is, that there can be a cultural level of analysis and interpretation but not a psychological level. They assume, further, that psychological accounts are always couched in the language of a presumed indigenous Western psychology that violates alternative indigenous self-experiences of public, social personas with culturally shaped emotions but at the same time imply that culturalist accounts do not suffer from pretheoretical Western assumptions. Thus, they treat culture as an analytic rather than a folk concept and do not question whether it can be used to understand "cultures." They show no recognition that cultural theory—the belief that culture, discourse, and pragmatic enactment are universal categories of investigation, whereas psychological theories can only be culture-specific—is itself a Western academic assumption. But in fact the writers on self and feeling and their cultural determinist colleagues are themselves operating in light of a Western cultural conception, one that opposes public to private and the cultural to the psychological or subjective. In this view, either there is a Western pristine individuality with private subjectivity— "the Western conception of the person as a bounded, unique, more or less integrated motivational and cognitive universe"—or the individual is completely culturally constructed. (The point that many who criticize psychoanalysis for its Western basis are also themselves operating within Western disciplines is made also by Obeyesekere, 1990, 219).

Part of the difficulty for the anthropologists of self and feeling (and indeed for many insistently cultural thinkers dismissive or critical of the psychological) is that they set the terms (or the terms have been discursively set) in a way that leaves them little alternative. The "other side," that is, has often argued against a particularistic cultural determinism, not from a specifically psychodynamic psychology of unconscious fantasy but from a universalistic bioinstinctual determinism, or from what Spiro (1984, 335–336) calls a generic cultural determinism—a claim that universal structural similarities in cultures and families, along with universal features of biology, create a generic human mind. Within this binary polarization, if affect and meaning are not entirely matters of cultural discourse, they must be entirely matters of natural hardwiring. The anthropologists of self and feeling thus compare claims for universal affects that can be physiologically read in facial expression, or Freud's drive theory, to a conception of emotions as "serving complex communicative, moral and cultural purposes rather than simply as labels for internal states whose nature or essence is presumed to be universal" (Lutz, 1988, 5). Lutz, for example, who opposes "historically specific social experience, received language categories, and speech traditions" to "the biological basis of human experience" (210), claims that "the prevalent assumption that the emotions are invariant across cultures is replaced here with the question of how one cultural discourse on emotion may be translated into another" (5).

Posing the dichotomy in terms of the cultural and ideational, against the precultural and physiological-affective, rules out by fiat a third realm, the psychic reality of introjective and projective-transferential shaping, enabled, certainly, by psychobiological capacities and taking into account through the transformations of unconscious fantasy the cultural and interpersonal. With regard to this third realm, emotions will be best understood, not "with reference to cultural scenarios and the associations they evoke" (Rosaldo, 1984, 141–142) or "prototypic or classic" cultural scenes associated with particular emotions (Lutz, 1988, 211), but through analysis of personal psychobiography and individuality. This personal meaning incorporates but is not shaped by cultural meaning; it is a particular person's creation. According to my argument, even emotion words and emotional concepts must have individual resonance and personal meaning. Anger, shame, hope, fear, envy, love, and hate may be evoked in particular ways in different cultures and in reaction to culturally typical experiences, but these emotions are also evoked differently by different members of the culture and differently for the same member in different internal and external contexts. Some cultural commonality may be found among Ilongot or Ifaluk that I do not share, but it is equally the case that each of my American patients, as well as my non-American patients currently speaking English and living in the United States, experiences particular emotions differently, in a different web of personal historical and transferential meaning. If I do not explore these individual meanings, I cannot understand my patients. And if we do not look at an individual Ilongot experience of anger, or Ifaluk experience of compassion and nurturance, or any other "cultural" emotion, we also do not understand that cultural affect. There is no direct relation between experience and emotion such that for all members of a culture, a particular situation "shapes" a particular emotional response. To understand cultural selves and feelings fully, culturalists need to theorize about personal psychology as a separate area of analytic interest. Rosaldo rightly notes (1984, 141) that just as culture is not personality writ large, neither is personality culture in miniature.

This assertion does not mean that an anthropologist studying another culture does not need to learn to "translate" emotional meanings and understand emotion in context, or that "tears and other gestures" (Lutz, 1988, 8) might not be infused with cultural as well as individual meanings. It does mean that a full understanding of "bursts" of self, emotion, or other "intensely meaningful" experiences requires going beyond cultural shaping and determination, and it means that individuality and agency are not purely pragmatic or strategic. What is missing from the approach of doing things with emotion words is an understanding of what exists between universal human instinctuality or panhuman culture and universal cultural particularity, and how this in-between develops and is experienced in particular interpersonal and intrapsychic settings to which projection and introjection, and transference and countertransference, give personal meaning.

That thoughts and feelings are entangled and that thoughts are thought in culturally specific languages—these ideas do not mean that there is no private feeling or that any particular thought has only a public cultural meaning. Culturally recognizable thoughts or emotion terms can also be entwined in a web of thought-infused feelings and feeling-infused thoughts experienced by an individual as she creates her own psychic life within a set of interpersonal and cultural relations. In the symbolic-culturalist tradition, a theory of personal meaning is missing both as a conception and as a process lived by the individual actor. When Rosaldo, in a both-and formulation, claims, "Feeling is forever given shape through thought and . . . thought is laden with emotional meaning" (1984, 143), she has no fully psychological theory, besides the implicit psychoanalytic theory that she explicitly eschews, that can keep her from returning to the view that thoughts and emotional meanings are entirely cultural.

The anthropology of self and feeling conflates, it seems, two levels of argument. On one level, its spokespersons are comparing ethnopsychologies, or folk theories of the psyche—"ours" against those of the cultures they study. Rosaldo, for example, points out that Americans conceptualize the self and emotions in line with a psychoanalytically derived theory of instinct, while Ilongot hold a different theory. On another level is the clearly implied universal psychological theory of how emotions and selves work. According to this theory, the analytic domain of psychological experience is discursively and culturally constructed; if Ilongot do not conceptualize an inner self, this means that they have no depth psychology or depth-psychological experience. Concordantly, if Americans hold an instinctually determinist theory, then for Americans, instinctual repression leads to psychological disaster. It is supposed that in cultures that do not recognize levels of consciousness as known or unknown or that do not name a particular emotion, these do not exist for people in that culture. Paradoxically, we are back with a version of culture and personality that the anthropology of self and feeling intended from the outset to avoid: Americans, Ilongot, and Ifaluk all have their own cultural construction of concepts of selfhood and notions of how emotions work, each pattern embedded in the particularities of a respective culture. Emotions here are no longer a felt experience, nor do they develop in reaction to experience. They develop as a direct outcome of cultural socialization.[13]

The anthropologists of self and feeling make a double and in some ways contradictory argument. They wish on the one hand to establish that it is important to study emotions, persons, and selves, but on the other, that emotions and selves are exclusively culturally constructed, no different from any other aspect of cultural systems. In elaborating this Geertzian aspect of their argument, they find themselves with Geertz's blind spots: a unidirectional cultural determinism or an account of emotions that simply brackets out or ignores theoretically aspects of observed and experienced emotional reality and sense of self. By assuming that a psychoanalytic or psychological view requires a belief in the determination of culture by personality or psychobiology, by maintaining an attachment to professional purview rather than substantive inquiry and to a theoretical assumption of cultural primacy, and by seeing the culture and personality debate in terms of inadequate oppositions, these accounts miss not only the ways in which cultural forms can express or respond to psychological conflict but also and especially the emotional, psychodynamic experience cultural meanings have for the individual.

Ironically, it was Renato Rosaldo's tragic personal experience, described in "Grief and a Headhunter's Rage" (1989), that provides the most powerful substantive critique from within the discursive, culturalist perspective on self and emotions. Renato Rosaldo, along with Shelly, had studied Ilongot headhunting; like her, he puzzled about the cultural meanings of passion and anger that led to the taking of heads. Rent with grief after his wife's sudden accidental death, Rosaldo describes how he came to feel directly what Ilongot mean when they talk of an anger generated by grief so powerful that only a killing can reconstitute emotional equilibrium—can "throw away" the anger. According to Rosaldo, no amount of extended investigation into the cultural meaning, in all its polysemic symbolic complexity, its embedding in a thickly described web of meaning, and its imbrication in a never-ending chain of signifiers, enabled him to understand an Ilongot man's claim that "rage, born of grief, impels him to kill his fellow human beings" (1).

Rosaldo describes how, as his own personal animation of the external world changed as a result of his devastating loss (and, we could add, as his internal world also shifted), he was able to reconstruct, emotionally and not only cognitively, his understanding of culturally described Ilongot emotions: "My use of personal experience serves as a vehicle for making the quality and intensity of the rage in Ilongot grief more readily accessible" (11). Against a focus on the language of emotion or on terms for emotion that are seemingly like all other words, and against generalization about feelings in common or patterns of personhood in common, he writes of "powerful visceral emotional states" (9) by which he personally was overwhelmed. The statement that rage born of grief leads to headhunting must, according to Rosaldo, be understood to mean what it says. It is a claim about straightforward emotional force, and it directly describes the personal experience, at the death of an intimate relation, of finality and rupture. As he puts it, "The rage born of devastating loss animates the older men's desire to raid. This anger at abandonment is irreducible in that nothing at a deeper level explains it. . . . Although certain analysts argue against the dreaded last analysis, the linkage of grief, rage, and headhunting has no other known explanation" (18).

Rosaldo argues, then, that we need to focus on the force of the signified—on referential meaning—to understand cultural behavior: "The concept of force calls attention to an enduring intensity in human contact that can occur with or without the elaboration conventionally associated with cultural depth" (20). (In psychoanalytic terms, we need a Kleinian or object-relational, not a Lacanian, theory of emotional meaning for cultural as well as for personal meaning.) Rosaldo also suggests that you cannot understand culture if you do not seek to describe and explain intense emotions in themselves. Anthropologists, however, have avoided such a project. Most anthropological studies of death, Rosaldo points out, do not look at feelings of loss and bereavement and are not concerned to understand death itself. We do not find in these accounts "the deep cutting pain of sorrow almost beyond endurance, the cadaverous cold of realizing the finality of death, the trembling . . . , the mournful keening . . . , the tearful sobbing" (9), the "agony" (13). These studies, rather, following their Durkheimian lineage, are studies of mourning rituals geared toward understanding social structure.[14]

Renato Rosaldo's account directly documents the intersection of personal meaning and cultural meaning, but it does so not so much by retheorizing as by offering an emphatic demonstration. By making so clear empirically that personal and cultural meaning cannot be separated, he does not need to elaborate a new psychology (though he is contributing to a nonexclusively culturalist anthropology). He poses the issue of the relation between personal and cultural meaning in a way that bypasses questions of universalism versus particularism or panhuman commonality versus cultural uniqueness. Emotion is a question of personal force as well as cultural meaning. By experiencing his own grief, Rosaldo finds that he can understand Ilongot grief.[15]

The anthropology of self and feeling developed out of the ostensibly nonpsychological traditions of interpretive and symbolic anthropology. Along with the traditions of culture and personality and psychological anthropology, it provides persuasive testimony to the great cultural variety in construals of emotion and conceptions of self. Some anthropologists in this tradition, like Geertz and Michelle Rosaldo, assumed familiarity with Freud and took certain psychoanalytic insights for granted, even as they generally considered psychodynamics either uninteresting or ultimately cultural. Others, like Lutz, occluded all hints of emotional dynamics outside linguistic practices and meanings.

In asking how feelings and their labels, and selves and their definitions, are culturally specific, and in comparing claims for a universal human psychology with the particularities of cultures, the anthropology of self and feeling is, perhaps reluctantly, also part of the psychological anthropology dialogue. The investigators of self and feeling raised questions of personal psychology that were for some time taboo in most of the discipline. But the more these anthropologists leaned toward exclusively culturalist, linguistic, and discursive positions, the more they were left with contradictions and tensions, both in their theoretical accounts and in the ethnographic descriptions that their theories were meant to contain.

I argue throughout this book that if cultural meanings matter, they matter personally. They are projectively construed, animated, and created. Reciprocally, selves and emotions, however culturally labeled, are, like gender, introjectively reshaped partially through unconscious fantasy, through the unconscious inner world that develops from birth onward. Emotions may be culturally recognized or unrecognized, but they are also directly felt and become implicated in unconscious aspects of self and world. Psychological force drives the experience of culturally recognized emotions just as cultures help to shape emotional life.

The very theorists who were insisting on the polysemy, historicity, changeability, indeterminacy, and multivocality of meanings were also insisting that meaning was exclusively collective, political, and culturally constructed. They implied that the multiplicity of meaning could not also contain elements individually created through emotion, fantasy, and intrapsychic process. But to any reader who had or could recognize strong feelings, as well as to any reader who read both the claims and the counterclaims and evidence, this anthropology described something so palpably real and recognizable that an argument for exclusive linguistic or discursive determinism was not persuasive. In short, the anthropology of self and feeling lacked a viable psychology.

6 The Psyche in the Field

> Not only may individuals differ among themselves,
> but also any one individual may differ from himself
> or herself at different points in time. . . . The "same"
> value may be psychodynamically different and may
> play different roles in the psychic economies of
> different individuals, or for the same individual at
> different points in the life cycle—or even at different
> moments in the day—because it is associated with
> different tangles of experience.
>
> JEAN BRIGGS
>
> "MAZES OF MEANING"

RECENT ANTHROPOLOGY HAS ARGUED FORCEFULLY AGAINST A holistic view of culture as a seamless web of complementary, mutually reinforcing significations and has taken issue with Durkheim-derived views that culture, language, and social structure exist in a timeless way before, during, after, and apart from individual lives. Instead, culture is seen as historically evolving, local, and contested, and cultural patterns, discourses, and narratives are seen to depend on how any cultural actor's age, gender, race, class, sexuality, generation, kinship position, and so forth, create intersecting, positionally based perspectives and understandings. But this reconsideration nonetheless retains many traditional anthropological assumptions. Even though culture is now seen in these complex ways, the notion persists that meaning is entirely cultural—that culture, however contingent, historicized, and characterized by contradictory elements, entirely defines what provides meaning and order for the individual. Culture still constitutes individuals as subjects, and perspective still comes from (multiple) positions in the social structure.

I have suggested, rather, that we need to cross what might be called the horizontal view of cultural meaning—thick description, multiplicity, polysemy, webs of meaning, forests of symbols—with a vertical view, in which each individual's internal history is its own emotionally polysemic web of continually created unconscious and conscious personal meaning, animated by fantasies, projections, and introjections. This psychobiographical personal meaning calls on, intersects with, and itself helps shape the complex web of culture.

Thus, feelings, selves, and other "forceful" cultural concepts are not entirely cultural, but neither are they unvarying universal, natural essences "inside" the person that are irrational, uncontrollable, unintended, or purely physical. Self and feeling, and meaning in general, are inextricably cultural and personal. An adequate conception of culture and cultural meaning should also include an account of historicized, biographical, intrapsychic meaning: people obtain meaning and order not only from culture and social structure but also from their own psychological capacities to accord personal meaning, to experience conflict, to create and live in an internal world of fantasy. Each of us creates psychological meaning throughout life. This individual psychological meaning is an equal constituent of any person's experience of cultural meaning and may even take precedence over cultural meaning in creating individuality. If the meanings of particular feelings and the experience of self, personhood, tribe, group, class, or nation, gender or sexuality are important and culturally charged, it is also because they are individually charged, through those interpersonal processes and emotional contexts, verbal and nonverbal, in which they are given meaning, and as individuals throughout life bestow on them their own set of personal meanings in addition to experiencing the rich, polysemic meanings of culture. People avail themselves of cultural meanings and images, but they animate and create them through unconscious fantasy processes of projection and introjection in accordance with their own unique biography or history of intrapsychic and interpersonal strategies and practices. A clinical, psychodynamic perspective thus offers enormous room for the individual construction of meaning and experience, which reduces neither to a universal theory of drives nor to a psychobiological universalism, and which is compatible with cultural variation.

In this chapter, I explore the contributions within psychoanalytic anthropology that in my view most successfully elaborate a theoretical and empirical account of personal individuality as it enters into the experience and creation of cultural meanings. As I do so, I select and privilege one segment of the psychoanalytic anthropological endeavor. Specifically, because this book is about individual subjectivity and the realm of personal meaning, I do not consider psychoanalytic anthropological interpretations of cultural symbolism or symbolic practices like myths, folklore, religious beliefs, rituals, stories, dramas, or other collective symbols and symbolic practices, unless these studies explicitly concern themselves with or describe how individuals in particular cultures experience cultural symbols.

Such studies can be fascinating and illuminating, and they are often, just because of their creative and original insights, a pleasure to read and ponder (see, e.g., Dundes, 1984, 1997, and other works; Paul, 1996; or the implicitly psychoanalytic Jay, 1992). At the same time, my own propensity is to believe that we may not be able fully to analyze the psychodynamic meanings of cultural practices and beliefs on the purely collective, cultural level. We must have in mind the meaning (however contradictory, multilayered, condensed, partial, and evanescent) *to someone* or to some people. Without the evidence provided by studying those people, the interpreter's account remains to some extent projective, suppositional, and of necessity based on previously held psychoanalytic assumptions about symbols, fantasies, and their meanings or about archetypal developmental scenarios. I differ theoretically, then, even as I admire and enjoy their accounts, with those who in their psychoanalytic analyses of symbolic systems explicitly treat culture as "an autonomous sui generis system" (Paul, 1982, 300) in which the psychodynamic meanings of cultural practices and beliefs can be analyzed exclusively on the cultural level and without regard to individual psychology or motivation. (See also Paul's argument, 1987, for analyzing structure rather than history and events.) My argument throughout this book is that cultural meanings, like personal meanings, may be analytically separable, but they are empirically intertwined. They can be sui generis but not autonomous. In this context, analyses of psychoanalytic symbolism and meaning in myths, folklore, stories, and so forth, are incomplete insofar as they reveal complexity and variation in culture but not in the psyche.

Studies of cultural symbol systems have contributed to rethinking of and debate over universal contents of psychic fantasy and structure. On the one side, we find such studies claiming support for universal symbol systems tied to species-specific phylogeny or bioinstinctual-bioevolutionary necessity, following Freud's (1905c) account of a universal developmental unfolding of libidinal phases and erotogenic zones, and affirming a universal psychosexual meaning of symbols or the universality of oedipal myths (see, e.g., Dundes, 1984, 1997; Johnson and Price-Williams, 1996). These studies may argue that core cultural problems and universal developmental problems demand resolution, symbolic elaboration, and psychological correlates—as Paul puts it, "objective structural requirements of culture arising in response to generic, species-specific conflicts" (1982, 303; see also Paul, 1987, 1996). On the other side, proponents argue that such symbol systems document basic variation. They entail the necessity for culturally and psychodynamically specific analyses of, for example, myths about generational conflict that might otherwise be subsumed under the single universal ur-category or archetype of Oedipus, and for particular family structures and cultural patterns that give rise to culturally particular myths and beliefs (see, e.g., Kurtz, 1992; Obeyesekere, 1990; Spain, 1994, who cites Okonogi, 1978, 1979).

In this last debate about cultural universality and variation, psychoanalytic studies of cultural symbolism overlap with a second area of psychoanalytic anthropology that the present chapter addresses only briefly. That is, several leading psychoanalytic anthropologists argue, like Freud in some of his writings, for a psychoanalysis rooted in evolutionary and instinctual views of mind and psychological development, for recognition of features of family structure and characteristics of human infancy that universally determine a nuclear fantasy, Oedipus complex, or incest taboo, for universal symbol systems tied to bioevolution, phylogeny, or universals in family structure, or for a theory of cultural universals thought to solve necessary functional or structural problems of culture. (For strong statements of this position, see, e.g., Paul, 1982, 1987, 1996; Johnson and Price-Williams, 1996; Spiro, 1982, 1987. Spain, 1988, 1994, takes a carefully delineated middle position on universality.) As should be clear by now, a bioevolutionary position is to my mind precisely an understanding of psychoanalysis that does not accord sufficient recognition to psychic life as a separate, sui generis realm of ongoing, unconscious, affectively infused meaning creation. It perpetuates, from the biological side, the polarized biological-cultural divide that has made psychoanalysis seem so incompatible with contemporary feminist and cultural understandings. Thus, when the self and feeling anthropologists, or cultural thinkers more generally, challenge psychoanalytic understandings of selves and emotions by pointing out that these tend to derive from universalized bioinstinctual or bioevolutionary assumptions, or from assumptions about universal psychosexual stages and outcomes that do not sufficiently respect and recognize cultural particularity, they have accurately pinpointed particular tendencies in psychoanalytic anthropology.

I certainly do not pretend here to evaluate these particular texts or arguments extensively, even as I disagree with their general position. In fact, it is not clear that such evaluation can be useful. Because evidence (from neuroanatomy, primate or family studies, and so on) can be marshaled on either side in questions of bioevolution and instinct, because one side does not think bioevolutionary evidence is relevant to cultural questions in the first place, and because the two sides use the same cultural data to support or refute claims for the universality of the Oedipus complex, it seems to me that a more extended evaluation would change nobody's mind: bioevolutionary and bioinstinctual positions and their critique or dismissal seem to be a matter of theoretical preference.[1] I hope, however, that calling attention to the psychological in-between might do something to alter the terms of debate.[2]

If they do not assume that psychoanalysis entails universal bioinstinctual stages (as do both the pro-bioinstinctual psychoanalytic anthropologists and the antipsychological cultural anthropologists), most anthropologists assume that psychoanalysis requires an ego-psychologically interpreted structural theory favoring an autonomous ego and superego. This assumption, along with a privileging of the cultural, has meant that anthropological investigation of emotions has focused disproportionately on guilt and shame—on superego-generated emotions that correspond to cultural expectations and signal social misdemeanor. Thus, cultural scholars have long contrasted "shame cultures" with "guilt cultures," and more recently they have compared different kinds of shame and questioned whether the internalized self and the shame-guilt dichotomy are Western constructions (see, e.g., Levy, 1983; Rosaldo, 1983). All these questions focus on how people are socialized to meet cultural expectations and on emotions that control and channel behavior toward cultural norms. The structural theory of id, ego, and superego—read especially though Freud's account (1930) of how the superego enforces social norms by heightening the sense of guilt, and perhaps through Talcott Parsons' argument (1952) for the convergence of Freud and Durkheim on the internalization of moral rules—implicitly underlies and elicits such preoccupations, even as anthropologists, in their critique of the Western universalizing of the bounded individual, challenge it.

Culturalism, along with a reading of psychoanalysis emphasizing the structural theory, leads to an exaggerated focus, from the point of view of psychic functioning, on emotions that control behavior and adherence to norms. Interest narrows to how emotions function not for the individual but for culture and society, to how culturally patterned "moral affects" help construct a cultural self. The task then becomes not to start from personal psychology or subjectivity as it helps to shape and give meaning to culture but, rather, to find other emotions, if shame and guilt won't do, that control and channel behavior. Robert Levy (1983), for example, suggests that shame or embarrassment is a lexically more prevalent non-Western emotion than shame alone; he cites hunger and lassitude in one culture and horror in another as emotions that control or evaluate individual behavior and isolate nonsociality (131–132). These accounts sacrifice an understanding of individual experience of any cultural form to analysis of "culture" itself and sacrifice personal meaning to cultural meaning. Their authors understand more about behavioral and emotional control than about emotional meaning.[3]

Anthropological readings of psychoanalysis that emphasize, whether explicitly or not, evolving, situated processes of transference, projection, and introjection enable psychoanalytic anthropologists, like psychoanalysts, to avoid universalized claims about the contents of fantasy or about necessary developmental stages or tasks and to avoid psychological or bioinstinctual determinism and reductionism. They make possible an account that recognizes fully how psyches actually shape and create meaning from within: the most psychoanalytically sympathetic social scientist, I believe, finds it hard not to conceive that a creative psyche chooses from among cultural ingredients which are, finally, given. A psychoanalytic anthropology of personal meaning also helps to address more fully the psychoanalytic question of "external reality," thereby greatly enriching psychoanalytic conceptions that relegate the psychic role of culture to the internalization of values by the superego. Such an integrated conception of psyche and culture argues that individual, personal, charged psychological motivations can be based on an inner world continuously created through unconscious fantasy, motivations that come neither from a universal instinctual or structural base nor from cultural shaping.

Quite a few ethnographies and theoretical accounts move toward such a view. A contemporary culture and personality anthropology, variously called psychocultural anthropology, psychodynamic ethnography, and person-centered ethnography, overlaps with the anthropology of self and feeling in its interest in cultural emotions, selves, and experiences of self.[4] Psychoanalyst-anthropologists construct theoretical formulations that integrate their understandings of psychic reality and of culture, and ethnographies document and theorize about individuality in culture and transference and countertransference in the ethnographic encounter.

Psychocultural anthropology explores, among other interests, personhood, selves, emotions, sexuality, dreams, and prevalent psychological conflicts in particular cultures. Unlike the anthropology of self and feeling, it begins from a direct interest in the psychodynamic level of experience—that is, from a referential rather than an exclusively discursive view of the psyche. These ethnographers assume that emotions, selves, and other especially meaningful or powerful experiences are there to be described. In this sense, they worry less than the self and feeling anthropologists about how to justify what they are choosing to study and whether by doing so they are importing Western assumptions. At the same time, like the anthropologists of self and feeling, they pay special attention to how natives describe personal emotional experience and experiences of self. Accordingly, although they have selected a domain of study with "Western" conceptions in mind (as do most ethnographers, of course), they are unlike the earlier anthropologists of culture and personality in that they are also fully socialized, as contemporary symbolic and interpretive anthropologists, to embed their accounts much more completely within a cultural perspective. Cultural meaning systems are preserved, and universalized or psychiatric evaluative terms are used only with the greatest caution.

Not surprisingly, sexuality provides one favorite topic in the contemporary study of culture and psyche. Thomas Gregor (1985), for example, claims that sex for the Brazilian Mehinaku sustains and forms kinship groups, defines human and tribal identity, serves economic functions, and supports the sexual division of labor, but his *Anxious Pleasures* more particularly describes a preoccupation with sex as sex in Mehinaku society. He focuses on the central metaphors of sexuality—in particular, eating—so that sex, or a particular person's genitals, are "delicious," "delightful," or "disgusting," and one gender's genitals are "food" for the other's.[5] He describes the prohibitions on sexual partners or sexual appetite enforced by graphic cautionary or humorous tales and myths, sexual intimidation and warning in rituals, and numerous cultural expressions of conflicted masculinity. These expressions include beliefs about dirty, disgusting female genitals, male rituals like ear-piercing or couvade, which are explicitly identified with menstruation or childbirth, myths of origin in which women had male genitals, and so forth. Gilbert Herdt's studies of the Sambia (1981, 1987) show how a complex intertwining of symbolic and psychological beliefs and fears about masculinity and heterosexuality is expressed in secret male initiation rites that include homosexual fellatio on the basis of the belief that taking in semen orally from an older male is a necessary route to strong heterosexual masculinity and an ability to wage war.

Like other psychoanalytic anthropologists, Herdt and Gregor take for granted that sex, sexuality, and gender identity are conflictual, powerful, and important to psychological, cultural, and social life. They use psychodynamic interpretations rooted in early childhood patterns to explain the extensive cultural preoccupation with actual physical male genitality as well as with masculinity more generally in the societies they study. Both Gregor and Herdt illuminate personal and cultural meanings of sexuality and the way that myths in one case and initiation rites in the other address (masculine) childhood experiences and their psychodynamic sequelae.[6]

As in clinical psychoanalysis, the study of dreams provides another route into understanding cultural psyches. Waud Kracke (1979, 1987b, 1987c, 1991, and elsewhere) has studied extensively dreams and dreaming among the Brazilian Kagwahiv. In comparing cultural beliefs about dreaming (1991), he notes that some cultures elaborate dreams and treat them as arenas of action as real as waking life, whereas others minimize their importance. A culture's conception of dreaming will affect the meaning and significance of a dream for the dreamer. Everyone dreams, but dreams will always draw upon and incorporate specifically cultural images and metaphors (we dream in a particular language), and dream construction itself may also depend partly on how a dreamer's culture conceptualizes dreams and their function and significance (an observation daily observable in the psychoanalytic consulting room, where patients know that dreams and dreaming are significant).

The question whether cultures, like individuals, create more or less distance between conscious and unconscious—between reality and dream—can be generalized. Kracke has studied a culture that experiences dreams and waking life as equally important and meaningful, and he also notes (1987a) that sexual fantasy, metaphor, and behavior are much less covert and tabooed as topics of interest, conversation, and attention among the Kagwahiv than in American culture. Extending this view, Obeyesekere (1990) suggests that Freud's early topography of the systems of unconscious, preconscious, and conscious may be universal, or at least consonant to a degree that the structural theory and its later ego psychological extensions are not, with the great variation in the extent to which cultures recognize unconscious processes and enable their psychological expression. (He also notes that the early topography receives empirical support in Freud's own work: the case studies, *The Interpretation of Dreams,* the studies of jokes and slips, and the papers on technique were written before the development of the structural theory.) Playing ethnographer of psychoanalysis, the Sri Lankan Buddhist Obeyesekere claims,

The idea of unconscious and preconscious motivation and "thought" is, in my view, consonant with forms of thought in many non-Western societies, whereas the personology of ego, superego, and id is far too rooted in Western language games and philosophical speculations. Both Buddhism and Hinduism clearly recognize unconscious motivation, and indeed delve more deeply into such processes than Freudianism, though they both lack the special theoretical slant that Freud gave it. It is indeed possible that a future psychoanalysis might well incorporate these Hindu-Buddhist insights. I also think that shamanism, spirit possession, and other kinds of hypnomantic states are widespread forms of life that recognize implicitly the centrality of unconscious motivation. . . . The second topography [he means the structural theory] . . . is consonant with Western philosophical traditions because it fits neatly with the Western preoccupation with the self, the ego or the transcendental or reflective consciousness. [1990, 253][7]

Obeyesekere points especially to cultural assumptions in the conceptualization and role of the superego. He notices Freud's unselfconscious use of Kantian terminology as Freud claims that the ego must submit to the "categorical imperative" of the superego (Freud, 1924, 48), and he reminds us that Freud's superego expresses a Judeo-Protestant conscience emphasizing punitive morality and internalized guilt. Superego development depends on a conception of family process and structure anchored to a punitive paternal authority who himself is further linked with a "higher being," the Judeo-Christian god (see especially Freud, 1913, 1939). Obeyesekere notes that Freud, as he moves from *The Ego and the Id* to *Civilization and Its Discontents*, frames his conception of the superego more and more in terms of punishment and internal and external violence and aggression, and that this framing is again tied to a culturally and historically specific family process: "What is missing is any discussion in Freud of the 'positive' aspects of this conscience; that it can be moved by compassion or kindness, irrespective of the negativity of guilt acting as a sanction. I suspect that this is due to Freud's neglect of the introjection of *maternal* values in the formation of the conscience (and possibly in the Oedipal resolution) in his cultural setting" (1990, 252).[8]

Obeyesekere's claims about Freud's Western Judeo-Protestant conception of the superego seem to me irrefutable, but I do not think he recognizes sufficiently the clinical basis and utility of some elements that the structural theory—and the late dual-instinct theory— try to take into account. The centrality of anxiety as a motivational source that must be recognized clinically and forms the basis for much analytic work is not adequately spelled out until *Inhibitions,*

Symptoms and Anxiety (1926a), after *The Ego and the Id* established the structural theory, and the unconscious sadistic, self-punishing attitudes and fantasies that Freud tried to capture in his conception of the superego are often a central focus of clinical work. These psychic experiences, however, do not need to be tied to the structural theory as it has been elaborated. We do not need to think of the ego as the "seat of anxiety" or to conceptualize excessive guilt and rage in terms of a punitive, "primitive" superego, as if each of these were a fixed entity in a tripartite mind. (Fairbairn, 1952, made an early critique of the mixed metaphors and arbitrariness of the tripartite division; see also Schafer, 1976.) Obeyesekere, by persuasively showing how the structural account itself is deeply embedded in European culture and thought, adds a distinctly cultural and historically specific conscience, based on a specific religion and family structure, to the less culture-bound claims of the first topography. Ironically, Freud's specifically cultural agency, the superego, turns out to be the most embedded culturally.

Obeyesekere's critique of the Freudian concept of the superego suggests that Westerners of particular times and places may be more likely to experience particular forms of superego guilt and a particular superego structure. Similarly, other psychoanalytic anthropologists, like anthropologists of self and feeling, pay attention to the cultural shaping of emotions and selves more generally. In his classic *Tahitians* (1973), Levy develops an account of how, in different cultures, some emotions are "hypocognized"—that is, not recognized—and others are "hypercognized"—that is, overrecognized and elaborated. Culturally recognized, or hypercognized, emotions can be subjectively labeled. In Tahiti, for example, sadness and depression are not culturally recognized emotions, so that when a Tahitian feels what a Western observer would call sadness, she labels it as something else— for example, spirit possession, physical illness, or fatigue. "Covert" knowing of one's emotions is thus distinguished from "overt" knowing. Levy follows Schachtel (1947) in suggesting that by providing particular emotion and sense categories and not others, cultures foster some linguistic, conceptual, and memory schemata and "starve" others. Even the quality of felt pain seems culturally specific, so that Levy observes that Tahitians seem actually to feel less pain from illness and injury than Americans would feel.

Levy wishes to develop a middle position between universalist, psychogenetic, panhuman views of the emotions and the view of Geertz and M. Z. Rosaldo that passions and affects are as cultural and public as institutions and beliefs (Levy, 1984, 217). He suggests that personal feeling is an organizing tool for perception and cognition and that, as cultures hypocognize and hypercognize different emotions, personal feeling also becomes organized symbolically. He draws on Klein and Devereux to stress the importance of this symbolization: "Feeling has something essential to do with the encounter with the world as represented cognitively. . . . Only the emotional-laden symbolic processing of percepts gives the infinite number of pieces of the perceived world some kind of integrated unity. . . . Symbolization [is] the process by means of which the infant apprehends reality and endows it with value" (218).

Levy thus pays close attention to the cultural labeling of emotions and "private experience," but he also moves definitively beyond analysis of discourse: it is actual feeling and emotion that are affected by the "cultural structuring of knowing" (218). Unlike the anthropologists of self and feeling, Levy is not saying that Tahitians can feel only what has been culturally labeled and relates to other public social and cultural forms. He notices flat affectivity and believes (though he is almost apologetic as he says so) that some cultural emotion schemata—say, the Tahitian denial and somatic displacement of sorrow over loss—"*may in some transcultural sense be wrong*" because they do not label what is "really" there (1984, 226). He also claims that Tahitian emotion labels refer to feelings "similar" to those we label (see especially 1973, chap. 9).

Culture, then, can help make some emotions more salient consciously and also, as it were, invest these emotions with emotional and fantasy meaning, thus shaping how they are experienced. It can also make some emotions harder to label and experience consciously. Several anthropologists follow Levy in this kind of investigation, showing how cultures conceptualize selfhood, identity and personhood, mental states and processes, and important interpersonal relationships (see, e.g., Hollan and Wellenkamp, 1994; Poole, 1991, 1994; Ingham, 1996).

Contemporary psychodynamic ethnographers rely on traditional psychodynamic and emotional categories and are less exclusively interested in language than are the anthropologists of self and feeling. They are certainly a step ahead of thinkers who hold that only the social and cultural side of life matters and who ignore the personal, emotional realm. At the same time, as anthropologists, most focus only or especially on shared categories that have general prevalence in a culture—looking at specific, culturally recognized psychodynamics, aspects of self, and emotional stresses, and bracketing or ignoring what is individual and idiosyncratic within this experience. (Marcus and Fischer, 1986, 50, also make this point.) The psychodynamic ethnographers retain a view that the cultural is by definition collective and consists of shared meanings.[9] Levy, for example, claims: "I am not concerned here with the more idiosyncratic components of an individual's personality, those components presumably determined by the fine details of his constitution and his developmental adventures, by his responses to the unique reality of his experience. The markedly different stylistic, ethical, and psychological qualities of my respondents, their colorful individualities, are background, as is their evident common humanity. . . . I am interested here in their *experience as Tahitians.* . . . My interest in *Tahitian* qualities produce[s] a partial portrait" (1973, xxiv; see also Hollan and Wellenkamp, 1994).

The desire to generalize and the attempt not to pathologize cultural variation lead many contemporary anthropologists of culture and personality not to pay much attention to people who react to emotional shaping and feeling rules, who resist them, feel impoverished when feeling finds no label, or try to create individual meaning that resonates with individual experience in spite of cultural hypocognition. Levy, for example, recognizes exceptions to his characterization of flat affectivity among Tahitians and finally takes a clinical as well as an ethnographic stance, speculating that hypocognized emotions may be particularly distressing. But these acknowledgments are not stressed. Rather, as these ethnographies persuasively address cultural difference and variation, they pass over individual differences and the way the culturalized psyche interacts with the personal psyche in an individual. They criticize traditional psychological anthropology and psychoanalysis for abstracting from cultural context and meaning that which fits preconceived Western-identified behaviors or dynamics and traits of personality, but the studies themselves abstract those behaviors, dynamics, traits, concepts, and meanings that are held in common and are therefore cultural.

These accounts, which portray a person in relation to culture, may or may not be based on a complex view of culture, then, but they tend to offer an unelaborated concept of the psyche—of an internally differentiated self, an inner world, or complex unconscious mental processes. By looking only at elements of meaning that are culturally shared and not at those which are individually particular, they cannot portray the personal experience of meaning. They skim off one part of experience, so that experience becomes less rich than it actually is. In the process, they lose understanding of how individual psychologies enact or express cultural forms and give them psychological force, depth, and complexity. Examination of exceptions, variations, and emotional dissonances would, I believe, give us greater insight into that very "experience as Tahitians" that Levy wishes to depict. As it is, part of what seems to sustain Levy's claims for the flattened, casual Tahitian emotionality is that, in his account, all Tahitians are alike. Where traditional theorists of culture and personality cut across cultures to retain universal assumptions about personhood, contemporary approaches do the reverse, cutting across persons to retain universal assumptions about culture.

Several formulations attempt to wrestle with this great difficulty in holding both culture and psyche fully in view. A prevalent solution for psychoanalytic anthropologists is to construct a doubled view of meaning. Robert LeVine (1984), for example, compares the distinction between cultural and individual meanings to a cognitive-developmental distinction between reflective and intuitive understanding (also to Turner's conceptualization of the poles of ideological and sensory meaning of cultural symbols). He uses as a metaphor a building or house. A house can have many reflective meanings, depending on whether you are its builder or architect, another architect, an engineer, or someone who lives in it and uses it functionally. If you live in the same house in childhood and adulthood, it will by adulthood have acquired functional and organizational meanings. Such multiple meanings are like the multiplicity of meaning that anthropology has discovered in cultural symbols, but LeVine wants particularly to stress the developmental changes in the experience of meaning from childhood to adulthood: reflective consciousness will overlay the more intuitive, lived, emotionally powerful sense of the house, just as the "same" cultural symbols will be known differently by child and adult. But the emotionally powerful childhood resonances will nevertheless still be there: "Earlier meanings are not lost but form the intuitive basis for emotional responsiveness to symbols even after the latter have been understood at a reflective level. . . . The multiplicity of experience over time has produced a multiplicity of meanings" (1984, 85–86).

In a similar vein, Spiro (1984) wishes to formulate an integrated psychodynamic and cultural account of emotions and the self. He distinguishes between the public, collective meanings of cultural symbols and the meanings they have for social actors, arguing that thoughts, as well as feelings, are by definition private and experienced by a person. "These meanings . . . do not constitute the (conventional) meanings *of* symbols but are rather the meanings that social actors, consciously or unconsciously, *intend* them to have." The meanings thoughts and emotions have for people are " 'located' not in the symbols themselves but in the minds of social actors" (325–326); they are properties of people, not cultures. Cultural propositions have unconscious as well as conscious meanings, and the "emotional action of symbols" lies in these unconscious meanings. Spiro's view is that those who study other cultures learn only conscious, conventional meanings. Such meanings are not full of the unconscious resonances that someone socialized in a culture will have as a result of the many contextualized and personally biographical settings in which such meanings are communicated: "The range of meanings that a culture has *for* social actors is much broader than the range of meanings *of* (conventional) cultural symbols" (326).

In arguing against accounts that rely on what he calls "particularistic cultural determinism"—that particular cultures entirely shape human activity, emotions, meaning, and interaction—Spiro, as I have indicated, tends to turn to a "generic cultural determinism" that considers how the mind works as a product of "culture in general." He emphasizes how "culture in general" acts on the unformed human to shape the generic culturalized human; in this context he returns to a cultural determinist account, albeit in universalistic rather than particularistic terms: "A set of universal culture patterns, . . . in interaction with a common biological heritage and common features of social interaction, creates a generic human mind" (335). Such an account makes the psychological once again derivative.

But Spiro also makes a different argument against particularistic cultural determinism. He not only argues for a generic cultural determinism but also makes claims for "transcultural characteristics of the human mind" (330). Spiro himself links these two formulations, implying that many of these transcultural characteristics of mind result from generic cultural determinism; at the same time he implies that these characteristics arise from and constitute a separate, undetermined realm of psychic meaning. In this latter view, the psychological, coded as "imagination and fantasy," is an independent level of reality—a transcending potential not "shaped" by biology, culture, or social relations but potentially autonomous. In arguing for the influence of biology and social relations, in addition to culture, on "action, growth, and understanding," he asks, "Is there nothing in imagination and fantasy that might also affect the way we feel about and live our lives? . . . Do our egos never transcend the constraints of all three determinants—the biological, the social, and the cultural alike—and thereby achieve some degree of autonomy, if only in fantasy and imagination?" (330). He accomplishes here what other accounts do not, by building psychological—personally interpretive and creative—agency into meaning. And he transcends the polarized limits set by those who oppose instinctual universals to culture.

Levy (1984), finally, distinguishes two different kinds of learning or knowledge. Children initially have "relatively random experiences" with others in a culture and learn a variety of relational lessons, and "later learning must operate to modify and control this primary knowledge." The individual comes to apply a cultural program to the primary reactivity established in initial experience. Early experience is "rich and diverse," and later experience is "starved" but cultural; early experience is perceptual, later experience conceptual. Like Freud's repressed unconscious, "the 'starved schemata' are left as a basis for creativity, dreams, humor, and transcultural understanding" (225).

Levy, then, tries developmentally and conceptually to sort out primary (random, personal) and secondary (cultural) awareness, primary and secondary feelings, first- and second-order knowledge, and personally random and culturally systematic experiences and knowledge. For Levy, emotions are more than ritual or linguistic attitudes, but his account of the cultural constructions of emotions is not accompanied by a psychodynamic theory of self. Instead, he returns, unavoidably, to a universal human mind "outside" culture. This "mind" has an initial "feeling," itself outside both person and culture, which the "person," who may or may not act in terms of her internalized "culture," then reacts to. Culture becomes a "system of control" to produce appropriate behavior. Emotional feeling "activates" a cultural response or label, even in the "internalized culture" of the individual; but the feeling is in the " 'human mind' . . . that cultures everywhere . . . have to deal with" (232). Such a view leads to unnecessary polarizations, as Levy grapples with the incontrovertible implication of his primary/secondary schema: that some senses of an emotion, because they do not label what's "really" there, "*may in some transcultural sense be wrong*" (226). What is really there developed during childhood interactions and is therefore primary, or "precultural" (Spiro, 1984).

All these formulations, put forth by psychoanalytically or psychiatrically trained anthropologists, struggle to move beyond a dualistic view of meaning but cannot quite succeed. The anthropological view expressed is that culture consists in supra-individual, collective, consensual, symbolic, cognitive, and linguistic meanings. These are the meanings that anthropologists learn, and they are thinner, not full of the personalized and individualized resonance that someone socialized in a culture has, as a result of the extensive contextualized events through which such meanings are communicated. Culture in this view can be studied apart from the meanings it has for particular actors. The intense, personalized meanings of culture are a thing apart, characterized as primary, sensory, full of surplus, and not just core, meanings. These meanings are originally the province of childhood but continue to be found in the unpredictable creativity of "imagination and fantasy" and "intuitive emotional responsiveness" that, growing from childhood, persist throughout life. Contextualized childhood social and interpersonal experiences, imagination, and fantasy cause a culture whose meanings exist apart from the individual to be "internalized" as personal belief and experience.

Such formulations make sense from the point of view of the observer, but they miss, even as they extensively theorize, the point of view of the subject. As observers or theorists, we can certainly distinguish analytically and conceptually those webs of meanings which are cultural (shared, related to other cultural meanings), and those which are intrapsychic, within one person. For the subject, however, there is a fusion of cultural and personal meaning in any emotional or cultural response or thought. Any cultural meaning, as it is conveyed and as it is experienced, is infused with emotional particularity in complex, indeterminate ways, as well as with particulars of discursive context, social setting, and so forth. Correspondingly, as Klein's transferential "doubling" suggests, unconscious fantasy meanings hook onto and into cultural and social realities and gain meaning from them, also in indeterminate ways. Psychoanalytic ethnographic accounts of the psychological meanings of cultural symbols and practices for particular individuals in specific contexts enable us to see how this complex double reality works. Like Rosaldo's "Grief," such accounts document emotional investment in cultural practices and beliefs and the cultural infusing of psychodynamic experience. These accounts go further than Rosaldo, however, in that they also give us a theoretical understanding of the processes they describe.

Anthropologist-psychoanalyst Kracke's *Force and Persuasion*

(1978) investigates patterns of leadership in an indigenous Brazilian community, comparing two settlements organized around two different leaders. He wishes to show how different leaders operate and how their different personalities make them more or less suited to particular historically situated political and economic conditions. He also uses psychoanalytically derived interviewing techniques to investigate the life histories, fantasies, dreams, conflicts, and defense configurations of these leaders and several of their followers. Kracke shows how their particular psychodynamic organizations, histories, and motivations draw particular men to follow one or another leader and how each leader himself, as a result of his own psychic conflicts and fantasies, organizes his group and develops his form of leadership. In arguing theoretically that leadership fulfills both social and psychological prerequisites and in demonstrating how the duality works empirically, he thus carefully keeps in view both the social and the psychological without letting one determine or explain the other. In order to understand leadership and organization in any setting, both must be investigated.

Kracke thus documents the lack of determinism in social form and the intrinsic involvement of personal psychology in any social outcome. He also argues against the notion of some simple cultural shaping of personality in early childhood. For him, "each individual must select from his experiences—some of which are bound to be 'atypical'—those to emphasize and those to pass over in his own personality integration" (27). Prevalent cultural practices and patterns have "quite different personal significance and relative emphasis for different individuals" (29). Although Kracke is interested in emotional style and concepts of emotion in Kagwahiv culture, they are not a central part of his inquiry. Instead, he argues that a description of social norms and social structures cannot predict social process, because personal choice, itself based on unconscious as well as conscious factors, along with the much more widely studied ambiguities that inhere in cultural meanings and social practices, always plays a part. Kracke pays particular attention to the fact that people can invoke norms to cover behavior motivated by personal rather than normative factors.

Kracke is not afraid that a focus on individual difference detracts from an understanding of culture. He argues against an approach to culture and personality based on a "replication of uniformity" (252) and emphasizes that the individuality he found in his informants is one that all anthropologists see but many pass over (xii). Thus, although his research focuses on personality and psychodynamics, Kracke argues directly against the tradition of culture and personality (and implicitly against the ethnographers of self and feeling as well). For him, cultural personality is a limited concept: "The personality sketches . . . bring out the diversity of character, conflicts, and defenses to be found in a group of Kagwahiv individuals, of a range and variety similar to what we might find in a comparable group among ourselves. This is not to say that there is nothing distinctively Kagwahiv about their personalities; one may find a number of common patterns in their mode of emotional expression and conceptualization of emotions, such as Robert Levy describes for Tahiti. But when we focus on individual motivations in specific situations and on the configuration of needs and defenses that make up individual personalities, we find the same sorts of differences among people that are familiar in our own society, and the same range of personality configurations" (237).

Obeyesekere further portrays and theorizes the individual-culture nexus. In the concept of personal symbol, he captures both how cultural symbols can ground and organize psychological conflict and the nondetermined individual creativity in this personal evocation of cultural meaning. He develops this concept in *Medusa's Hair* (1981), a study of Sri Lankan Buddhist priestesses with matted hair who enter a trance. Obeyesekere shows how the public symbolism of the matted hair becomes "infused with personal meaning" for the priestesses, thereby enabling intrapsychic conflicts, personal psychodynamics, and private meanings to be expressed in this cultural idiom. Intrapsychic pain and conflict here can be integrated and transcended, as it is recognized and given meaning by others as well as by the self.

Obeyesekere notes that for a cultural symbol to be also a personal symbol, it must be accorded a personal psychodynamic meaning by the actor; in this sense, he takes issue indirectly with anthropologists and others who interpret cultural symbols psychoanalytically without reference to their meaning for particular individuals (see also Kracke, 1994, 210, on wild cultural analysis). Ostensibly psychologically meaningful cultural symbols that do not have meaning for particular people are psychogenetic symbols, symbols that may once have carried unconscious symbolism but no longer have psychological resonance or personal meaning for the user.

Obeyesekere implies that particular symbols, like matted hair, signifying castration, have potentially universal unconscious meanings that resonate for certain people because of their own intrapsychic conflicts. These people, for psychodynamic reasons, then reproduce and enact these symbols. But his account does not require such universalism. We could also suggest that particular cultural symbols appeal to particular individuals not necessarily because their psyches resonate with universal meanings but because they can personally infuse these symbols with their own psychobiographically particularized unconscious fantasies and emotions. They create meaning from within rather than latching on to a universal meaning because of the coincidence of the given meaning with their own inner world. In a particular cultural setting, it is not unlikely that practitioners might have some similar unconscious fantasies and emotions that imbue cultural symbols: for reasons of common life experience, these symbols serve in some ways as collective evocative objects, but symbols do not in themselves necessarily have universally given meanings.

Personal symbols operate simultaneously on both the cultural and the personal level; neither can be reduced to the other. They enable personal psychodynamic expression and cultural intelligibility at the same time, uniting rather than opposing symptom and symbol. Accordingly, priestesses in trance cannot be seen simply in Western psychiatric terms as mad, psychotic, or sick. Their apparently symptomatic behavior expresses unconscious fantasy and an unconscious inner world, but it is also interpersonally intelligible and culturally validated as meaningful. Although in a trance, they are at the same time aware of participating in a cultural practice. As Obeyesekere (1981, 105) puts it, trance possession may be ego-alien, but it is not culturally alien. Obeyesekere gives us what he would call a Weberian psychoanalysis: personal symbols, like culture in general, help to satisfy what is almost a Weberian species-drive for meaning and coherence. Symbols can have cultural meaning in relation to other cultural meanings, but some will also be personal symbols whose primary significance and meaning lie in the life experiences of individuals. Cultural ideas and experiences are filtered through personal meaning, or given personal meaning that is at the same time cultural.

Personal symbols, in this view, have the characteristics of transitional phenomena that link inner and outer. They are given as cultural and presented from without—products of specific historical interactions and institutions, gaining meaning within particular networks of meaning. But they are also created through personal fantasy animation from within—individually created anew, not just once for all, but each time an individual experiences them with personal psychological force. In this account, both an individual, intrapsychic invocation and a putting together of cultural categories (that are themselves also emotionally laden and embedded) create cultural meanings for any individual. As with transitional phenomena, if we try to give one of these determinations priority over the other, we lose the very both-and object we are trying to describe. When we look at the concept of personal symbol and its application by different ethnographers, we can see how intuitively right is Winnicott's claim that the transitional object expands into the location of cultural experience, how culture is a product of potential space and has a transitional character.[10]

When we look at the priestesses in *Medusa's Hair* or the two leaders in *Force and Persuasion,* we can see that there is never a single way in which a cultural meaning is personally construed. Anthropologists, like other cultural thinkers, have in recent years stressed how complex, contradictory, multiple, and situated cultural meanings are. From psychoanalysis and psychoanalytic anthropology, we also can see how cultural meanings, like any dream image or other psychological symbol or fantasy, are also personally multiple, individualized, and situated, with no fixed and unchanging meaning. In addition, contemporary accounts stress that the relations between cultural meanings and personal meanings, and between culture and personality, are not so seamlessly intertwined as psychological anthropology once affirmed. There is no simple internalization of culture, no single way in which psyches hook onto culture. Rather, the same disjunctions, contradictions, and tensions that inhere in meaning in general also inhere in the various relations between culture and psyche.[11]

Fitz John Porter Poole also investigates these disjunctions. He is interested in "how what is culturally constituted and socially negotiated can become personally significant and endowed with psychological force" (1994, 854), and he shows in case studies how particular children's conflicts, fears, and anxieties can be partially expressed and made sense of intrapsychically through personal symbols that are also cultural symbols. But he is also attentive to those elements of fantasy and fear that do not find such integration and that, even if they draw on cultural meanings and images, remain on the level of individual, often painful, fantasy and symptom (1987, 1992). Thus, not only are cultural meanings and culture contextual, embedded, and ambiguous, but among members of one culture individual understandings of cultural forms and practices are not automatically congruent. "Personal construals of cultural schemata of personhood, selfhood, and individuality" (1994, 852) do not always work emotionally and intrapsychically.

In a similar vein, Herdt (1987) suggests that the public, cultural meanings of a symbol or ritual and its private, personal meaning might be diametrically opposed. The secret ritual flutes of Sambia male initiation, for example, are publicly conceptualized as masculine, powerful, and aggressive, whereas their meaning as personal symbol to participants involves femininity, powerlessness, and vulnerability. Robert Stoller and Herdt (1982) investigate the case of a Sambia man who does not "complete" his socialization and move from homosexual to heterosexual desire.

Kracke does not deny that in some ways culture provides meaning and context for individual personal development ("this is not to say that there is nothing distinctively Kagwahiv about their personalities"), but with Poole and Stoller and Herdt, he claims that the founding culture and personality conception of a close parallel between psyche and culture is empirically incorrect as well as distinctly unpsychoanalytic: "Were we all perfectly shaped by our upbringing, life would be much simpler, and desire less prone to conflict. On the contrary, what Freud showed was precisely that adult designs for child rearing are bound to come up against the child's own construction, shaped by fantasy and stage-specific needs and desires, and by efforts to fulfill forbidden desires despite all adult efforts at socialization. Individual differences in temperament, in relative strength of desires and endowment, and in a whole host of endogenous factors, make it impossible to predict how a given individual will resolve a given conflict, let alone how a group of people will respond if faced by the same socialization demand" (1994, 215).

Another form of tension and disjunction within cultural psyches and psychologically imbued culture is described in Obeyesekere's *Work of Culture* (1990). The work of culture consists in "the process whereby symbolic forms existing on the cultural level get created and recreated through the minds of people," but Obeyesekere also notes that personal symbols can vary in their distance from the intrapsychic stress or conflict that they enact and draw upon, in a process he calls symbolic remove.[12] Thus, he describes how one participant in a culturally recognized ritual involving self-mutilation has in fact only a thin hold on the cultural veneer of his practice: these practices bring some control and order to a chaotic and conflictually driven inner life, but this practitioner does not have the flexibility or distance to enact the ritual fully as a ritual. Unlike the priestesses in *Medusa's Hair,* this man "has not exorcised his own past, the pressures of his infantile history have not been resolved through the symbol system, and they continue to exercise control over his everyday existence" (11). For this practitioner, participation in cultural symbolic practice leads to regression and even symptom formation, whereas in cases of greater symbolic remove, the use of personal symbols extends progressively in more creative and flexible directions.

The concept of symbolic remove allows us to extend Winnicott's claim about the transitional location of cultural experience. Grolnick (1987) claims that a concept like Obeyesekere's symbolic remove needs to be introduced if we are to understand how transitional phenomena become culture. He distinguishes "potential space" (also Winnicott's term) from transitional phenomena and argues that potential space is a "more abstract, nonprimitive illusional heir to the *pre*symbolic concept of the transitional object and phenomenon. In transitional space, only partially differentiated symbols and referents live and are played with in the service of development, socialization, and acculturation. In potential space, more grown-up, hopefully multivalent symbols with roots in the bodily self, or drives if you will, reach up to the anagogic" (139). Both these conceptualizations—symbolic remove and the change from transitional phenomena to potential space in the symbolic realm—draw confirmation also from Klein's (1930) and Segal's (1957) insistence on the importance of symbolization to psychic health, as well as in some ways linking Winnicott to Freud's concept of sublimation.[13]

In my view, Jean Briggs (1991, 1998, and elsewhere) provides the most persuasive and extensive account of the multiplicity and personal individuality of cultural meanings and the disjunctions between psyche and culture, of the way that culturally infused psyches and psychologically infused cultural meanings (all terms comprising a modifier and a noun seem to privilege one direction of construction over another) express uneasy compromises and contradictions. Since *Never in Anger* (1970), Briggs has turned her attention to the minidramas, or "games," involving cultural emotional and interpersonal values that Inuit adults play with children. Although she found living up to Inuit values very difficult and conflictual, it did not at first occur to her that the Inuit themselves experienced mixed feelings about the emotions they were expected to portray (1982, 1987). Her observation of these games—games about anger, possessiveness, who belongs to whom, sibling jealousy, being loved, humiliated, or abandoned—leads her to propose that personal commitment to cultural values and meanings and making these one's own are strengthened to the extent that the emotions that sustain and invest them are contradictory, complex, and ambivalent. Learning cultural meanings is not simply a matter of straightforward socialization; rather, conformity to cultural expectations arises from a sense of internal conflict and danger. Thus, Briggs stands the debate about internalization and cultural conformity on its head, in arguing that it is those very cultural values and meanings that matter that are most likely to be inconsistently internalized. It is the fact of their being emotionally charged and continually invested with fantasy, conflict, and shifting private meaning that keeps cultural meanings alive for the individual and thus for the culture.

Briggs asks, "What can a study of the individual contribute to the anthropological enterprise?" (1991, 111), but she immediately recognizes that in referring to "the" individual, she is already homogenizing many individuals and abstracting from them: "It is not *the* individual that creates meanings, it is individuals who do so."[14] Her goal is to show how "culture operates in persons and how persons operate with culture, each creating the other" and she chooses the case study method to do this (112). Accordingly, Briggs follows one little girl, Chubby Maata, as the child creates the meanings of herself, her family, and her cultural environment. Briggs thus learns about this one little girl's psyche (Briggs is interested in the personally psychological as a register in itself) and also about the multiple, shifting, ambiguous, situated complexity of each cultural meaning, practice, and rule that this little girl grapples with (Briggs is interested in the constitution and experience of culture). She documents how a child's early experiences are themselves fusions of cultural and personal meaning, as patterns of interaction and shared emotional experiences come to form a self in relation to others who are themselves culturally and personally actors and experiencers.

Briggs describes not only the learning and acquisition of culture in general but the learning and adoption of particular cultural-personal meanings. She is an anthropological observer of children who, intuitively and through her research, understands the complexity of inner worlds of meaning. We do not elsewhere have such extended naturalistic accounts of, for example, how children come to a conscious and unconscious gendered subjectivity, of how "we" experiences, as described by Emde and his colleagues (Emde, 1991, Emde and Sorce, 1983), are created between mother and child, or of how language, as Loewald (1978a) holds, arises originally in the interpersonal maternal matrix and always has idiosyncratic, situated unconscious emotional and fantasy meaning as well as culturally recognized public meaning.

Briggs goes back to the games and problematized questions that a child participates in: "Every time the question occurs, it will resonate with other occurrences, so that each plot will provide additional clues to how to deal with the problem. Meanings will cumulate, and in this way, little by little, children will create for themselves worlds that contain variants of plots of their parents' worlds." These many occurrences will be linked by affective as well as cognitive plot: "It is also possible to find links among interactions by tracing the tones of voice in which messages are delivered. . . . tracing out all these interrelationships, recognizing at the same time that there must be many others that I cannot trace, which are created by associations in other communicative modalities—facial expressions, gestures, touches, smells— . . . a labyrinth of potential meanings that children have to thread their way through, meanings that they have to trace out repeatedly, and repeatedly try to make *temporary* sense of, by selecting links, codifying perceptions, forming and revising hypotheses about relationships, consequences of action, and so on" (1991, 147). Briggs's modesty about her claims, I believe, should be heeded by those clinicians who, as they analyze an adult, claim to know exactly how that adult thought and felt as an infant: "Of course, my image of the world that a child is building will never match exactly that of the child. . . . I can never have access to all the material out there in the world that the child has to build with; I can never see, hear, smell, and feel all that happens to the child. Secondly, and more fundamentally, I am not that child; I do not have the child's accumulated store of thoughts and feelings with which to meet events, react to them, create them, and build on them. Moreover, not only do I not have the child's thoughts and feelings, I have a great many of my own, which interfere" (1991, 147–148).

Briggs's research on one individual's richly textured, complex, many-storied experiences of "culture" leads her to change her conception of culture to one surprisingly in accord with postmodern conceptions. Culture, like psyche, comprises multiple, shifting meanings, "a mosaic of dilemmas, which echo, cross-cut, confirm, and negate one another; which are never totally resolved, and which always have to be juggled, rearranged, repeatedly dealt with and redealt with" (1991, 148). This mosaic is "organized and created in the minds and bodies of those who participate in it" (148). Culture consists of a great many "ingredients" that individuals actively "select, interpret, and use in various ways as opportunities, capabilities, and experience allow" (112). This selection from the mosaic, however, is not only practical, institutional, cognitive, or strategic but also affective and personal: ingredients are "available for being invested with affect, hence meaning" (148).

This approach is a tricky business. Although Briggs's case study keeps an individual, Chubby Maata, in full view in all her complexity, the "culture as a bag of ingredients" formulation threatens to lose the role of affective and personal meaning in actually creating cultural meanings, rather than simply selecting among them. Briggs tries to avoid this anthropological pitfall. Much as LeVine, Spiro, and Levy do, she differentiates the "substance" of culture from the "experience" of culture, the "overt substance of values, attitudes and behavior—'Inuit are generous'; 'Inuit value autonomy'—from their psychodynamic functions and meanings, that is, the emotional resonances and motives" that underlie and give meaning to substantive culture (1991, 150). Just as cultural stories about gender, as well as a multiplicity of affective, bodied, and other sensual communications, help to create a child's sense of gender, Briggs shows how the games and dramas put forth "in emotionally forceful ways" (149) for a little Inuit child (and other Inuit children) make particular emotional dilemmas and cultural values visible to children. Much as I argue earlier, Briggs notes that she can generalize about how these processes probably work but not about the specific content of the fantasies and conflicts that will emerge for each child, in her own particular family, with her own particular daily experience, and her own particular potential.[15]

According to Briggs, when you study individual experience, the almost definitional "shared" nature of culture becomes problematized. Neither the overt substance of culture, its underlying psychodynamic meanings, nor the processes of acquisition of either cognitive or emotional elements of culture can be assumed to be the same; when they seem to be shared, it is an empirical matter for investigation, not a definitional one. Like interpersonal transferences and projective investments of the outer world with unconscious fantasy and meaning, any individual's involvement with a cultural identity or value, her unconscious and conscious, emotional and fantasy investment and interpretation of elements of culture differ at different points in time. Danger and conflict, rather than unproblematic internalization, help to fix and create the emotional importance of cultural values for the individual. Briggs's claim that "the 'same' value may be psychodynamically different and may play different roles in the psychic economies of different individuals, or for the same individual at different points in the life cycle—or even at different moments in the day—because it is associated with different tangles of experience" (1991, 151) almost echoes Klein's account (1952 and elsewhere) of the rapid-fire projective and introjective shifting of inner and outer worlds. More than anyone, Briggs documents Loewald's claim (1951 and elsewhere) that for the individual, ego and reality are created at the same time.

Anthropologists do not just study the psyche of the native. Like contemporary psychoanalysts, they stress the role of the ethnographic encounter in the generation of anthropological knowledge, and they draw on their own reactions. As Obeyesekere puts it, "Ethnography highlights, more than any other human science, the intersubjective relationship between the scholar and the subject of his study, by focussing on a single individual, or a couple at most, hopelessly trying to make do in an alienating field situation" (1990, 225). Obeyesekere might have included psychoanalysis with ethnography here: his description (225–236) of what he calls the "second intersubjectivity" of the ethnographer's participation and observation could stand almost verbatim for many contemporary psychoanalytic descriptions of the psychoanalytic encounter and the psychoanalyst's role, knowledge, and self-knowledge within it.

But it is not only psychological anthropologists who make such observations. Ortner, for example, claims that ethnography means many things, but "minimally, . . . it has always meant the attempt to understand another life world using the self—as much of it as possible—as the instrument of knowing" (1995, 173), and Rabinow writes of the "mutually constructed ground of experience and understanding" in ethnography (1977, 39). The sociological ethnographer Stacey claims that the new ethnography emphasizes the "interactive and subjective character of ethnographic knowledge" (1990, 36), and Riesman (1974) calls his book an "introspective ethnography."[16]

In Chapter 5, I pointed to the remarkable convergence of method, epistemology, attention, and experience in the clinical consulting room and in the field. Of all the "applied" fields of psychoanalysis, only in psychoanalytic anthropology do we find the actual intersubjective encounter, the processes of transference and countertransference, and the attempt to understand another (or many others) directly as a result of interaction with them that we also find in the psychoanalytic clinical encounter. Just as psychoanalysts have discovered that some of their greatest and deepest insights—those most attuned, perhaps, to unconscious life—come from analysis of countertransference, projective identifications, and other moments that feel not as though one is figuring out an intellectual puzzle about a patient's psyche but, as though, in some sense, one is experiencing something in relation to that psyche, so it seems that self-scrutiny within psychological anthropology provides persuasive insight into the native's psyche. Although many anthropologists recognize that ethnographic knowledge emerges from intersubjective encounters and from introspection, psychoanalytic ethnographers offer the most theorized account of these observations. They document inextricable connections between the reflective psychodynamic awareness of the anthropologist, her participation in the ethnographic encounter, and her understanding of the dynamic processes that create cultural and emotional meaning for the native.

But these parallels have not been noticed by psychoanalysts (at least not since the 1930s). We could speculate about this peculiar omission among practitioners normally so self-reflective about the nature of their discipline. In general, it seems that when psychoanalysts extend their interests in nonbiomedical directions, they extend it toward the humanities and arts. Without minimizing the intrinsic interest and fascination of psychoanalytic literary and art criticism, psychobiography, psychohistory, and psychoanalytic interpretations of texts, stories, and myths, we can note that analysts can claim to do the same kind of applied psychoanalysis as scholars trained in these other fields. But without further professional training, psychoanalysts do not have the same investigative access to people in general, and especially to peoples of other cultures, that they have to texts and other arts and artefacts. In addition, it may be the case that concern (if not obsession) with defending psychoanalysis as a science leads most psychoanalysts to shy away from comparing their field to an assertively nonscientific social science. For these practitioners, by contrast, it is clear that one is doing something entirely different in interpreting a text. Accordingly, those psychoanalysts who have turned toward a hermeneutic-interpretive perspective have done so via philosophy and literary interpretation; their interest in hermeneutics and interpretation has not led to knowledge about or interest in the social sciences.

Psychoanalytic anthropologists both theorize the ethnographic encounter as a clinical encounter and describe the empirical understanding they gain by so doing. Kracke (1987a) argues that an anthropologist's emotional engagement with another culture is central to successful cross-cultural understanding. Just as the topics of study that interest him have to do with unconscious fantasies, psychic processes like dreams and emotions, and the way people in different cultures use cultural beliefs and practices to express unconscious fantasies or allay the anxieties that they generate, he also claims that his "view of the nature of ethnography is essentially psychoanalytic" (1994, 196). He notes that terms like "culture shock" attest to the emotional impact (in this case seen as negative) of cross-cultural experience. His own characterization stresses the rapidly fluctuating variety of emotional reactions—"an alternation of excitement, discovery, frustration, embarrassment, liberation, depression, elation, puzzlement" (1987a, 60), including the anxiety described by Devereux (1967) that is especially elicited by cultural practices or beliefs repressed and repudiated in the ethnographer's own culture.[17]

Kracke finds the conception of transference useful in encompassing the affective dimension of the ethnographic experience, both transferences to particular individuals with whom the anthropologist interacts and transferences to cultural themes as a whole. In the anthropological encounter, he notes, not only is present experience invested with unconscious meanings from the past and experienced in light of them—meanings that might, in some sense, distort or narrow one's vision and understanding—but the anthropologist's transferences also have broader import. Drawing upon Loewald and Bird, Kracke suggests that unconscious transferences are ubiquitous and give depth and significance to any relationship or experience. In this way, they create the emotional significance of the ethnographic encounter and make possible a complex, multilayered understanding of another culture and the individuals within it. Just as the analyst recognizes the patient's psyche partly by experiencing her own, so, Kracke suggests, the anthropologist's transferences—resonant creations of personal meaning—"may be an important vehicle for perceiving elusive—and especially emotionally toned—aspects of the present" culture (1987a, 65). "Self-understanding is not just a by-product of intercultural experience; it is the crucial tool of ethnography" (1994, 211).

Kracke is aware of a potential danger in assuming that the ethnographer's transferences necessarily describe and reflect another culture rather than projectively create it in the anthropologist's mind. But he suggests that the anthropologist's transferences, if analyzed and made conscious, will react to a cultural " 'hook' "—"a nucleus of real, if subtle, congruence between the current situation or relationship and the past one which makes it possible to experience them in the same way" (1987a, 65). Transference, he is suggesting, not only creates the unconscious personal emotional and fantasy meaning of inner life and an internal world; it is also elicited by objective assessments and perceptions of reality. His argument, then, accords with Klein's careful attention (1940) to the external world that partially creates and "doubles" the inner one, with Winnicott's understanding (1971) that the transitional object is, in part, objectively presented from without, and with Bollas's conception (1992) of the evocative object. Kracke's own self-analytic work in the field allowed him to see how evoked transferential fantasies (of rivalry with a sibling, of not feeling understood as a child, of being a helpless child with less knowledge and competence than grown-ups, of feelings about his father) shaped his emotional reactions to particular experiences and people and some of the emphases and interpretations in his writings and also how they helped him understand particular cultural themes, preoccupations, and personal interactions. As has been the case for other ethnographers, his freer emotional and transferential involvement also led him toward cultural themes, as he puts it, that were *"their* central concern" (1987a, 72) rather than his own. These data he gathered about others' emotionally charged concerns, he suggests, are probably better than those he gathered on his own explicit research topic.

In the classic psychoanalytic ethnography in which he develops the concept of personal symbol, Obeyesekere also illustrates Kracke's claims. Obeyesekere (of course, a different Sri Lankan native from the Sri Lankan natives he studied), turned to the study of "Medusa's hair" because of his own strong reactions, experienced as castration anxiety, on first viewing the snakelike matted locks of the priestesses. He draws on these countertransferential reactions but is careful not to impose them: "But could it not have been a *fantasy* of castration anxiety by an anthropologist sensitive to psychoanalysis rather than the real thing?" (1981, 7). Yet, while acknowledging that his personal reaction constitutes the anthropologist's projection of meaning, he nonetheless gives himself permission to study both the priestesses and their rituals for their own sake. He notes, moreover, as do recent psychoanalysts who write of attitudes toward countertransference in the past, that anthropologists almost never mention their personal projections or values and the cultural biases they bring to the field situation. "It is folly," he claims, "to imagine that the informant carries the burden of anxieties, cultural values, and personal idiosyncrasies and that the investigator is exempt from them" (8). He advocates using personal projections as a tool (see also Obeyesekere, 1990), not to assume similarity between one's psyche and those of one's informants but also not to rule out the possibility that personal preoccupations reflect those of informants.

There is a parallel, then, between analytic listening and clinical listening. As Kracke puts it, "the analyst, like the anthropologist, tries to be as open as possible to what is different about the structure of the other person's thinking, to keep to a minimum the intrusion of his or her own presumptions, preoccupations, or predilections" (1994, 199). Just as in psychoanalysis, ethnographic focus on conflictual topics brings the ethnographer closer to personal-cultural meaning. Ewing (1987) finds that in therapy, as in fieldwork, she learns best about the experience of cultural meanings from informant accounts that are ambivalent, emotion-laden, and conflictual rather than from seamless, narratively smooth cultural stories. In ethnography as in therapy, constructions of meaning are completely dependent on the interaction between anthropologist and informant, such that the anthropologist's own anxieties and confusions contribute to the quality of any interaction. Retrospectively, after clinical training, Ewing is able to analyze her own projections and constructions of psychodynamic meaning that interfered in earlier ethnographic research and to hear the many levels of communication conveyed by her informant as she speaks about conflictual and difficult issues. Ewing learns about cultural beliefs by listening not only to how a person construes these beliefs but also to how her own countertransferences and projections shape her listening and the other's sense of freedom to communicate.

Just as Rosaldo's "Grief" provides a paradigmatic argument from outside psychological anthropology for the importance of drawing on the anthropologist's emotional experience in cultural understanding, Briggs provides the complementary, and considerably more extended, argument from within. Briggs was one of the first ethnographers to insist on the cultural shaping of emotions, and to do so through her own experience, although it is not until her later writings that she theorizes her clinical method. In her now classic *Never in Anger* (1970), Briggs describes how she came to understand Inuit rules of emotion and what it feels like to act, feel, and interact within them. As she tells it, Briggs set out with the intention to study shamanism, but there were no acknowledged shamans in the community. At the same time, she found that her relations with her Inuit family were extremely difficult, and as a result she often felt irritable and depressed. At one point she was ostracized from the community for, in her view, trying to defend it against exploitation by Canadian hunters. Her acute personal pain and jarring, when her too quick temper, emotional outbursts, and general irritability were absolutely unacceptable to her hosts, and her descriptions of being alone, cold, and desolate in a tent for days without visitors give us a sense of what interpersonal contact means in such a setting. She was treated in these situations, she says, like a recalcitrant child, and she often felt like one—unsocial, annoyed, not wanting to help, wanting to be alone.

Briggs is, of course, not from the Inuit culture, but we begin to see from her experience and self-observations what the costs and difficulties might be of acting "never in anger." We also see this in her detailed, carefully rendered observations of interactions with children as they are slowly socialized into controlling their emotions. She describes a four-year-old girl forced, once again, to accede to the demands of her three-year-old sister, still considered a baby: "I had never imagined that sulking could be such an aggressive act, that one could feel so directly attacked by inertness" (138). And she closely observes individual differences in adults' abilities fully to master anger. But the real persuasiveness of her account comes from her own story of the way she participated, and not as a detached anthropological observer, in the emotional interactions and rules that she also describes. There is no question in *Never in Anger* that Briggs was more than a cultural actor with a translation problem. She gives us a here-and-now, immediate rendering of the quality of emotional expression in a setting distant and unfamiliar to us.

Although it is based on careful, extensive field observations, conversations, formal interviews, life with an Inuit family over a long period, and other traditional ethnographic practices, Briggs's first study of Inuit emotional self-construction really derives, as she acknowledges, from analysis of her own experiences: "My first view of Inuit interpersonal relationships . . . derived from that first field problem: how to figure out what was wrong with my relations with the Inuit" (1987, 9). In her later research, although her direct, first-person voice remains, so that we always have a sense of Briggs as a participant in any setting or interaction she observes, Briggs does not explicitly describe and draw upon her own reactions as a key to cultural understanding. The subsequent focus of her inquiry, her methods, and her theory, however, derive from this first experience, indirectly if not directly, as Briggs continues to focus on the personal force of cultural processes. Her ethnographic understanding of Inuit emotional values and practices has developed through her own interpersonal and intrapsychic experience of these values.

We come back, finally, to the issue of how to theorize about this ethnographic encounter, for those who study the cultural psyche and psychologically infused culture within it; how to capture the contribution of the anthropologist's observations, transferences, and anxieties and the projections and projective identifications directed toward the anthropologist, in relation to the informant's expressions, described experiences, and accounts of culture and life history. Kracke, Briggs, Obeyesekere, and others describe important elements in such encounters; Crapanzano (1980) tries to show how it is finally put together. His *Tuhami: Portrait of a Moroccan* defines the terrain for contemporary self-reflective ethnography. Other psychoanalytic anthropologists have stressed the potential space in which culture, or personal symbols, are created and expressed and the cultural evocative objects that the ethnographer's transferences adhere to. Crapanzano brings a similar conception to the ethnographic encounter itself. He claims that anthropological knowledge—whatever the anthropologist subsequently claims to be the reality of a culture—has been misrepresented. This knowledge itself is part of a potential space, or what we might call, following Ogden's conception of an analytic third (1994), an ethnographic third. It can be reduced neither to the informant's perspective and experience nor to the ethnographer's but is entirely relationally based and created: "The ethnographic encounter, like any encounter between individuals or, for that matter, with oneself in moments of self-reflection, is always a complex negotiation in which the parties to the encounter acquiesce to a certain reality. This 'reality' belongs (if it is in fact possible to speak of the possession of a reality removed from any particular social or endopsychic encounter) to none of the parties to the encounter. It is—and this is most important—usually presumed to be the reality of one's counterpart to which one has acquiesced, to expedite the matter on hand" (Crapanzano, 1980, ix).

Crapanzano follows Devereux in attributing the need to deny the negotiated nature of reality to the anxieties of full recognition of the mutual construction of reality and "the burden that encounter imposes on the psyche of the investigator" (xiii). Like Devereux, he points to the varieties of methods used to ensure purported objectivity and generalizability (for instance, repeated questioning, focusing on consistency and patterns, multiple modes of research) and claims that these methods, and even extensive self-reflection and evaluation, "serve as rationalizations for the objectification of the negotiated reality and its attribution to the Other" (x). Like other contemporary ethnographers, and like contemporary psychoanalytic thinkers, Crapanzano is critical of the professional tendency to present a culture and its members as if they exist out there to be studied: "In the ethnographic encounter, where the matter at hand is the knowledge of the Other and his reality, there is a very strong compulsion to attribute the negotiated reality to one's informant" (x). The pull he describes is very much like the analyst's pull to conceptualize her discoveries as inhering in the analysand: "By eliminating himself from the ethnographic encounter, the anthropologist can deny the essential dynamics of the encounter and end up producing a static picture of the people he has studied and their ways. It is this *picture . . .* that becomes the 'culture' of the people" (ix).

Within the literature of psychoanalytic anthropology, we find increasingly complex accounts of the intersections of psyche and culture, neither one reducible to or determined by the other, but the content of each infused by the other. We also find that these accounts move away from universalist notions of psychic content or bioevolutionary and instinctual universals underlying culture. In this sense these accounts certainly address those social scientists who find it hard to conceive of an inner psyche that does not reduce to nature or who equate psychology with biology. Without always having the apposite psychoanalytic terms to formulate their conceptions, writers of these accounts see the psyche as constituted introjectively and projectively in the intersubjective (transferential and countertransferential) encounter and the intrapsychic here and now rather than primarily in the childhood past. They conceptualize the culture-psyche nexus in terms of live, fantasy- and emotion-imbued personal symbols, of transitional objects or potential space. Some take issue with and provide empirical arguments against Freud's universalism of psychic content—for instance, his notion of a universal Oedipus complex (see, e.g., A. Parsons, 1964; Obeyesekere, 1990), but at the same time they document empirically the pervasive importance to human life of sexuality, aggression, loss, attachment, and other fundamental psychic experiences.

The data of psychoanalysis and anthropology challenge both the Western conception of the individuated, bounded self most clearly reflected within psychoanalysis in ego psychology and psychoanalytic tendencies to see guilt as a universal prime motivator of feeling and conflict. In so doing, these data implicitly and explicitly point up the Western slant of some versions of the structural theory. Yet psychoanalysts and anthropologists implicitly and explicitly recognize that the topography of conscious and unconscious shapes human psychological life everywhere, even as they note that many cultures openly incorporate unconscious life and grant much greater recognition to dreams, fantasies, myths, and altered states than does the Western culture whose psychology has theorized the division between these and conscious waking states.

Psychoanalytic ethnography, like clinical investigation, shows that feelings and selves are both given and created, naturally, culturally, and individually, and that projective and introjective recastings of interpersonal experiences, cultural categories, social processes, bodily experiences, and perceptions are found whenever meanings are accorded to people and situations. As human beings, we have the innate ability to create cultural meanings, social formations, history, and patterns of social practices, and to engage in those unconscious, fantasy- and emotion-laden projective and introjective constructions that create personal meaning. These innate abilities, whatever their biological basis, sustain the capacity to create both cultural meaning and psychological meaning.

Thus, psychobiological possibility enables us to have unconscious feelings and fantasies and to develop a particular response pattern for these in relation to our early caretakers and in later encounters. As we develop this response pattern, we create a sense of self and self feeling through projections and introjections that we continue to employ throughout life, in transferences that accord emotional meaning. At the same time, we acquire and employ cultural meanings individually, both because capacities for processing and interpretation are psychobiologically given and because a "cultural" meaning is always individually communicated and emotionally particularized. Meanings and meaning systems are not merely shared and cultural. Cultural patterns of emotionality and meanings of self enter in, as some emotions are more precisely labeled, as caretakers themselves express them, as narratives and stories elaborate them, as patterns of emotional interaction and mutual according of emotional meaning begin in infancy and continue throughout life, but these patterns do not exclusively determine or take priority in shaping an individual's sense of self, emotion, or cultural symbol or meaning. For the individual, meaning is always as individual as it is cultural.

Freud (1911) divided the world into psyche and reality and considered that psychological development consisted in coming to terms with a previously given reality, the "external world." This external world has been conceptualized as physical materiality, frustration resulting from parental admonitions and behavior, as society or culture. In the account I have been developing, by contrast, reality is constructed by the individual as she creates self and world. From the point of view of the subject, ego and reality, or psyche and culture, are constructed at the same time, rather than the individual's being inscribed into, taking in, or accommodating to a given reality or culture. Both the clinical encounter and the ethnographic encounter document this individual shaping and reshaping of the self and the object world, of personal and cultural meaning. The cultural and linguistic world exists for us as and because we invest it with unconscious, emotion-laden, fantasy meanings.

This reading, in which unconscious creation of emotional and fantasy meaning is an ongoing individual process, suggests that if we are as interested in the experiencing individual as we are in culture, we need to recognize that generalizing about shared meanings is not enough, even if these shared meanings include psychodynamic as well as cultural meanings, and even if we constantly keep in mind that these days when we talk about shared culture, we no longer mean a seamless, holistic web of cultural meanings. The process of meaning creation is not just a matter of overlaying idiosyncratic meanings developed earlier in life with shared meanings developed after a person has been socialized, or of separating out idiosyncratic meanings from psychological meanings held in common. Even those who transmit cultural practices or meanings have themselves already given a personal, idiosyncratic cast to those practices and meanings. Even as we can generalize about cultural phenomena, it is also the case that there are as many individual interpretations of cultural categories and practices as there are people. Personal meaning cannot be seen in purely cultural terms.

It is very hard for social scientists and other contemporary cultural thinkers to accept this view. Even those interested in both culture and psychic or emotional life do not problematize culture as they do the psyche. Psychological meanings may infuse or enliven cultural meanings and enable the expression of culture, but they do not shape, modify, or create cultural meanings in the way that cultural meanings and culture are thought to shape the psyche. There is a prohibition on psychological determinism or reductionism but not on cultural, discursive, social, or political determinism or reductionism.

In these chapters I argue that the psychological is just as irreducible as the cultural and has as much force and power in shaping and constituting human life and society. Clinical psychoanalysis and psychoanalytic anthropology document individual psychological processes that construct meaning for the individual in addition to, and in a different register from, culture, language, and power relations. A transitional conception of cultural and psychological meaning, both presented from without and created from within, and holding a unique character in a third space, describes the conjunction of the two registers.

Psychological life is not a seamless whole any more than culture is. Psychoanalysis documents the multiplicity of unconscious fantasies and conflicts and the complex internal worlds that characterize psychic life for the individual. Such multiplicity and complexity do not bifurcate according to cultural versus private resonance. Just as psychological theorists have been criticized for chopping up culture into nonculturally attuned categories, cultural thinkers have tended to dissect the psyche to fit their ideas of culturally and socially relevant meanings, emotions, or aspects of self or identity. In the idiosyncratic totality of psychodynamic meaning and experience, however, we cannot separate that which is connected in some way to culture from that which is not.

But, as the anthropological project makes clear, a recognition of the psychological as a separate register, sui generis, does not mean that culture has no input into meaning, self, and emotion. I am in agreement with culturalist and social-scientific criticisms that psychoanalysts often mistakenly reduce social and cultural forms to the psychological, rely on a theory of universal developmental stages that is not congruent with cross-cultural empirical observation, and apply a theory of universal symbolism that ignores cultural particularity and embeddedness. Both shared and idiosyncratic constructions of cultural meaning and cultural constructions of selves, emotions, and meaning become important in the clinical consulting room.

7 Coda on Culture: Preliminary Thoughts on Culture in the Consulting Room

> The historical prototypes which determined
> infantile ego-identity crises appear in specific
> transferences and in specific resistances.
>
> ERIK ERIKSON
> "EGO DEVELOPMENT AND HISTORICAL
> CHANGE"

THE ANTHROPOLOGICAL THINKING I HAVE BEEN DESCRIBING goes well beyond putting cultures on the couch, imposing psychological universals out of cultural context, or generalizing about "external reality." Anthropologists who study the psyche in the field may need to inform themselves continually about contemporary psychoanalytic theory and clinical understanding, in order both to understand their ethnographic findings and experience and to give their writing appropriate theoretical elaboration, but they have learned their psychoanalytic lessons well. Reciprocally, psychoanalysts should not ignore anthropological theories, findings, and epistemological reflections, which have profound implications for a clinical understanding of culture in the consulting room. Culture in many forms confronts us daily in clinical work (as in everyday life). The short reflections in this chapter, derived from my more extensive considerations of the importance of personal meaning to an understanding of culture and cultural meaning, constitute a preliminary attempt to assess what such a confrontation might entail.

Culture is a ubiquitous presence in the consulting room and yet goes almost unnoticed and unexplored, at least by Western analysts. Just as feminism has affected our clinical and theoretical understanding of gender and sexuality, however, it seems to me that psychological anthropology, the anthropology of self and feeling, and the generative reflections of those few analysts who are culturally and historically attuned should also influence our understanding of self, identity, psyche, and culture in the consulting room. The analytic encounter itself and the psyches in that encounter are culturally presented as well as created from within. Just as Freud once argued that a study of pathology illuminates normality, so anthropological studies suggest that we are always interacting, not just with a generic universal oedipal or preoedipal psyche, but with an Ilongot headhunter, a little Inuit girl, a Brazilian Indian political leader, or a confused and upset little boy from tribal New Guinea. Clinically, we all treat strange natives whose psyches, families, and cultures we do not at first know at all.

This is no easy challenge. Anthropologists, I have suggested, fall into an intuitive cultural determinism, an insistence on the emics of culture—analyzing webs of cultural meanings—even if such a position leads to an occlusion of the continuity and integrity of all aspects of one individual's psychic experience or to ignoring the psyche altogether. By contrast, analysts think in terms of an emics of the psyche—analyzing webs of psychic meaning—and are often barely aware of culture as a psychological force. By character, perhaps, those who become social scientists tend intuitively to be paranoid externalizers who projectively see troubles and opportunities as coming from without; those who become analysts tend intuitively to be omnipotent (or depressive) narcissists who see the world as created from within. Analysts by training and perhaps character thus downplay historical, social, and cultural forces.

In thinking about culture in the consulting room, we can borrow Fast's (1984) distinction between observed and subjective gender. In the case of gender, the two are overlapping categories rather than a hard-and-fast distinction, yet heuristically it is useful to conceptualize those psychological patterns that characterize the sexes as distinct from unconscious fantasies and conceptions of self that are linked to a person's sense of gender. A similar distinction clarifies psychological culture. Anthropological thinking focuses on both observed and subjective culture—prevalent psychological processes and patterns within cultures, on the one hand, and the cultural (and individual) sense of what constitutes a person, self, reasons, and emotions in a particular culture or group, on the other. We also observe subjective culture when members of cultural groups themselves develop a sense of who they are in contrast to other peoples with whom they interact. And in our own multicultural society we can distinguish patterns of observed culture (with different ethnicities different family norms and living arrangements prevail) from subjective culture—the cultural identities held by members of ethnic and racial groups that are important politically and theoretically in the current period.

With the exception of the psychoanalytic bioinstinctual universalists, the anthropologists discussed in the preceding chapters and those few psychoanalysts who notice culture clinically (e.g., Doi, 1973, 1990; Erikson; Kakar, 1990) make it clear that when we are in the arena of observed culture, we are not talking about cultural differences superficially imposed on underlying psychological universals. As described earlier, they make us aware of the very different culturally prevalent links between consciousness and unconscious processes and the sharpness of the culturally created boundaries between the two. These distinctions between cultures include the extent to which dreams are thought culturally to be important and interpretable, how they are experienced, and whether they are available to the dreamer in waking life. Anthropologists describe variations in the openness, repression, and cultural shaping of sexuality as well as cultural patterns in gender conflicts. They investigate the cultural recognition of trance, possession, and other forms of altered consciousness, hypercognized and hypocognized emotions and their lexical availability, prevalent cultural life narratives, and varying conceptualizations of self and self-other boundaries. They describe culturally variable responses to loss and patterns of mourning, cultural patterns in psychological disorders and crises, and the ways in which culturally diverse spousal and parenting relations seem to shape and reflect different constellations of emotionally charged inner worlds and cultural stories.[1]

Analysts, it would seem, need to be aware of these fundamental cultural differences that help to constitute self, unconscious fantasy, and emotion. Obeyesekere suggests that the structural theory of id, ego, and superego already gets us unwittingly into cultural assumptions about psychic functioning. This book suggests that universalized accounts of the content of psychic fantasy, structural requisites of development, and assumptions about necessary childhood developmental tasks do so as well. (Notably, the structural theory and universalized psychoanalytic assumptions about development meet in Freud's later argument for the Oedipus complex as the nodal complex of neurosis.) I have also noted, in this book and elsewhere, that similar considerations require a rethinking of development and gender. Attention to unconscious transferential processes that create personal meaning and an inner world, along with adequate recognition of variation in observed culture, enables us to recognize how cultural meanings, symbols, and processes are expressed and help to shape the analytic encounter. We should then expect culturally specific tendencies in fantasy, in defensive processes, in expressions of shame and guilt, in forms of individuation and relatedness, and in many other spheres.

We can find in the analytic literature the beginnings of such rethinking, mainly in writings that consider the cross-cultural assessment of psychopathology. In an early paper, the anthropologist-clinician Anne Parsons presented the challenge of these issues in their starkest form. In the case investigation reported in "Expressive Symbolism in Witchcraft and Delusion" (1969c), she asks how the clinician can distinguish paranoid delusions in one person when the belief in witchcraft is culturally accepted by all members of that person's culture. In another prescient article, "Cultural Barriers to Insight and the Structural Reality of Transference" (1969b), she points to the cultural specificity of particular transference attitudes toward the therapist, problematizing analytic expectations and interpretations of transference that do not acknowledge the cultural meaning of the analytic encounter for some patients or the importance for some patients of real cultural and class differences between them and the analyst.[2] Recently analytic attention paid to shame has increased, explicitly as a result of clinical interest in narcissism but also, perhaps implicitly, as analysts become intuitively more aware of the cultural specificity of oedipal guilt. Shame, as the literature on shame and guilt would predict, is personally specific also in the extent to which cultural conceptions for patients of different backgrounds connect who they are with what they do, and the extent to which they consider that what they do brings honor or shame to their family. In the context of cultural considerations about shame, cross-cultural education for clinicians must sometimes include recognition that a focus on status is not simply defensive or superficial. Western notions of authenticity or of a true or inner self apart from profession, family, role, or status are historical and cultural constructions.

A few non-Western analysts (Kakar, 1995; Akhtar, 1995; for an earlier psychiatric account, see Doi, 1971) point, like Geertz, to prevalent cultural differences in self-other boundaries and intrapsychic and interpersonal self-other relations. They argue in this context for a rethinking and cultural situating of psychoanalytic assumptions about individuation and individuality as well as about analyzability. (Kakar, as I note in an earlier chapter, also questions the cultural norms that go into psychoanalytic assumptions about normal gender.) Kakar puts his concerns forcefully, as he warns against imposing culturally specific individualist views clinically: "I wonder how much of this kind of psychoanalytic expectation that Pran [his patient] is sicker than what I believe to be actually the case is due to a cultural contamination creeping into the clinical judgment of his sexual differentiation and separation-individuation processes" (1995, 279). He concludes: "Clinical work in another culture, however, does make us aware that because of the American and European domination of psychoanalytic discourse, Western cultural (and moral) imagination sometimes tends to slip into psychoanalytic theorizing as hidden 'health and maturity moralities.' . . . Cultural judgments about psychological maturity, the nature of reality, 'positive' and 'negative' resolutions of conflicts and complexes often appear in the garb of psychoanalytic universals" (280–281).[3]

Finally, Kakar brings this clinical attunement to the specificity of his Indian patients back to the general psychoanalytic project. He notes that both hyperindividuation and hyperrelatedness may be strengthened in particular cultures at the expense of the other pole: "In spite of the cultural highlighting of the inter- and transpersonal, I found my traditional Indian patients more individual in their unconscious than they initially realized. Similarly, in spite of a Western cultural emphasis on autonomous individuality, my European and American patients are more relational than *they* realize. Individual and communal, self and other, are complementary ways of looking at the organization of mental life. They exist in a dialectical relationship to each other, although a culture may . . . stress the importance of one or the other in its ideology of the fulfilled human life and thus shape a person's *conscious* experience of the self in predominantly individual or communal modes" (274).

I consider myself fortunate to have worked clinically with people from a variety of cultures and countries, but I think that such a practice is probably, though unacknowledged as such, historically the analytic norm rather than the exception. Freud and the early analysts have been repeatedly criticized for their rootedness in and unwitting generalization from a particular culture of Mitteleuropa, but in fact Freud's patients came from several countries (among his classical cases, at least the "Wolf Man" and "Miss Lucy R."; by the end of World War I, many people came from the United States, England, and many other European countries, both as patients and as would-be analysts). After World War II and the psychoanalytic diaspora, it must also be the case that large numbers of analyses took place in which neither analyst nor patient spoke in his or her first language (for further discussion see Amati-Mehler, Argentieri, and Canestri, 1993; Akhtar, 1995). In my own experience, moreover, I have found that once I began to notice the cultural specificity of thoughts, expressions, fantasies, and conflicts in patients from "other" cultures, it became impossible not to notice cultural specificity in every patient. Patients supposedly from my own culture (unmarked white American) were also specific cultural products and had their own specific cultural location.

These observations do not undermine my previous arguments, nor do I mean them in a culturally deterministic way. People create cultural selves and emotions and animate cultural meanings and interpretations individually and idiosyncratically, but it is nonetheless specific cultural selves, emotions, and meanings that they animate. Specific cultural patterns are always given an individual cast. As

Kracke reminds us, even if we can generalize about the Kagwahiv, the Viennese, and New Yorkers, different members of any culture will be just as individual as each of Freud's turn-of-the-century Viennese patients or any contemporary New York analyst's patients.

Culture in the consulting room is expressed and experienced not only in accordance with the observed cultural patterns I have been describing: the recognition that different cultures have different prevalent constructions of self and other, ways of thinking, fantasies, and so forth. We also find subjective culture in the consulting room. People create a cultural subjectivity, consciously and unconsciously, and, in my experience, they also use culture consciously as a defense against thinking. Since its inception psychoanalysis has been centrally interested in subjective gender and sexuality, assuming these to be fundamental to unconscious fantasy and mental life, but it has virtually ignored subjective culture. To rephrase this, psychoanalysis has itself created a cultural blind spot against noticing the psychic centrality of conscious and unconscious fantasies about culture, race, ethnicity, nationality, or place of origin. As in Freud's treatment of gender, we can see a contradiction between theory and case. All of Freud's cases are saturated with cultural and historical observations, with observations about cultural consciousness, and with (Freud's and his patients') cultural conceptions of gender, Jewishness, and other cultural identities (on fin de siècle politics and culture in the *Interpretation of Dreams,* see Schorske, 1979). Insofar as subjective culture generates or gets rooted in specific senses of self and identity and particular internal worlds of conscious and unconscious fantasy, we need to be able to analyze these just as we analyze gender, sexual identity, family history, and other aspects of subjectivity.

Among analysts, only Erikson seems to have analyzed or even considered subjective culture in any thoroughgoing or systematic way. Erikson gives persistent and insistent attention to the intertwining of psychological and cultural life. He provides clinical and psychohistorical documentation of the inextricable involvement of history, society, and culture as constitutive in the fundamental organization and experience of self and psyche and shows how culture, history, and ethnicity enliven unconscious fantasies, symptoms, and conflicts.

Erikson wants to keep psyche and history equally in view. In *Childhood and Society,* in implicit conversation with psychoanalysts, he claims: "If psychoanalysis as yet differentiates the psychosexual from the psychosocial, I have endeavored . . . to build a bridge between the two" (1950, 108). Also writing for clinicians, he opens *Identity and the Life Cycle:* "Men who share an ethnic area, a historical era, or an economic pursuit are guided by common images of good and evil. Infinitely varied, these images reflect the elusive nature of historical change; yet in the form of contemporary social models, of compelling prototypes of good and evil, they assume a decisive concreteness in every individual's ego development" (1959, 18). He calls on psychoanalysts to theorize about this "bridge," this "decisive concreteness." At the same time, he makes a corresponding demand on historians and social scientists: "On the other hand, students of history continue to ignore the simple fact that all individuals are born by mothers; that everybody was once a child; that people and peoples begin in their nurseries; and that society consists of individuals in the process of developing from children into parents" (18).

Such general claims about the intrinsic relatedness of psyche, culture, and society are offered also by many writers contemporaneous with Erikson, who wrote during a period of efflorescence of psychoanalytic social thought, but Erikson's vision and insight hold a unique place because of his repeated and fruitful clinical attention to these matters. Like cultural-school psychoanalysts and anthropologists of culture and personality, Erikson argues compellingly that particular cultural and caretaking arrangements have an impact on culturally prevalent defenses and forms of self. Not only, however, does he claim that there are observable differences among cultural personalities, he also documents incontrovertibly (and until very recently, almost uniquely among psychoanalysts) that the multiple sociohistorical constituents of identity need continually to be addressed clinically. Psychoanalysts are used to addressing questions of gender and sexual identity; they have virtually ignored cultural identity. By contrast, Erikson found himself, forty and fifty years ago, interpreting an unconscious Wandering Jew in a successful Midwestern businessman (1964, 87–88), and finding in the rigidly erect stance of a small, dark ballet dancer not only an unconsciously gendered—phallic—identification with her father, but also, even less accessible to consciousness, an ethnic—blond, upright, military, German—father identification (1959, 29–30).

Not without justification, widespread criticism has been voiced about the psychoanalytic imposition of normative white middle-class psychological standards and of psychoanalytic inattention to the great variety of sociocultural differences and related aspects of identity that help to form subjectivity. But it is not an exaggeration to claim that Erikson was as obsessed as any multicultural postmodern academic with the question of cultural identity and its conflicting unconscious and conscious manifestations; indeed, his attention is especially notable in the face of these critiques. The very writers who make such criticisms are, like Erikson, consumed by concerns with identity—whether sexual, gender, racial-ethnic, cultural, national, or class identity. Indeed, "identity" is one of the most widely used and debated terms in the academy today, but contemporary academics seem not to recognize their debt to Erikson in these matters: "identity" has, as it were, lost its own historical identity and roots.

Specifically, Erikson describes his patients' symptoms, unconscious conflicts, and identities in terms of their place of origin—whether they are Southerners, Midwesterners, or Westerners, Europeans or Americans. He focuses on their caste, class, and race, their parents' country of origin, their religion and ethnicity (see Erikson, 1950, 1959). He investigates clinically, in chapters with titles like "A Combat Crisis in a Marine" and "Son of a Bombardier," how World War I, World War II, and immigration are drawn into unconscious fantasy life and meet patients' inner worlds and identities (1950).

Especially but not exclusively, Erikson is attuned to the impact of unconscious elements of identity and psychic conflict that stem from minority ethnicity. Sam, the little boy with convulsive symptoms whose case opens *Childhood and Society,* is affected psychodynamically by shifts and contradictions generated by his grandparents' immigration from an Eastern European shtetl, his father's upbringing among a group of ethnically diverse roughnecks, and his own early childhood, split between the streets of New York and the small, quiet, Bay Area town in which he was supposed to "become quickly what the Gentiles of the middle class would call 'a nice little boy, in spite of his being Jewish'" (1950, 28). Erikson shows how this specific familial history and the generational transmission of unconscious fantasies and apprehensions are further sustained by cultural mythologies and fears.

For Erikson, ego identity—sameness and continuity in one's own and others' view—is a foundational basis of psychic health. Identity depends not simply on identifying with others but on being confirmed and recognized by others as a particular individual in a particular universe. Erikson draws upon sociohistorical as well as clinical examples to make his point. He describes (albeit in ways that we— with fifty years of twenty-twenty hindsight—might consider stereotyped and occasionally condescending) the difficulties in constructing a positive black identity in a white society and of straddling the margins between Indian and white society. He claims that immigration challenges basic trust, recognition, and identity. In "Identity and Uprootedness in Our Time," he notes that uprooted people face the very difficult challenge of preserving identity in the face of radical historical change. To the immigrant, history does not facilitate the continuity of generations and tradition. As he puts it, uprooted people have a "basic hope for recognition and [a] basic horror of its failure: the dead, the still-born identity" (1964, 95).

Erikson's clinical accounts document that these sociocultural identities are not simply secondary, conscious add-ons to a more fundamental psychic structure and unconscious life that will emerge when "real" analysis begins. These individualized historical and cultural contributions to identity are deeply implicated in unconscious selfhood and fantasy, personalized through parental identifications, related in complex ways to ego ideal and that which the ego ideal rejects. They are tied up with affects like shame, guilt, and fear. That is, they build personal meaning into cultural categories.

In each case, Erikson is no cultural or historical determinist. He does not claim that being the son of a bomber pilot bestows on a boy a particular identity, fantasy, or emotional conflict. He claims, rather, that his patients (and people in general) bring personal psychodynamic interpretations to unconsciously as well as consciously transmitted cultural and historical circumstances and to parental fantasies and identity. In each individual case, such personal interpretations help generate symptoms and character. People projectively enliven aspects of cultural meanings and social identities. Their introjection of these cultural identities is also conflictual, emotionally charged, and filtered through fantasy. Thus, the oedipal identification he describes is not a generic, abstract identification with the father. Rather, it consists in an individualized, emotionally charged identification with an individualized, historically and culturally individual particular father. He concludes, "problems of patienthood are caused by outer and by inner conditions" (1964, 89).

In *Identity and the Life Cycle*, Erikson warns of the countertransferential blocks, the "unconscious resistances," among analysts to acknowledging the impact of changing historical reality. "Such resistances," he claims, "must be located and appraised in the observer, and in his habits of conceptualization, before their presence in the observed can be fully understood and effectively handled." He goes on: "It is a commonplace to state that the psychoanalyst in training must learn to study the historical determinants of what made him what he is before he can hope to perfect that human gift: the ability to understand what is different from him" (1959, 45). According to Erikson, however, psychoanalysts have not been able to apply this commonplace understanding to their own specific historically determined situation and to the historical determinants of the theory with which they work. He reproaches Hartmann, Kris, and Loewenstein for suggesting that, beyond preliminaries, the analyst's "common sense" is enough to allow her to understand the impact cultural conditions have on both her and her patient. In response to the claim of these three theorists that as an analysis progresses, unconscious intrapsychic material will emerge culture-free, he "ventures to suggest that rather central problems of ego development, which are, indeed, 'accessible only to an analytic investigation,' demand that the psychoanalyst's awareness of cultural differences go well beyond that 'common sense' which the three authors (being themselves outstanding cosmopolitans) seem to find sufficient in this particular area of observation, while they would assuredly urge a more 'analyzed' common sense in other areas" (152).[4]

Erikson's concern with locating the psyche within a particular cultural-historical cohort and generation is in itself one of his great contributions to psychoanalytic thinking. This contribution becomes all the more remarkable because it arose so directly out of Erikson's own life story and he greeted it with an acknowledgment rare in contemporaneous psychoanalytic writings. Fifty years before the current focus on the analyst's subjectivity, Erikson's own particularized personal, generational, cultural, historical "I" seems ubiquitous, even in his claims about universal aspects of identity and self-development (in other words, Erikson makes his own identity and self present in his writings about identity and the self). In whatever we read, we have a sense of Erikson the person, as he works with a child in psychoanalysis, as he describes the conflicts expressed by an adult patient, as he writes about and then reflects on men like Luther and Gandhi, who exemplify for Erikson personal and historical struggles with identity and social transformation. In "Identity and Uprootedness in Our Time," for example, Erikson places himself as an immigrant: "I cannot offer my contribution to these problems, however, without one word of remembrance for those who could not join us in migration: the dead. The very worst conditions of migration would yet have offered them their naked life, and a flicker of hope in a possible humanity. But to them even flight was denied; and our image of man must forever include the hell which was their last experience on earth" (1964, 85).

Along with his autobiographical "I," Erikson's insistence on the intrapsychic significance of historical reality and of unconscious subjective constructions of culture contrasts strikingly with the writings of most members of his psychoanalytic generation. Even in the current period, few analysts follow his lead, and these very exceptions may warrant renewed attention to the concerns he raised. Neil Altman (1995) and Kimberly Leary (1995, 1997), for example, explore unconscious and conscious class and racial constructions that enter the psychoanalytic situation between analyst and analysand and become linked to the internal senses of self and other and to intrapsychic splitting and projection. Akhtar, himself an immigrant, writes of the "third individuation" experienced in immigration (1995). His study ranges across loss, mourning, and idealization, the effects on id and superego of different cultural standards of (especially sexual and interpersonal) behavior, and the potential splitting off of psychic elements that the analysand experiences in the native language and of unconscious emotions and preverbal experiences rooted in the childhood spent in another culture. He considers analysis in a non-native language and notices many other experiences that shape an immigrant's psychic life and affect the analytic process.

Unlike Kakar, Doi, and others, Akhtar tends to accept universalized, normative ego-psychological conceptions of a psychic structure that is located, somehow, beyond culture. Yet such a perspective enables him to label and recognize clinically instances where his patients use culture as a defense against anxiety or guilt or as a projective cover for other conflicts and splits. Problems in self-other relations, for example, inside and outside analysis, can be consciously couched in terms of cultural dissimilarity. People can allocate disavowed elements of the self alternately to the country of origin or to the adopted country.[5] They can sustain and deny oedipal splitting or mother-father splits, libidinal or aggressive conflicts, and dictates of the superego by conflating them with one side or the other of the cultural divide.

In my experience, the analyst walks a fine line in such a situation. I have found myself caught between what I consider a necessary cross-cultural sensitivity and a recognition that, historically, psychoanalysis has turned cultural norms into scientific claims and, concurrently, a specific clinical assessment that a patient is drawing on culture to move away from personal insight—caught, that is, between cultural imperialism and clinical assessment. For the analyst, this dilemma is perhaps worst when ostensible cultural communication generates negative countertransference or moral condemnation. I think of one patient who came from a culture where the divide between rich and poor was profound. She continually expressed outrage at having to earn money and at not having a husband who provided totally for her. She explained her reactions as cultural: "I do this because I'm from X [her country]. I need pampering and attention, because that is how I was brought up. Women of my class don't work. That is why I am angry." As she put it, she divided the world into commanders and commanded, masters and servants. She herself hated not feeling like a master. Conversely, I often felt treated like a servant: her unreflected-upon assumption and consciously held belief were that doctors were there at her behest, hired, like servants, to do what she wanted done. When I tried to explore this construction, she insisted that this was how the world was. If pressed, she would acknowledge that this was how the world was in her country of origin.

This patient had many memories of her mother and father screaming at, criticizing, and punishing servants, and she identified consciously with such power and was excited by it. As a child, she was proud to be the daughter of her parents and expected that she would come into such power. But she also became furious when she remembered that her parents often found her behavior, like the behavior of their servants, wanting. Clearly, my patient was describing behavior and attitudes that were cultural and familial, but also personal. For her, it may not have mattered much: whatever their origin, her interpretations of the world and her feelings about her situation brought her nothing but grief. In me, however, her claims to be special, her melodramatic self-pity, and her merciless and relentless criticism of me in the name of culture did not exactly generate or reinforce a strong commitment to cultural relativism.

In many other cases, patients may convey cultural beliefs that are less charged and self-destructive—for example, a different sense of time or of polite or expected behavior. Cross-cultural knowledge, or at least diffidence about cross-cultural knowledge, is useful in all these cases. To take a particular example, when a patient from a culture that veils women feels naked and vulnerable on the streets, or feels shame and vulnerability in the consulting room, she is expressing, on the one hand, a personal sense of shame and self-criticism for her sexual and exhibitionistic desires and on the other a cultural norm that she has absorbed since early childhood. Neither the one nor the other is the "real" reason for the feeling. We need to analyze both, together and apart.

Observed culture, then, helps constitute many elements of psychic reality, prevalent affective patterns, and aspects of psychic structure and process. Subjective culture likewise enters into many elements of psychic fantasy and sense of self and into the construction of an inner world. Patients consciously and unconsciously introduce cultural elements that have become psychically theirs into what they say and do, and the clinician needs to recognize and understand them, as well as to monitor her own cross-cultural transferences and reactions. Although most psychoanalysts have traditionally ignored the contributions of culture to psychic life, we can nevertheless draw on the clinical writings and theories of a few non-Western analysts whose own experiences compelled them to notice the cultural biases of psychoanalysis and the cultural inflections of the psyche, as well as on the remarkable and prescient writings of Erik Erikson on this topic. For all of us, culture in the consulting room is experienced daily and shapes the clinical encounter in many ways. This chapter opens a discussion of how we might not only recognize the pervasiveness of culture in the psyche and the clinical encounter but of how we might analyze it.

PART 4   CONCLUSIONS

8 Psychoanalytic Visions of Subjectivity

I shall be concerned particularly with layers which
may underlie our conscious experience, giving it an
added glow.

ROBERT DONINGTON

OPERA AND ITS SYMBOLS

Our present, current experiences have intensity
and depth to the extent to which they are in
communication (interplay) with the unconscious,
infantile, experiences representing the indestructible
matrix of all subsequent experiences.

HANS LOEWALD

"ON THE THERAPEUTIC ACTION OF
PSYCHOANALYSIS"

I HAVE CALLED THIS BOOK *THE POWER OF FEELINGS*, BUT I DO
not mean feelings in the sense of emanations of raw affect. The
feelings that concern psychoanalysis are always feelings enmeshed
within stories. A particular feeling condenses and expresses an unconscious fantasy about self, body, other, other's body, or self and
other. Unconscious fantasy projectively endows the world with personal meaning, filtering the world through an emotionally laden
story, and it affects and shapes the introjective construction of an
inner object world. Through the power of feelings, unconscious fantasy recasts the subject—emotions and stories about different aspects

of self in relation to one another and about the self and body in relation to an inner and outer object world. In these senses, unconscious fantasy creates both the external and the internal world.

When we look at the affects that psychoanalysts discuss, we can see that they have everyday, life-constructing meaning. They are never simply technical terms, and the point is never to reduce them to simple components but to investigate them in their richest complexity. We think of anxiety, envy and gratitude, lust and desire, love and hate, hope and dread, a sense of aliveness or deadening. And each experience of anxiety, envy, gratitude, lust, and so on, tells its own unconscious story. In turn, these stories are passionate and have dire consequences. They may concern destroying the self or the other, patricide and matricide, atoning for or repairing the results of one's destructiveness, fears of merging with or invading another, feeling devitalized with a devitalized other or devitalized with a vital other who has usurped all one's vitality. The stories may have to do with a sense of being punished for wishes or deeds or a belief that a particular accomplishment or relationship will bring bliss. These are the personal meanings that constitute psychic life and that also shape interpersonal relationships, personal projects, work, and constructions of cultural meanings and practices.

If psychoanalysis as a theory describes how we create personal meaning, then psychoanalysis as a practice and process has as a goal an expanded understanding and awareness for the analysand of the personal meanings she creates. Psychoanalysis has a vision as well as an understanding of subjectivity. Freud first captured such a vision when he claimed that "where id was, there ego shall be," and that psychoanalysis would "make the unconscious conscious," but such phrases barely tap the sense that Freud and his colleagues had, both of the terrible suffering that their work was meant to ameliorate and of the psychic possibilities for a "well-analyzed" person.

Yet, although psychoanalysis holds out a hopeful vision of subjectivity, analysts have for understandable reasons focused more on the ways that unconscious reactions, symptoms, character problems, neurosis, deficits, inhibitions, anxiety, depression, and other forms of psychic difficulty have hampered or limited human lives. They, along with many others, have taken psychoanalysis to be a theory primarily about problems in human functioning. Freud describes the ego as not being master in its own house, driven as it is by unconscious forces beyond its control—on the one hand sexual and aggressive drives, on the other a relentless superego. "Where id was, there ego shall be" very much advocates not only the integration but the overcoming and banishing of these unconscious id forces. Especially in the structural ego-psychological tradition, "making the unconscious conscious" seems to elide with "where id was," implying that the unconscious, like the id, is best done away with. For Freud, dreams were the royal road to the unconscious, and dream analysis was very much meant to bring unconscious nighttime wishes to the light of day. As psychoanalysis developed, transference became the royal road to the discovery of unconscious fantasies, fears, and wishes. And as we saw earlier, transference was originally seen as an impediment to psychoanalytic progress. The assumption was that once transferences or dreams were analyzed, the unconscious fantasies they expressed would no longer affect the person. To the extent that we follow Freud's two well-known dicta, then, psychoanalysis seems to have as its goal the substitution of the rational for the irrational and the erasing of unconscious life in favor of consciousness.

Repressed or split-off unconscious fantasies and unknown or unacknowledged but powerful feelings, wishes, or interpretations of self and object can certainly lead a person to put herself repeatedly into difficult or disastrous situations and to feel anxious, depressed, fearful, or out of control. Throughout this book, however, my account suggests that such a view of transference and fantasy is insufficient. Since Freud, many psychoanalysts have articulated their intuition that psychoanalysis is much more than a theory of neurosis and treatment: that it provides insight into human life in general.[1] Interleaved with accounts of development or pathology, one finds conceptions of how psychic life ought to be as well as writings that make central the project of describing a psychoanalytic vision of subjectivity. A focus on the psychoanalytic encounter, located both in the intrapsychic field of projection and introjection and in the intersubjective field of transference and countertransference, moves us toward such an expanded view.

About fifteen years ago, I began to keep track of particular psychoanalytic formulations that I called "meaning of life" statements. These were rarely topic statements of articles or books—they were more often buried within paragraphs—yet they summarized an entire conception of how life is or should be. I found them in formulations concerning the intrapsychic goals of analysis, in conceptions of the psychoanalytic encounter, and in accounts of individual development within an interpersonal matrix. I had first, while a graduate student, noticed Loewald: "The deepest root of the ambivalence that appears to pervade all relationships, external as well as internal, seems to be the polarity inherent in individual existence of individuation and 'primary narcissistic union'" (1962, 264). As I began to keep track, I came across Margaret Mahler: "Here, in the rapprochement subphase, we feel is the mainspring of man's eternal struggle against both fusion and isolation" (1972, 231). Michael Balint: "The ultimate aim of all libidinal striving is thus the preservation or restoration of the original harmony. . . . This *unio mystica,* the re-establishment of the harmonious interpenetrating mix-up between the individual and the most important parts of his environment, his love objects, is the desire of all humanity" (1968, 74). Ella Sharpe: "The people who enjoy the greatest ease, and to whom work and conditions in life bring the greatest internal satisfaction, are those who have justified their existence to themselves. They have won through to a right to live, and a right to live means a life in which physical and mental powers can be used to the ego's advantage and well-being, which means to the advantage and well-being of the community. For a 'right to live' is only ultimately based on the right of others to live. I believe 'justification for existence' is the very core of our problems" (1930, 81).

In an era wary of universalizing claims about human life and skeptical of unabashed humanism, any vision of subjectivity will be suspect. Contemporary intellectuals, followers of postmodernisms and Lacanian theory, often believe (and may even idealize their belief) that our psyches are inevitably split and alienated and that the multiple positions we take in discourse shape a fragmented, unstable subjectivity that has no center.[2] Ironically, Freud was one of the main spokespersons to decenter and destabilize modern individuality, yet psychoanalysts could not do their work without a hopeful sense of human possibility. This book participates very much in the critique of universalisms and essentialisms, but I wish at the same time to put forth a consistent vision of a desirable life. In this conclusion, I consider the clinical goals of psychoanalysis and outline some of the elements that I believe go into psychoanalytic visions of subjectivity, the analysts' hope of turning lives limited by personal emotional construction into lives enriched by such construction. I cannot, of course, address the work of every analyst who engages in this endeavor. Instead, I point to a number of organizing themes and to the writers who to my mind most fruitfully or fully articulate them.

Although by definition psychoanalytic practice always concerns itself with psychic change, during certain periods in the history of psychoanalysis analysts have tended more to develop conceptions of a desirable life and during other periods they have tended to focus almost obsessively on questions of clinical technique and process. A number of the writers who most influenced my own thinking (for example, Loewald, Winnicott, Erikson, and Schachtel) developed their ideas in and around the 1950s (also a time when psychoanalytic social theory flourished). In recent years, another generation (perhaps especially Benjamin, Bollas, Mitchell, and Ogden—and I am of course very much a member of this generation) has taken up the challenge of formulating psychoanalytic visions of subjectivity.[3] In overlapping conceptualizations, they query the uses and possibilities of unconscious fantasy and transference, address questions of self-recognition and (re)discovery, investigate determination and cause, reflect on individuation and the nature of relatedness, consider what it is to be psychically alive, and assess forms of intersubjectivity and object-relations. They describe, finally, the power of feelings.

Winnicott has been almost lionized for his contribution to psychoanalytic visions of subjectivity, but I begin with Loewald.[4] Loewald, followed especially by Bollas and Mitchell, develops an interpretation of the relations of unconscious and conscious that turns Freud's work (and a rationalist ego psychology) on its head. For Loewald, a meaningful human life is founded not on the absence or overcoming of the influence of the unconscious but on its presence and integration. Unconscious fantasies expressed in dreams and transferences enrich life and give it meaning. If, as Freud puts it, the psyche is composed of two records, one unconscious psychic reality and fantasy and the other conscious, rational, pragmatic life, then the classical position wishes to replace the former by the latter, whereas Loewald advocates a constant intertwining of conscious and unconscious, of transference and reality, such that in the desirable case, any single thought or feeling simultaneously creates and embeds itself in both realities.[5]

In his influential paper "On the Therapeutic Action of Psychoanalysis," Loewald notes that Freud used transference in three ways. Conventionally, transference refers to the transfer of relations with infantile objects onto later objects. A second meaning involves the transfer of libido from ego to objects. Finally, transference refers to the way that unconscious ideas transfer their intensity to preconscious and ultimately to conscious ideas. Dreams, which allow unconscious, intensely charged thoughts to enter consciousness through their connection with day residues, provide a model for this third process. Loewald claims that transference in all three senses is normal and desirable, but it is the third meaning that most concerns him. Although psychoanalysis discovered through the study of neuroses and dreams how preconscious and unconscious interact, the ways they do so "are only the more or less pathological, magnified, or distorted versions of normal mechanisms" (1960, 248).

Loewald takes the position that without transference—the same processes of attribution and affective coloration that were originally seen as problematic in the psychoanalytic situation—there would be no personal meaning. Precisely through the infusion into the present moment of our unconscious as we have created it and our past as we have experienced it and made it ours, we most fully live our present and are conscious. Loewald's formulations seem particularly capable of capturing how unconscious processes resonate with conscious ones, and how, when they are integrated rather than repressed, they give conscious life depth and richness of meaning. As he, most radically, puts it: "The integration of ego and reality consists in, and the continued integrity of ego and reality depends on, transference of unconscious processes and 'contents' on to new experiences and objects of contemporary life. . . . There is neither such a thing as reality nor a real relationship, without transference. Any 'real relationship' involves transfer of unconscious images to present-day objects. In fact, present-day objects are objects, and thus real, in the full sense of the word . . . only to the extent to which this transference, in the sense of transformational interplay between unconscious and preconscious, is realized" (1960, 252, 254).

In his famous analogy for the gains that come from the transference of unconscious meanings to conscious phenomena, Loewald describes the turning of ghosts into ancestors. Ghosts of the unconscious will "taste blood" and awaken when they sense something familiar in conscious and preconscious life—the day residues that enable dream formation, for example. But, as Loewald puts it, "those who know ghosts tell us that they long to be released from their ghost life and led to rest as ancestors. As ancestors they live forth in the present generation, while as ghosts they are compelled to haunt the present generation with their shadow life. Transference is pathological insofar as the unconscious is a crowd of ghosts . . . : [In analysis] ghosts of the unconscious, imprisoned by defenses but haunting the patient in the dark of his defenses and symptoms, are allowed to taste blood, are let loose" (1960, 249).

Although transferences, like ghosts, need to emerge and become visible, they are not something to be gotten over, something that interferes with the reality of daily life. Loewald (1960) makes a strong case for transference:

Far from being . . . "the enduring monument of man's profound rebellion against reality and his stubborn persistence in the ways of immaturity," transference is the "dynamism" by which the instinctual life of man, the id, becomes ego and by which reality becomes integrated and maturity is achieved. Without such transference—of the intensity of the unconscious, of the infantile ways of experiencing life that have no language and little organization, but the indestructibility and power of the origins of life— to the preconscious and to present-day life and contemporary objects— without such transference, or to the extent to which such transference miscarries, human life become sterile and an empty shell. [250]

Loewald thus makes our capacity for transference into a virtue. Transference—our psychological shifting between past and present or unconscious and conscious—gives vibrancy to life. The role of trans- ference is not mainly to limit, drag down, or negatively shape expe- rience, though of course it can do so, and clinical psychoanalysis addresses largely this negative shaping. Transference also makes experience fuller, as it helps to shape and give meaning to interpersonal and intrapsychic experiences and encounters. What matters is not the presence of transference but whether transferences are incorporated into psychic life in a way that gives texture and richness to experience, whether one lives one's transferences or is lived or driven by them. At the same time, Loewald provides an argument against idealizing the unconscious—as many psychoanalytic social critics have. When he says, "The unconscious needs present-day external reality (objects) and present-day psychic reality (the preconscious) for its own continuity, lest it be condemned to live the shadow life of ghosts or to destroy life" (250), he has clinical as well as visionary goals in mind.

Loewald revalues fantasy as well as transference. For Kleinians, transference is the vehicle for expressing unconscious fantasy, those constructions of self and object that we create through projections and introjections and other modes of mediating and shaping experience. In the ego-psychological view, unconscious fantasy opposes reality and intrudes into conscious life (as well as into psychoanalytic theorizing). It is mainly a derivative of drives that expresses instinctual wishes, though it also receives some input from ego and superego reaction, and its existence is evidence of repression and psychic conflict (see Arlow, 1969). In both views, an important goal of analysis is to reestablish the linkage between fantasy and reality. As Loewald puts it, "In the analytic process the infantile fantasies and memories, by being linked up with the present actuality of the analytic situation and the analyst, regain meaning and may be reinserted within the stream of total mental life" (1975, 362–363).

Reality, then, is not intrinsically meaningful. In Loewald's view, unconscious fantasy gives this reality personal meaning: "Fantasy is unreal only insofar as its communication with present actuality is inhibited or severed. To that extent, however, present actuality is unreal too. Perhaps a better word than 'unreal' is 'meaningless' " (362). The point, therefore, is not to overcome fantasy: "At the same time as the present actuality of the analytic situation is being linked up with infantile fantasies, this present gains or regains meaning—i.e., that depth of experience which comes about by its live communication with the infantile roots of experience" (363). There comes to be a resonance between fantasy and reality, then, the former deepening and enriching the latter, the latter keeping us rooted and connected in the world.

As with transference, ghosts haunt us, but the ancestors are there to quicken us. In contrast to those psychoanalytic cultural thinkers who suspect that claims for psychic health or integration through analysis may become socially normative and who prefer Freud's theoretical pessimism, Loewald makes direct, optimistic claims about psychic health: "Psychic health has to do with an optimal, although by no means necessarily conscious, communication between unconscious and preconscious, between the infantile, archaic stages and structures of the psychic apparatus and its late stages and structures of organization" (1960, 254).[6]

Like transference and unconscious fantasy, projective identification is a vehicle for understanding and change and a continuous part of life itself. Patterns of projective identification may shift, and some will come to be recognized, but projective identification is not something that an analysis will finally do away with. The question is not whether projective identifications will be there or not, but the extent to which a person uses her capacities to project and to create projective identifications in a rigid, driven, repetitive, and controlling way and whether, as parts of the self are assigned to the other, they are forever lost to experience. Projective identification, putting aspects of the self or the self's internal world into the other, can enrich the experience of self and other and give aliveness and meaning to both (see also Caper, 1988). Alternatively, if projective identifications are rigidly maintained, they can drain aspects of the self of affect and meaning.

Psychoanalytic visions of subjectivity advocate, along with the integration of unconscious and conscious, the integration of past and present. Earlier, I suggested that we needed a both-and view of the relation of past and present in psychic life. In creating a story or set of stories about inner life and its development, psychoanalysis lends personal meaning by helping to create continuity, both historical continuity and continuity between psychic elements. Psychoanalysis enables us to see how patterns from the past affect, shape, and give meaning to the present and enables the present to reshape memory and the past. In the analytic process, present-day experiences, behaviors, feelings, and apparently disconnected fears and anxieties, experienced initially as discontinuities, come to be seen as continuous with internal representations of the past and with each other. At issue here is not an absolute truth but a sense of a coherent and plausible storyline that makes sense of life history and memories and a person's current senses of self. This is not to say that any story is acceptable, but we can say that several psychoanalytic stories—several plausible reconstructions and ways of making a life coherent—can be told about any one person.

Recognition and self-recognition seem particularly crucial to the integration of unconscious and unconscious, including past and present (in calling this realm recognition, I am indebted to Benjamin, 1988, 1995). Making the unconscious conscious is a first form of recognition if we are clear that such recognition is not a form of replacement. In Freud's initial conceptualization, the unconscious, though partially a product of primary repression, is composed mainly of thoughts that have been secondarily repressed and can be rediscovered; the unconscious internal world described by Kleinian theory seems also to be waiting to be discovered. With an increasing understanding that the analysand's internal world is being created in the psychoanalytic encounter and not simply discovered by the analyst, the question of recognition and discovery becomes more complex. Bollas (1987), with his felicitous conception of the "unthought known," perhaps best captures the process and product of recognition and (re)discovery in analysis, but years before, the phenomenological psychoanalyst Ernest Schachtel, in "Memory and Childhood Amnesia" (1947), also expanded on our sense of the elements in unconscious life that could not be recognized or that waited to be discovered. Schachtel makes his point through a cultural critique of childhood, whereas the more classically psychoanalytic Bollas makes his through a consideration of development in the individual parent-child matrix.

Schachtel extends Freud's concept of infantile amnesia, by claiming that our inability to experience fully (indeed, to feel fully alive) arises from a lack of schemata that makes certain experiences unlabelable. According to Schachtel, early childhood is a time of an incredible richness and variety of experiences, new sensations, and new feelings. These experiences come through all five senses but especially through the proximal senses of smell, taste, and touch. They have a global rather than a differentiated feel. (With more access to infant research, Stern, 1985, also describes these early sensual experiences.) In the process of enculturation and language learning, however, only some experiences are categorized and labeled; Western society, moreover, privileges and elaborates culturally the distal senses of seeing and hearing. As a result of these shifts, the mode of experiencing shifts. The ability to take in new experiences with vibrancy and openness is curtailed, and the ability to remember the richness of early childhood experience becomes restricted. Proximal sense experiences and memories of early childhood, Schachtel claims, are not simply repressed; they are starved away. Repression is like a nightstick, "the psychological cannons of society" (321), whereas normal childhood amnesia—in which schemata do not allow the preservation and remembering of nonschematic experience—operates more like a blockade and slow starvation.

Schachtel is making a point here about some inevitabilities of development. As many cultural theorists argue, linguistic schemata themselves shape experience and make it recognizable, and memory comes more easily with the "I" that language brings. In this sense, he is describing the inevitable difficulties of being human: as a child gains a sense of continuity as experiences become familiar and recognized linguistically and she develops a sense of self, as she can deepen experience through the ability to communicate and share intersubjectively, at the same time she loses a certain capacity to experience intensely.

But Schachtel is also suggesting that this sense of loss and the inability to remember are not an inevitable cultural product. They result (as Briggs describes in detail) from fitting the individual child into a social process. Depending on the extent of schematic starvation, the psychological result may be an uneasiness, a listless dropping of curiosity, a sense of futility and boredom. Memory, Schachtel suggests, becomes utilitarian, oriented toward conscious social stories— where we grew up and with whom, where we went to school, or our career and life-cycle achievements. Like other analysts, however, Schachtel has hope. Starvation never works completely; memories and possibilities of trans-schematic experiences remain as an intrapsychic tension. In his moving conclusion, Schachtel claims: "Memory cannot be entirely extinguished in man, his capacity for experience cannot be entirely suppressed by schematization. It is in those experiences which transcend the cultural schemata, in those memories of experience which transcend the conventional memory schemata, that every new insight and every true work of art has its origin, and that the hope of progress, of a widening of the scope of human endeavor and human life, is founded" (1959, 322).

Since his critique is mainly cultural and social, Schachtel does not investigate the analytic possibilities of retrieving starved-off experiences from current life and memory. Bollas, following Winnicott and other object-relations thinkers concerned with futility and un-ease (see also Guntrip, 1969), does. Bollas's description of the "un-thought known" mirrors and extends Schachtel's conceptualization of nonschematized primary experience, and he also describes the uneasy sense one can have of the self striving for articulation (see also Phillips, 1993). Bollas takes as his starting point Freud's claim that "the shadow of the object falls on the ego." This shadow, he claims, is an "unthought known" that influences and structures the self but is unavailable to consciousness. Bollas derives his conception from Winnicott's idea of a true self and adds to it the intersubjective perspective (also following Winnicott) that the unthought known integrates an internally generated idiom of true self with maternal care. Developmentally and experientially, the unthought known pre-cedes the development of the self or subject (or the many different aspects of self, or subject, and other that constitute being). It is the person's basic way of "being and relating" (1987, 9) and arises from an inherited or constitutional inner psychic idiom, in inter-action with the character of the earliest relation to another. The unthought known is "the human subject's recording of his early expe-riences of the object," or "the mental representation of the mother's logic of intersubjectivity" (1987, 3, 279).

Crucially, the unthought known is not represented in language; it is "known, but not yet thought" (4) or capable of being thought. Bollas describes how this unarticulated, undeveloped, but totalizing unthought known is expressed, how it develops out of the earliest relation to the other but precedes unconscious fantasy and an inner self-object world. As he puts it, "We are in possession of complex rules for being and relating, processes that reflect the dialectic of the inherited and the acquired. In the primary repressed unconscious we know these rules, but as yet only some of them have been thought. A very significant portion of our existence is predetermined by this unthought known" (9). Unconscious fantasy first begins to articulate the unthought known: "Phantasy is the first representative of the unthought known in mental life. It is a way of thinking that which is there" (279–280). As Bollas puts it, and Schachtel as well as contemporary infant researchers would agree, "In the beginning there may be the word, but there is also the wordless" (281).

Clinical psychoanalysis has the goal of understanding the unthought known, of "bring[ing] the unthought known into thought" (9)—in my terms, of recognizing or discovering it. Bollas asks, "In what ordinary way . . . does the unthought known become thought?" He answers that it becomes thought as it developed, through object relations. It emerges, and becomes recognized and elaborated through projective identification and the use in transference of the analyst both as an internal object and as an intersubjective other. Transference-countertransference enables "the emergence into thought of early memories of being and relating" (3), but at the outset, in any analysis, this being, relating, and using is felt first through the analyst's countertransference and can be only tentatively articulated. For Bollas, as for other Kleinian and Independent analysts, anything the patient talks about is a part of herself or her conception of the other, and how she uses the analyst expresses the unthought known of self-other relations. By recognizing patterns of projective identification, the analyst gives back these parts of the patient's self, articulated, transformed, and available for recognized (re)integration into the self. In his later work (1992), Bollas describes how throughout the natural, cultural, and interpersonal world the idiom of self can meet "evocative objects" that elicit self-enriching projective identifications of meaning.

Psychoanalytic visions of subjectivity put forth another form of recognition. Erikson's concept of ego integrity, I believe, most precisely articulates it. For many people, this is the form of recognition most difficult to attain. Recognition traverses many of Erikson's life-cycle stages and begins in the earliest stage of basic trust and mistrust. In this stage, the infant depends on the recognition by another of her agency, being, and drive. Although Erikson ties infant trust and mistrust to Freud's oral stage and an oral incorporative mode, recognition is not oral. (Bowlby's claim, 1969, 438, that Erikson is trapped theoretically is apt.) Recognition is an affirmation, actually or metaphorically gained through the eyes and face. Erikson sounds Winnicottian (or the reverse: Erikson's writings on these matters probably precede those of Winnicott) when he describes the infant's capacity "to let the mother out of sight without undue anxiety or rage because she has become an inner certainty as well as an outer predictability" and the development of "consistency, continuity, and sameness of experience" (1950, 247). He sounds Kleinian when he claims that ego identity depends "on the recognition that there is an inner population of remembered and anticipated sensations and images which are firmly correlated with the outer population of familiar and predictable things and people" and describes "the early process of differentiation between inside and outside" when "in introjection we feel and act as if an outer goodness had become an inner certainty [and] in projection, we experience an inner harm as an outer one: we endow significant people with the evil that actually is in us" (247, 248–249). Trust is intrinsically relational, not a matter only of individual development, and this relational basis explains why issues of trust resound throughout the life cycle.

Another of Erikson's major concepts, ego identity, is likewise not mainly a matter of identifying with others or of a sum of identifications. Ego identity requires one's being confirmed and recognized by others as a particular individual in a particular universe. As I noted earlier, Erikson uses both personal and cultural examples to document problems in ego identity, in the latter case the difficulties faced by minority outsiders and immigrants in finding interpersonal confirmation and recognition. Erikson notes that uprooted people look for recognition: they do not "hear what you say, but 'hang on' to your eyes and your tone of voice" (1964, 95). Finally, recognition reappears in Erikson's conception of ego integrity. For Erikson, the problem of ego integrity and despair is the last challenge of the life cycle. Ego integrity involves, he claims, "acceptance of one's one and only life cycle as something that had to be and that, by necessity, permitted of no substitutions" (1950, 268).

When I was younger, the concept of ego integrity gave me a great deal of trouble. Erikson seemed to be suggesting that a person had passively to accept as inevitable whatever social, cultural, and personal evil befell her. But Erikson is talking about recognition. Knowing, as he puts it, "that an individual life is the accidental coincidence of but one life cycle with but one segment of history" (268), he is saying that however painful, traumatic, and difficult one's life has been, whether because of external economic, historical, or political forces, racism or war, abuse or mistreatment or because of one's own internal conflicts, inhibitions, and neuroses, however much it is not the life one would have wished to have, it is one's life. The goal at this stage is, finally, a matter of internalizing basic trust, taking the early maternal function of recognition—when the mother recognizes the child's continuity and sameness or engages in what Winnicott describes as maternal mirroring—into the self. This is a more painful process if interpersonal or cultural-historical factors have made for a tragic and unfulfilled life, but the goal must be the same. Like Schachtel, Erikson looks not only toward the intrapsychic or the intersubjective relationship with parents ("it thus means a new, a different love of one's parents" [268]), but also, in *Childhood and Society* and elsewhere, toward cultural and social factors that might enable ego integrity to develop more easily.

At the end of an analysis, just as at the end of a life, a person, if all goes well, comes to recognize herself for who she is and has been. Winnicott makes this point when he claims that one goal of psychoanalysis is to gather impingement into omnipotence: "In psycho-analysis as we know it there is no trauma that is outside the individual's omnipotence. . . . The patient is not helped if the analyst says: 'Your mother was not good enough' . . . 'your father really seduced you' . . . 'your aunt dropped you.' Changes come in an analysis when the traumatic factors enter the psycho-analytic material in the patient's own way, and within the patient's omnipotence" (1960, 37). In analysis, then, even as a patient may acknowledge difficult experiences and traumas in her past and present, she has to come to see that she has lived these, to see herself as an experiencing agent who cannot intervene in or alter the lived, external past, but who is capable of intervening in and altering the current experience and understanding of this past.

Winnicott makes this claim not because he is unaware of impingements on the infant's existence. To the contrary, just as Erikson extensively describes the personal, cultural, and historical impediments to a good life, Winnicott's entire developmental account acknowledges the extent to which impingements potentially threaten the development of a true self in potential space and must be warded off by maternal protection. Like Erikson, Winnicott means that development, whether infantile or analytic, requires that the person experience the environment as coming from herself, that she own the experiences she has had. Winnicott calls this owning projection, and he notes: "The paradox is that what is good and bad in the infant's environment is not in fact a projection, but in spite of this it is necessary, if the individual infant is to develop healthily, that everything shall seem to him to be a projection" (1960, 38). Psychoanalysis concerns itself not with what Oedipus *did* but with his recognition of and insight into his actions, not with what a person does or has done to her but with her recognition and insight into these events.[7] As Schafer puts it, "What, after all, did Freud show in the *Studies on Hysteria* . . . but that a neurotic symptom is something a person *does* rather than *has* or has inflicted on him or her? It is a frightening truth that people make their own mental symptoms. It is an unwelcome insight that if neurosis is a disease at all, it is not like any other disease. It is an arrangement or a creation, an expression of many of an individual's most basic categories of understanding and vital interests" (1976, 153). Not to recognize this activity, according to Schafer, is to disclaim action and parts of the self.

The self-recognition that Erikson and Winnicott describe is also a form of individuation. It is not the individuation of an autonomous ego and superego or of a one-sided separation from the mother, but it is nonetheless a kind of internalization of a maternal function. These are also the individuation and internalization that engage Loewald when he describes the inevitable growing-up experience of parricide and atonement. In "The Waning of the Oedipus Complex" (1979), he asks whether we can rethink the Oedipus complex in a way that makes it interesting and relevant; whether, given our new understandings of psychic life, the Oedipus complex is still relevant for us to think about at all. Like Winnicott, who points to the need to destroy the object in fantasy in order to create it in interpersonal reality, Loewald suggests that growing up inevitably involves destroying not our parents but our early relationship to them. In order to take responsibility for our lives as our own, we must, by definition, replace the people who once had responsibility for us.

Complementing Erikson's and Winnicott's focus on the mother-child realm, Loewald describes the oedipal emancipation necessary to individuality: "In the oedipal struggle between the generations, the descendant's assuming or asserting responsibility or authority that belonged to ascendants arouses guilt in the descendant. It looks as if opponents are required with whom the drama of gaining power, authority, autonomy, and the distribution of guilt can be played out. . . . In an important sense, by evolving our own autonomy, our own superego, and by engaging in non-incestuous object relations, we are killing our parents" (389–390). In this view, autonomy and agency are forms of responsibility for self rather than a rejection of dependence on or involvement with others: "Responsibility to one-self . . . is the essence of superego as internal agency. It involves appropriating or owning up to one's needs and impulses as one's own, impulses or desires we appear to have been born with or that seem to have taken shape in interaction with parents during infancy" (392). Loewald here is very much in the realm of ego integrity and the gathering of impingement into omnipotence, of accepting one's life as the life one has lived, however contingently or accidentally, fortunately or unfortunately, it was created: "Such appropriation . . . means to experience ourselves as agents, notwithstanding the fact that we were born without our informed consent and did not pick our parents" (392).[8]

In other words, creating personal experience, making one's life meaningful, comes through the recognition of that life. Experience here has transitional features. Something happened and came from without, but in order for it to be personally meaningful, it must also be created from within at the same time. Whether formulated as the gathering of impingement into the realm of omnipotence, the achieving of ego integrity as a task of the entire adult life cycle, or the experiencing of ourselves as agents, such recognition is among the most difficult tasks of analysis. This is because inevitably, unless you are very young, it involves recognition of internal as well as external processes that have hitherto shaped and constrained your life. Although all lives are contingent and all lives, in some sense, could have been other than they are, ego integrity requires seeing this as not the case. Such recognition is tied not only to personal but even to biological history in that it involves not only gathering past impingement into omnipotence but also, sometimes painfully, recognizing what now can never be. This may be something absolute—one of the most difficult recognitions for some women in their forties and fifties is that, even if they have now in some way resolved the personal conflicts and anxieties that kept them from having children, they are, simply, biologically too late—but it may also be the recognition of having in some sense "wasted" years in suffering rather than living. Although it would seem, "rationally," that a person would want to seize the time left, as ten, twenty, or thirty years seem to have been lived in a driven or unfulfilling way, there can also be an internal push not to acknowledge fully that time really has passed but to engage in a particular kind of negative therapeutic reaction. A patient says, with wonder and amazement, "I've just discovered how hard it is for people to let themselves change and be happy."

We are again in the arena of past and present. None of this means that everything can be made all right or that conditions or circumstances have no bearing on what we do or think. We cannot remake the past if it has been painful, traumatic, or inadequate. But in analysis, we can come to recognize what our life has been and to see that our subjective experience of this past life is part of what we have made into our present. To return to earlier themes, such a view requires a conception of emergent meaning. By contrast, a theory that correlates early childhood with adult life and subjectivity, rather than looking at continuities and discontinuities of subjectivity itself, may paradoxically promote retention of discontinuity rather than recognition of the relation of past-to-present lived experience. Such a strategy makes it seem that elements of behavior or subjectivity which in fact connect to one another do not. The recognition specified by ego integrity, by gathering impingement into omnipotence, or by experiencing agency, requires moving beyond the belief that the past causes the present, rather than becomes imbricated within it.

In describing psychoanalytic visions of subjectivity, it is hard not to fall into accounts of fixed successes or goals. None of the so-called goals of analysis, however, is meant to be, or is conceptualized as, permanent. Both in analysis and throughout life, that which makes life meaningful—a desirable interchange between fantasy and reality, unconscious and conscious, self-recognition and (re)discovery—is not a once-and-for-all achievement. Conceptions of psychic life stress the continual nature of psychic activity, psychic life as a process rather than a product. Loewald (1951, 1962, 1979) describes how externality and internality and the boundaries between them are continually re-created, and he writes of the oscillation between the "psychotic core" of fusion and merging and oedipal individuation and difference. He argues for moving beyond associating one tendency with regressive and the other with progressive moments in human development and psychological life. Especially, he wants to valorize what we derive from the earliest period of development, before the subject-object distinction. For Loewald, "oedipal" projects of individuation and morality and "preoedipal" concerns with boundaries, separation, connection, and the transitional space continue throughout life: psychoanalysis "seems to stand and fall with the proposition that the emergence of a relatively autonomous individual is the culmination of human development. . . . On the other hand, owing in part to analytic research, there is a growing awareness of the force and validity of another striving, that for unity, symbiosis, fusion, merging, or identification—whatever name we wish to give to this sense of and longing for nonseparateness and undifferentiation" (1979, 401–402).

Kleinians, as I have noted, also show how psychological life involves continuous projections and introjections, continuous attempts to repair destruction and undo the consequences of envy, and continually shifting transferences as people create new selves and objects. Although Kleinians generally advocate a move from paranoid-schizoid functioning to depressive functioning and psychic integration (and all analysts would agree that on balance, depressive functioning and integration are less destructive of self and other), they also argue, like Loewald, that an oscillation between the two positions continues throughout life, and the paranoid-schizoid splitting, destruction, and change are as necessary to full experience as are depressive integration, reparation, and wholeness (see, e.g., Ogden, 1989). Of course, there can be in all these oscillations and changes activity that is not lively, that repeats itself over and over. Benjamin (1995) calls this subject-object complementarity—an apparently lively and moving activity that is in fact only a continual reversal of the same fantasized positions.

Psychoanalysis, as these considerations on activity and change make clear, is, finally, talking about the sense of being alive, and some analytic writers take the risk of claiming that psychic aliveness is what is at stake in their vision of subjectivity. This forthright sense that psychoanalysis addresses basic questions of psychic existence, now almost taken for granted in analytic thinking, might have been a shock to Freud and was for some time the province of the British Independents and a few interpersonalists only. Winnicott (especially 1960, 1971; but see also Guntrip, 1969; Little, 1981, 1990; Milner, 1936, 1957, 1969, 1987; Sutherland, 1994) is the psychoanalyst best known for his formulations of the British Independent group's precarious proposition that the main goal of analysis is the sense of being alive, or even just of being. He formulates his views developmentally, in his conception that the infant is born in an unintegrated state with a core of potential, barring impingement, for a true self to develop. The true self elaborates from a kernel of spontaneous creative gesture that is appropriately responded to by the environment-mother-analyst: "A description of the emotional development of the individual cannot be made entirely in terms of the individual, . . . but . . . in certain areas . . . the behaviour of the environment is part of the individual's own personal development and must therefore be included" (1971, 53). Winnicott, along with his Independent colleagues, takes it for granted that some of the patients he talks about—and talks to—are not alive, in spite of their ability to walk into his office. His primary goal, as an analyst, is to foster aliveness—spontaneity, the ability to dream, create, play, and have a sense of inner vibrancy—in these initially dead patients.

A key element in the process that creates and expresses aliveness is the capacity for symbolization. Kleinians (Klein, 1930, Segal, 1957, Bion, 1961, and O'Shaughnessy, 1981) have extensively developed this argument, claiming that meaning exists only to the extent that symbols are open, that one meaning enables another, and that meaning is never final. In a detailed case study, Winnicott (1971) describes how fantasy, when it is split off and not amenable to change and development, is experienced on the level of concrete symbolization (Segal, 1957), when it does not stand for or relate to anything else but is simply a fantasy in itself. Such dead fantasy has an effect not only on a person's ability to live in the external world but, more important, on her ability to dream creatively, that is, to create a vibrant inner world.

Winnicott's formulations have been elaborated by contemporary followers. Mitchell (1993b) focuses on what he calls the authenticity of the true self and claims that psychoanalysis today is concerned with "people . . . who are missing something fundamental in their experience of living . . . whose subjectivity itself is understood to be basically awry" (1993b, 22). Bollas (especially 1987, 1992b) uses the notion of personal idiom to describe the true self or creative gesture, and he sees the fostering of the personal idiom as one of the main goals of psychoanalysis. Ogden speaks directly about the experience of aliveness as he elaborates on Winnicott's conception: "The goal of analysis from this point of view is larger than that of the resolution of unconscious intrapsychic conflict, the diminution of symptomatology, the enhancement of reflective subjectivity and self-understanding, and the increase of a sense of personal agency. Although one's sense of being alive is intimately intertwined with each of the above-mentioned capacities, I believe that the experience of aliveness is a quality that is superordinate to these capacities and must be considered as an aspect of the analytic experience *in its own terms*" (1995, 2).

In this chapter, I have deliberately avoided the one-person/two-person psychology debate, though my focus has been on psychological processes and psychic reality from the point of view of a single subject. I have done so even while arguing that all of these psychological processes and psychic realities emerge in, incorporate, and take their shape partially from a two-person (or more than two-person) matrix—ideal-typically in analytic thinking a matrix of mother-child relatedness or of analytic transference-countertransference and projective identification. Loewald and Klein, for example, have as much to say about transference and countertransference, projective identification, and the analytic encounter as anyone, but they put forward, finally, what is in current parlance very much a one-person psychology. This is not surprising. Loewald's historical and theoretical home is in American ego psychology, even if it is not the ego psychology favored by Hartmann, Arlow, Brenner, Rangell, or Gray; Kleinian theory focuses on the internal world, even though internal projective and introjective interchanges and splits within self and object world are its basic constituents.

Without underestimating the significance of intersubjectivity (a significance that has been described brilliantly by Benjamin, 1995) and the tensions between mutual acknowledgment and self-assertion in two independent subjects, whether in the infant-caregiver relationship, in the analytic encounter, or throughout life, I worry that two-person or relational psychologies seem sometimes to flatten and oversimplify inner life. They have had to sacrifice the attention to the richness of inner life that one-person psychologies retain (by contrast, contemporary focus on the analyst's subjectivity seems rather to assert that the analyst's complex inner life also inflects the analytic encounter).[9] I find myself, then, unlike many of my contemporaries, drawn to what must still be called one-person psychologies, where the central role of the other is played out in intrapsychic rather than intersubjective life.

Because psychoanalytic theory has its starting point in the psychoanalytic encounter, however, any conceptualization of psychoanalytic subjectivity must also encompass this fully two-person intersubjective encounter as a locus of personal meaning. Several formulations of the relation to an actual other and the intersubjective encounter are relevant here, but we begin where everyone begins, with Winnicott's account of the transitional object and transitional phenomena. A real teddy bear is given to the child and is treated by her as a separate object or possession in the outer world; at the same time, it is a subjective illusion created by the child from within. It stands for the mother but is also separate and in between mother and infant and as such is invested with its own qualities. As Winnicott puts it, it is a subjective object and also an object objectively perceived. Its amorphous and paradoxical status can become symbolically generalized to other phenomena and encounters, which are themselves then perceived and experienced as part of a presented world and as created, projected onto, given personal coloring, and shaped from within. These days, one has to be diffidently self-conscious when drawing on Winnicott's theory. Much like the beloved teddy bear, the theory of the transitional object has itself become a transitional object. Through use, Winnicott's writings on this subject are loved, mutilated, destroyed, and made into whatever a particular writer wishes them to be.

Analysts (as well as writers in many other fields) have drawn on Winnicott's account to conceptualize something that goes distinctly beyond the two subjects in the consulting room. (I believe that the early interpersonalists derived a related conception from Lewin's field theory, Lewin and Cartwright, 1964, but this was not picked up by analysts in other traditions.) Winnicott describes, mainly from the infant's point of view, the potential space between mother and infant that is outside both individuals. It is neither an inner psychic reality nor the external world but an in-between created by the interaction

of two people that is more than the interaction itself. Both participants invest this potential space with personal meaning, thereby
creating new meaning. The analytic interaction creates such a potential space, which Ogden labels the analytic third (1994).
Ogden (1994, 60) builds on Winnicott's claim that there is no
such thing as an infant but only a unit of infant and maternal care.
The infant as an infant, and the mother as a mother, can be created
only in the in-between space of their interaction, through many
different processes of holding, projective and introjective identification, mirroring, primary maternal preoccupation, object usage, and
feeding. Similarly, the analytic dyad begins with two individual people, each with her own psychological, professional, therapeutic, and
personal-cultural biography, but together they create an analytic
third in the potential space between them. All analytically relevant
processes take place in (or become) this analytic third, with its own
meaning that has been created through interaction: like the mother-
infant case, an interaction involving projective and introjective identification, object usage, transitional meanings and objects created by
one or the other person, mirroring, noticing together, and so forth.

The analytic third is created through the "interplay of individual subjectivity [two individual subjectivities] and intersubjectivity"
(Ogden, 1994, 64). Any object noticed by either analyst or analysand
during an hour becomes an "analytic object"; any event, whether
happening between analyst and patient or outside the analytic encounter and brought for discussion, becomes an "analytic event."
Like transitional phenomena, these objects or events are presented
from without, but they are also created and given meaning from
within. It is through this dual creation, in the intersection of the
intrapsychic and the intersubjective, that they become created in a
new way as part of the analysis. Schafer (1983, 127–128) similarly
suggests that metaphors in the analytic situation draw on old elements, thereby gaining power and persuasiveness from their history

and meaning, and are nonetheless created anew in that particular analytic encounter.

Ogden is describing the qualities that go into any meaningful intersubjective encounter. Anthropologists, as I have noted, describe what we might call an ethnographic third (see especially Crapanzano, 1980, but also Kracke, 1987a, 1994, and Obeyesekere, 1990). An ethnographic object is not that which exists or existed independently of the ethnographer "in" the culture; it is given in the culture and by the informant, but it is also created in the ethnographic encounter and given meaning by the anthropologist's subjectivity, the informant's subjectivity, and the intersubjective encounter that they both create. Such an intersubjective view of meaning complements an intrapsychic or internal view. In the intersubjective view also, meaning is not simply given from the cultural or interpersonal existing without; it is also created through projection, fantasy, and illusion from within.

Intersubjectivity involves recognizing the other as well as being recognized by the other, but with few exceptions, analysts are able to envision a mutuality in the potential space of the analytic encounter that they cannot envision in the potential space between mother and child. In most conceptions it is the infant that creates a transitional object and potential space between self and other. As potential space is extended into the realms of creativity and play, it is the infant— with the capacity to be alone in the presence of the mother—who can now play and create. Even "the location of cultural experience" and "the place where we live" are seen from the point of view of the baby rather than as a mutually created, intersubjective experience or place (Winnicott, 1971; see also Ogden, 1986, 1994, and Bollas, 1987). By contrast, Benjamin (1988, 1995), although she also derives many of her conceptualizations from Winnicott, has throughout her writings elaborated a vision of mutual recognition between mother and infant and argued that, developmentally, the baby's recognition of the mother as another subject and center of experience is an important developmental experience and goal. (For a related argument, see Chodorow, 1978, 1979. We are both indebted to Alice Balint, 1939.) Intersubjectivity, in Benjamin's view, is based on mutual recognition. It is a risky business developmentally, for it involves, in the moment and for the purpose, destroying the object as an internal object and according her full status as an external object—"an equivalent center of self" to the subject (Benjamin, 1995, 27, takes the phrase from George Eliot). As a projection, the object has to be intrapsychically used and ruthlessly destroyed, and there is always the danger that intrapsychic destruction will be the end of the matter, that the original external object—the person who provides the fuel for the intrapsychic representation—will not be able to survive and reappear in the external world. But intrapsychic destruction and external survival are not once-and-for-all projects. Every minidestruction of another as exclusively a projection is, it is to be hoped, at the same time a recognition of another as a subject.

Schachtel, in his conception of focal attention, provides, along with Benjamin, the most extensive account of the development of recognition of the other, but he gives a somewhat different picture of these processes. In the Winnicottian view extended by Benjamin, drive derivatives—specifically, simple, non-hate-filled aggression in the form of ruthless object usage—is key.[10] By contrast, Schachtel derives the recognition of the object as an independent center of experience not from drives but from the mitigation of drive determination. The capacity for focal attention requires the ability to center attention fully on the object, with the disinterest and wonder of a phenomenologist. It involves perceiving the object in its many aspects and from many sides. In the tension of need, the object is seen only insofar as it satisfies or does not satisfy. There is by definition a focus only on its need-fulfilling qualities. In the world of driven projection and introjection, the object is also seen only in part-object terms as bad or good. Thus, focal attention is possible only when the object can be apprehended apart from need. In this sense, for Schachtel as for other psychoanalytic theorists, what is important is not the external world or object as a given from out there, but the external world or object as it is created. With focal attention, the integrated, depressively conceived object can be seen in its many different aspects, not as bad or good in relation to bad and good aspects of the self, but with consideration for aspects that have an existence independent of the self and the self's needs.

Schachtel argues that the object world, or reality, can emerge and be experienced only in the context of relative freedom from the tension of needs or anxiety (in object-relations terms, in the context of relative freedom from anxiety-driven paranoid-schizoid splitting). Focal attention, like transitional experience in potential space, occurs in the realm of play, where it is possible to explore and experience first this, then that aspect of the other or of the self. Giving as a first example not people but objects, Schachtel describes the child's reaction to a beloved book. When you read to a child, you have to read the book exactly in the same words, over and over, and you cannot skip pages, because with each reading the child is able to attend first to one, then to another part of the story. For the bored adult reader, it seems to be the same story again and again; for the child, each reading enables a different phenomenological bracketing. Schachtel claims, "Objects become distinct parts of experience only when they are encountered in a field sufficiently relaxed from need tension to permit the infant to approach and explore the object *playfully*—that is, without having to incorporate it as nourishment. . . . His relative freedom from urgent need tension is the basis of the richness of his object world, which could not have developed if he had not been free, in play and thought, to explore objects without having to use them for immediate need satisfaction" (1959, 270, 272).[11]

Of course, a really external subject—another in whom the subject has no interest—does not much matter when it comes to recognition, focal attention, or potential space. The external world unambiguously experienced as external does not pose a psychological problem. In this context, Schachtel notes that it is much easier to attend focally to objects than to people and focal attention is easier to achieve with nonparental people than with parents, who are originally known under the tensions of anxiety and need. Reciprocally, the capacity for focal attention toward and appreciation of an other who is a subject enables the self to experience itself, in some sense, objectively. As Benjamin also puts it, the greatest difficulties in mutual recognition for anyone lie in sustaining the permanent, active paradoxical tension between sameness and difference: another subject is both a like subject and a love object, someone like you but also someone who is different (1995, 38). There is almost a reversal: the self comes to be seen reflexively as a subject that is known to have capacities and subjectivity, like the object; the object is seen in terms of its subjectivity. Focal attention is rarely fully achieved. The object actively matters only to the extent that relations to it oscillate between felt anxious need and focal attention.

Acknowledgment of the paradoxes of recognition or focal attention directs our attention to ambiguity and paradox in the object. Important objects, it would seem, always have a dual character. Winnicott has pinpointed the paradoxical dual character of the transitional object, and ambiguous duality reappears in the character of later objects as well. Loewald rethinks the character of oedipal objects to emphasize their ambiguous duality for the self rather than their specific role in libidinal development. Oedipal objects, he claims, must be moved beyond (and hence are necessarily subject to parricide), but they are also in some sense transitional in their incestuous nature. Oedipal objects inhabit a transitional realm and space of being both one with and different from, like and unlike the subject—part of the subject and yet an object. This is what gives the oedipal constellation its intensity, and intense love its charge. They are important because they are at the same time both extensions of the self—linked to the subject by preoedipal bonds of identification and oneness—and objects of sexual desire, both *identificata* and *objecta:* "The incestuous object is thus an intermediate, ambiguous entity, neither a full-fledged libidinal *objectum* nor an unequivocal *identificatum*" (1979, 397; in Benjamin's terms, they are by necessity both love objects and like subjects). Loewald uses his insight into the ambiguity of the oedipal object to move us into the third area, in which subjectivity and objectivity are endlessly negotiated: "If we exclude the whole realm of identification and empathy from normality, . . . we arrive at a normality that has little resemblance to actual life. Identification and empathy, where subject-object boundaries are temporarily suspended or inoperative, play a significant part in everyday interpersonal relations, not to mention the psychoanalyst's and psychotherapist's daily working life" (1979, 403).

Thus, although oedipal objects themselves must be given up and replaced by more distant sexual relations, any love object that matters will also be a like subject. Loewald suggests that oedipal engagement with someone who is an intermediate object, an object both of identification and of desire, expresses a long-deferred, deeply felt wish that accounts in part for the depth and richness of adult love relationships. Thus, just as Briggs suggests that cultural values that matter must be internalized with conflict, intensity, and ongoing engagement, so Loewald's point seems to be that persons who matter must also be taken in conflictually, intensely, and with sustained attention to their status as subjective object and objective object, as object noticed because of need and as object experienced through focal attention.

How do we reconcile our being driven by anxiety and conflict and the limitations and constraints posed by our personal emotional constructions with a vision of being enriched by such constructions—of living an integration of unconscious and conscious, of fantasy and reality? Rigid projective transference templates constrain our ability to apprehend the world; how do we reconcile this recognition with the understanding that without transference and projection, people and experiences cannot matter? Throughout this book, I have suggested that the goal of psychoanalysis is, broadly, to claim as one's own the power of one's feelings. One analysand described his need to "bleach" the feelings out of words, to hold his breath and be vague. He was well aware of the great threat that recognizing the power of feelings could pose. Understanding one's own psychic reality, the power of particularized feelings, gives coherence, continuity, and meaning to the self and the lived life. This coherence is not that of a unitary, unchanging ego or a single identity or self. It is consistent with, and even requires, multiple, shifting senses of self and identity, a shifting internal world, and a fluid process of lively interchange between inner and outer. It is consistent with and requires change and transformation in internal life and in relations with others, continual projective identifications that allocate parts of the self to the other and introjective identifications that draw parts of the other into the self. It assumes—rather than simplicity and rigidity—complexity and change, in which every experience and impression of the external world is transformed and created by psychic reality.

Just as coherence is not a rigid unity, so the aim of continuity does not call forth a seamless biography described in the language of one or another psychoanalytic theory of the childhood past and the present psychic life. A sense of continuity helps link elements of psychic reality and the sense of self into an alive "I." The power of feelings comes to be couched in terms of an individual's own history, but a history interpreted, absorbed, and actively created. It is recognized as one's own. Current feelings, a contemporary sense of self, passions, and felt needs and desires come not only from what really happened in the past but from a web of internal processes that construct the present.

According to one form of conventional wisdom, psychoanalysis is a determinist theory. I have suggested that it is often rather social, historical, and cultural critiques of psychoanalysis that are determinist. Arguments emphasizing the power of social forces, economic or political conditions, or cultural categories may mask determinist assumptions yet deprive the individual of interpretive as well as behavioral agency. Psychological schemata can also take agency and freedom away from the individual, when the psychological meanings are rigid and unavailable to the actor, when the unthought known determines action and the actor herself is unable to recognize and play with these psychological meanings. This is why Freud's claim that psychoanalysis makes the unconscious conscious remains so significant.

Psychoanalysis allows for a recognition and understanding of the personal meanings that create psychic life and give it an "added glow"; analysis enables an enfolding of the split-off or repressed aspects of psychic life into the centered and known, makes continuities of discontinuities. Schafer (1976) reflects on skepticism about psychoanalysis:

In this view, the problem is not only a disagreeable *reduction* of people's conception of their personal scope and influence; it is a threatening *expansion* of this conception. In a basic sense Freud extended people's narcissistic sense of themselves. He showed that people make their lives by what they do, and, for psychoanalysis, what they "do" includes all their mental operations and thereby all the circumstances they contrive and all the meanings they ascribe to their circumstances, whether contrived or imposed on them. People, thus, are far more creators and stand much closer to their gods than they can bear to recognize. I do not mean that most people consciously recognize this expanded idea of lives that is implied in psychoanalytic interpretation; but they fear it nonetheless. [153]

In another form of conventional wisdom, psychoanalysis threatens to take uniqueness away from individuals. People commonly express the fear that entering psychoanalysis will eventually stop a writer from writing or a painter from painting, that neurosis is the root of creativity, and that psychoanalysis wishes to remove the latter along with the former. But it is only split-off unconscious fantasy that cannot inform creativity or otherwise make life fuller. Unconscious fantasy if not split off has the potential to deepen experience and to enhance creativity. By centering ourselves in the clinical encounter and in clinical goals, we can understand more precisely how the dialogue between inner and outer, past and present, is accomplished daily and can be fostered; we see how the power of feelings provides or fails to provide what we experience as vitality and richness in our lives.

Loewald points out a paradox. More than any other field, psychoanalysis has focused on a rational understanding of the nonrational, unconscious, fantasy, and emotional aspects of the human mind. At the same time, it has also been the field that most cogently problematizes and challenges the very rational quest that engages it: "Psychoanalysis has always been in an awkward position. . . . While it has been its intent to penetrate unconscious mentality with the light of rational understanding, it also has been and is its intent to uncover the irrational unconscious sources and forces motivating and organizing conscious and rational mental processes. In the course of these explorations, unconscious processes became accessible to rational understanding, and at the same time rational thought itself and our rational experience of the world as an 'object world' became problematic" (1979, 402).

All of us who study and practice psychoanalysis confront this paradox. My own venture into understanding the power of feelings, like the quests for meaning of all thinkers, must itself be transferentially shaped by an unconscious psychic reality. My quest has been to direct the light of understanding toward the ways in which we create personal meaning and to explore the use and generation of intersubjective, cultural, and social meaning in that process of creation. The clinical goals of psychoanalysis, I have argued, are intertwined with images of subjectivity and intersubjective engagement. Against the generalizing and abstracting tendencies of both psychoanalytic theory and social science, the insistent, relentless, unique individuality of each of an analyst's patients, of a social scientist's informants, of a biographer's subjects, or of personal friends, teachers, students, children, spouses, and lovers, stands out. To know who a person is, it is never enough to know the externals of her history or the culture she comes from. Against postmodern and poststructuralist claims that selfhood and identity are fictions, and that destabilized, multiply shifting, split psyches are not only inevitable but perhaps desirable, I argue for forms of psychic wholeness and for depth of experience.

A psychoanalysis that begins with the immediacy of unconscious fantasy and feeling found in the clinical encounter illuminates our understanding of individual subjectivity and potentially transforms all sociocultural thought. It demonstrates that all theories of meaning must incorporate the unconscious realm. At the same time, feminist, anthropological, and other cultural theories require that psychoanalysts take seriously the ways in which cultural meanings intertwine with and help to constitute psychic life.

The psychoanalytic approaches I have discussed may reflect a variety of theoretical traditions, but each of them is dealing unabashedly with big questions about human nature and possibility that have challenged thinkers for thousands of years. In the tradition of analytic critics and visionaries, and with the same hopeful diffidence that my contribution can help to change self and world, I offer a way of looking at things.

NOTES

1. Robert Wallerstein, in a personal conversation in 1996 or 1997, pointed out to me that the tension I find between clinical particularity and general theory may be particularly acute within the history of American psychoanalytic ego psychology and thus partially an artefact of my having been trained as a psychoanalyst in the United States. Heinz Hartmann and his followers were especially insistent upon psychoanalysis as a general psychology, and they were particularly unlikely to include case examples in their writings. The great exception is of course Erikson, but his ego psychology was never fully accepted by the ego psychological lineage of either Hartmann or Anna Freud. By contrast, although Kleinians also have a universalized, general theory, Kleinian writing from the beginning

has been replete with extensive, particularized, unique, often named child and adult case examples. It is notable that Freud's classic cases all come from before the development of the structural theory. Although this imbalance is probably also a result of Freud's aging and illness, it is worth speculating whether the structural theory is further removed from clinical particularity than Freud's earlier formulations.

CHAPTER 1: CREATING PERSONAL MEANING

1. Klein originally distinguished between projection and projective identification, but today the corresponding terms tend to be used interchangeably, the former perhaps focusing more on the projective process from within, the latter more on the object or person receiving the projection and responding to it. Although the concept is not current, and perhaps not used at all, I believe that it is useful to conceptualize a corresponding process as introjective identification. By "introject," we tend to refer to an internal object; "introjective identification" allows us to describe more specifically the way that, for example, the analyst's analytic capacities and functions, or particular analytic identifications, can be appropriated internally by the patient. Just as in projective identification, parts of the self can be put into the other, so, in introjective identification, parts of the other can be taken away from that other and put into the self.

2. This book presents few case examples and no extended case histories. In each example, I have given as few recognizable external details as possible; I have disguised biographical details and facts that needed to be given; and I have sometimes combined the facts of two or more cases into one, or divided those of a single case among several persons. When I have altered elements of an interaction or a case, I have done so in ways that (I hope) preserve the point that I mean the example to substantiate. Suffice it to say that the question of the presentation of clinical facts, cases, and vignettes in the history of psychoanalysis is complex and unresolved, given the dual goals of preserving patient anonymity, confidentiality, and treatment and of presenting theoretical and technical claims to analytic and other colleagues with adequate empirical backing. The former goal must of course take priority.

3. Adler and Buie (1979) describe how overwhelming loneliness and emptiness—the loss of a two-person psychology—can lead to the disappearance of evocative memory and even recognition. Klein (1963) discusses how a "sense of loneliness" emerges when the integration of good and bad objects and self is not able to maintain enough idealization and enough assurance that one won't

destroy the good object, and Winnicott (1958) claims that the "capacity to be alone" requires the good-enough internal presence of the mother.

4. Loewald (1960, 251) makes explicit what Klein implies, that internalizations and externalizations are not just of objects in themselves, but always of an interaction process in which fantasied ego-object interchanges are involved. We find here echoes of a Meadian account of meaning creation (Mead, 1934), in which meaning for the self comes about through interactions with the other, but we also see, as we reflect on the ceaseless transformations of projections and introjections, how contingent, discontinuous, jarring, and fluid the creation of emotional meaning can be, within any person and as any person reacts to the same process within someone else. The great distinction between sociological constructionists or interactionists and psychoanalysts is that social constructionists do not have a place in their account for a complex, fluctuating inner world of objects, meanings, intrapsychic conflict, and anxiety. They also have no theory of how senses of self and other come from within as well as from without.

5. I am on shaky ground interpreting a philosopher. As I understand him, both in his 1990 book and in his article "The Introduction of Eros: Reflections on the Work of Hans Loewald" (1996, 678), Lear is trying to show how external reality exists (following Kant, he is an empirical realist) and at the same time can be apprehended by us only through our mind, which has its own organizing capacities and conditions (in Kantian terms, he is a transcendental idealist). Psychoanalysis, he claims, is a "science of subjectivity," whose interest is in the capacities and processes of mind that enable us to give meaning—"the perspective *from the inside,* from the ego"—to the world (1996, 680).

6. For Bird, Freud's discovery and resolution of his own transference neurosis vis-à-vis Fliess "constituted the actual center of his self-analysis, and it was this event that was the beginning of analysis as we know it" (1972, 271).

7. A history of analytic attitudes toward countertransference is beyond the scope or requirements of this chapter. Briefly, little attention was paid to countertransference other than as the mark of an insufficiently analyzed analyst, until the early 1950s. At this time, some British Independents, some Kleinians, and some Americans of the interpersonal school—relying as they all did on object-relational conceptions of psychic process and interpersonal understandings of the analytic encounter—tended to argue more strongly for the necessity and usefulness of the analysis of countertransference to the analytic process (see, e.g., Racker, 1953; 1957; Winnicott, 1949; Little, 1951; Heimann, 1950; Fromm-Reichman, 1950; Cohen, 1952). A few mainstream American psychoanalysts also

interested themselves, though with reservations, in the uses of the countertransference (e.g., Reich, 1951, Tower, 1956). Discussion of countertransference has accordingly been central to psychoanalytic training in England and in the American interpersonal psychoanalytic institutes, whereas it has not been central in most mainstream American institutes (but see writings by ego-psychologically trained American analysts Jacobs, 1991, and Renik, e.g., 1993a and 1993b).

Joseph notes: "Counter-transference . . . like transference itself, was originally seen as an obstacle to the analytic work, but now . . . we see it too, no longer as an obstacle, but as an essential tool of the analytic process" (1985, 157). Loewald concurs: "If we limit the term *countertransference* to reactions of the analyst to the patient, we make the implicit and untenable assumption that the analyst is devoid of transference to the patient. . . . When we further limit the concept to the analyst's unconscious reactions insofar as they *interfere* with analysis, we take the concept out of the proper context of transference-countertransference interplay in human relations" (1986, 279).

CHAPTER 2: THE ANXIETIES OF UNCERTAINTY

1. See also Bion (1967), urging the analyst to be without memory or desire, and Ogden (1989) on "Misrecognitions and the Fear of Not Knowing."

2. Heated intellectual and political debate concerning Freud's abandonment of the seduction theory as he came to formulate the theory of infantile sexuality has obscured what I take to be an equally important consequence of this theory: a move from the contingent psychological present to a universalized developmental past. With regard to the latter dichotomy, those who claim that actual childhood trauma causes neurosis and those who argue that the endogenous psychic reality of infantile sexuality is at the root of it are on the same side.

3. Citations here cannot be comprehensive. On developmental lines, see Anna Freud (1965); on interrelating systems and structures, Tyson and Tyson (1990); on rapprochement, Mahler et al. (1975); on mirroring, Kohut (1971); on the maternal holding environment, Winnicott (1965) and Bollas (1987). Coates (1997, 43) also suggests that the concept of developmental lines is implicitly tied to the structural theory of ego and id, which itself derives from and extends Freud's original theory of libidinal phases. Her critique is less about the incompatibility of the concept of developmental lines with a here and now view of transference and countertransference, and more about its "linear and normative presuppositions." Coates, herself a child researcher and clinician who treats children, wonders whether it is "time to put the concept of 'developmental lines' to rest" (1997, 42).

4. I have argued elsewhere (e.g., Chodorow, 1994) that psychoanalytic concepts often reflect unwitting culturally normative assumptions. On how the "natural attitude" becomes science, see especially Garfinkel (1967). On the profoundly different ways that cultures conceptualize personhood, selfhood, emotions, and lives, including the extent to which explaining a life is even a prevalent cultural or personal preoccupation, see Chapters 5, 6, and 7. On how cultural narratives affect what can and cannot be told about a life, see Heilbrun (1988).

5. See also Poland: "Transference, though its roots are in the past, comes into existence as it is actualized within the world of the present" (1992, 185).

6. Recent Anglo-American attraction to the originally Lacanian but now more generically French emphasis on the *après coup* (Freud's *Nachträglichkeit*) seems to me another related attempt to reconcile past and present. The après coup refers to the way that older experiences and memories take on new meaning after the fact in relation to new experiences and contemporary psychic realities or to fit in with them. Prager (1998) provides a fascinating theoretical investigation and case study of a past being created in the service of current transference.

7. Malcolm, more explicitly, claims that "the analyst, when formulating [interpretations], should keep in mind the notion that it is the patient's past that is expressed in his unconscious phantasies" (1986, 78), and she describes herself speculating during an analytic hour about a patient's early relation to his mother and imagines herself in the early maternal role. Joseph (1985) claims that the transference is both created in the present and based on the past.

8. Christopher Bollas and Thomas Ogden, in fact, seem stunningly able (to this mother and analyst) to know exactly what their patients' mothers were like, how they failed, and the ways in which good mothers should be able to maintain near-perfect attunement with their infants.

9. In their applications of psychoanalysis, writers in a variety of fields also tend to follow this model, in that they take it as their task theoretically or empirically to explain adult patterns in terms of childhood conflict and developmental stages. Psychobiographical treatments may follow Freud's psychosexual theory, focusing on fixation or regression, childhood sexuality, and the Oedipus complex, or they may employ post-Freudian theories, examining early object relations, early object loss, and separation and individuation. A particular biographical or literary character may be understood to be preoccupied with oral or anal issues or with identity (e.g., Erikson in his great *Young Man Luther,* 1958), or to be, like Hamlet, dealing with (and exemplifying) a severe unresolved Oedipus complex. Grand cultural accounts are built on theories about sexual repression in childhood or infantile repression of the recognition of death (see, e.g., Mar-

cuse, 1956, and Brown, 1959), or they argue that the culturally induced weakening of the father in childhood leads to the lack of superego formation or to an authoritarian personality (e.g., Mitscherlich, 1963; Horkheimer, 1936; Marcuse, 1970; Adorno, Frenkel-Brunswik, Levinson, and Sanford, 1950). Historians and anthropologists show how treatment of children in different cultures gives rise to different adult personalities and cultural patterns. It is not that these works, or this way of thinking, are entirely wrong; indeed, I have in mind some of the most important and original psychoanalytically based treatments in social and cultural theory (which I consider to be among the most brilliant social and cultural theories of the twentieth century) and in psychohistory, psychobiography, and literary criticism. I point only to the assumption that psychoanalytic explanation should look to the psychic and experiential past to the exclusion of the psychic present.

10. Loewald's interests in the cognitive establishment of ego and reality and in the differentiation and development of psychic structure are very much in the ego-psychological tradition: his first paper is titled, "Ego and Reality." But he also brings to bear object-relational questions of projection, introjection, fantasy, and the interpersonal mother-child matrix, drawing explicitly at times upon Klein and Winnicott (on Loewald's syncretism, see Fogel, 1991; Fogel, Tyson, Greenberg, McLaughlin, and Peyser, 1996; Friedman, 1996; and Kaywin, 1994). See also Lear (1990, 1996), who extends Loewald's account of the creation of inner and outer as a psychological achievement in which both self and world grow in complexity and in investment with psychological and affective meaning.

11. Loewald takes a position here apparently incompatible with current understandings of infantile abilities to differentiate between self and other (see Stern, 1985). I think, however, that in its substance his account is remarkably consonant with these. Loewald seems intuitively alert to the intermodal, configurative, vitality-driven, and global affective and perceptual experiences that Stern describes, as well as to the interpersonal matrix in which experience is given meaning. Primary process, for instance, is not distinguished primarily by being earlier but by being "unitary, non-differentiating, non-discriminating between various elements or components of a global event or experience. . . . the original uniform density conveyed in primary process" (1978a, 196). Secondary process makes a textured, differentiated totality out of what was a global totality. As he discusses why drives cannot originally be connected to objects, because objects have not yet been differentiated from ego, Loewald also speaks in Sternian terms: "A more appropriate term for such pre-stages of an object-world [before differentiation of ego and objects have occurred] might be the noun 'shapes'; in the

sense of configurations of an indeterminate degree and a fluidity of organization, and without the connotation of object-fragments" (1960, 236). He claims, "In one and the same act—I am tempted to say, in the same breath and the same sucking of milk—drive direction and organization of environment into shapes and configurations begin, and they are continued into ego organization and object organization by methods such as identification, introjection, projection" (1960, 238).

12. My account that follows draws more on Klein, but I put Klein and Fairbairn together to stress their notable commonalities in the matters of which I write.

13. Klein's and Fairbairn's view that a primitive ego and object relations exist from birth is more directly consistent with recent infant research than the accounts of Loewald, of ego psychologists like Mahler and Hartmann, and of Freud, who claims that the infant does not distinguish the mother's breast from the infant's own body. However, these contemporary researchers would probably not agree that the infant's relation to the outside world is initially constituted entirely by fantasy.

14. I am certainly imposing a reading on these theorists rather than taking them exactly at their word. As should be clear from my account of both-and approaches earlier, most psychoanalysts, including those whose developmental theories I claim are describing lifelong transferential processes rather than determining childhoods, themselves tend to assume a virtually direct correlation between the earliest infantile period and the basic adult stance and to believe that structures or psychic contents laid down in early childhood are indeed being replayed in the transference relationship (for a particularly striking example, see Bollas (1987), whose "unthought known," or "idiom," is a memory of the earliest period recorded in ego structure). These accounts ambivalently subvert but do not undermine the psychoanalytic insistence on the importance of early development.

15. Within developmental theory, what we might call the maternal countertransference experience is not extensively described. For exceptions, see Stern on "reciprocal fantasy interaction [and] created interpersonal meaning" and his claim that "intersubjectivity is an innate, emergent human capacity" (1985, 134) and Loewald's claim that the origin of consciousness is *conscire*—mother and infant's "knowing together," in which "parental recognizing care reflects more . . . to the child than he presents [and] the developing, internal conscire represents something other than an internal reflection of experience in the sense of mere 'reduplication'" (Loewald, 1978c, 13 and 15). See also Bassin, Honey, and Kaplan, 1994.

1. I have in mind here the entire corpus of feminist post-structuralism or post-modernism, making specific citation difficult. Founding texts include Butler (1990) and Scott (1988); Nicholson, ed. (1990) is a representative early anthology. In recent writings, Butler (e.g., 1995) has moved toward a more internalist and psychodynamic view, though she still, finally, seems to claim to privilege the discursive over the unconscious psychic reality of fantasy (Layton, 1997, provides an overview of Butler's shifts along with their continuing limits from the point of view of relational psychoanalysis; see also Butler's response, 1997). For a critique of the feminist tendency to reduce the cultural-linguistic to the political, see Bloch, 1993.

2. In now-classic articles that bring the insights of feminist postmodernism to the clinical community, Dimen, 1991, and Harris, 1991, give clinically based accounts compatible with this claim. Dimen describes the intertwining of gender not only with cultural representations but with aspects of self-experience. Harris argues for the complexity, the contextual and varying salience, and the multiple figuration of gender and sexuality in anyone's psyche (see also Goldner, 1991, who provides elegant documentation of the paradoxical relational injunctions and cognitive contradictions that create and sustain normal gender as a defense and advocates a psychologically nondichotomous, decentered gender).

3. I have in mind, for instance, Freudian stage theory and Lacanian theory, which categorize gender as an oedipal achievement, and the currently competing second-year genital phase or rapprochement theories, according to which feelings about gender and genitals first become significant in the second year (e.g., Roiphe and Galenson, 1981; Benjamin, 1989, Fast, 1984). At this point, even the timing of what has traditionally been called core gender identity, or what Benjamin (1995) has renamed nominal gender identification—the early cognitive self-labeling that almost everyone develops to refer to being female or male—is in question. Traditionally, it has been seen as developing gradually and consolidating between eighteen months and three years (see Stoller, 1968, and Money and Ehrhardt, 1972). For a recent empirical study that queries the relation between the development of genital self-recognition and gender self-definition, see de Marneffe 1997. In her "Commentary" on de Marneffe, Coates (1997) questions the continuing utility of psychoanalytic theories of libidinal phases, and developmental lines more generally.

4. Freud describes a third pattern, in which the girl gives up sexuality in general as well as the masculine identifications that might lead to achievement in non-

sexual spheres. She becomes generally inhibited in gender, sexuality, and sublimations. For discussion of the multiplicity of women in Freud's writings, see Chodorow, 1994.

5. Klein's suggestive writings on gender (Klein, 1928, 1945, and 1957) have, unfortunately, not been elaborated on by her followers (but see Birksted-Breen, 1999, and Chodorow, 1999). The direction modern Kleinians have taken in their investigation of the Oedipus complex is not to attend to or problematize gender but instead to look at the generalized child in relation to the (heterosexual) parental couple (see, e.g., Britton, 1992).

6. For an especially powerful account of the impact of differential valuation on girls' emotional and fantasied sense of gendered self and sexuality, see Benjamin, 1988, and 1991.

7. (Rendering to Hegel what is Hegel's) I paraphrase and disagree here with Marx's famous claim: "Life is not determined by consciousness, but consciousness by life" (1845–1846, 155). This much quoted claim has become the pretheoretical assumption that underlies the macrodeterminisms of most of sociology, the cultural determinisms of anthropology, the political-cultural determinisms of poststructuralism, and the varieties of feminism that derive from each of these.

CHAPTER 4: THEORETICAL GENDER AND CLINICAL GENDER

1. Although these latter theories, with the exception of Gilligan, are barely read or cited by academic feminists and are not part of the mainstream psychoanalytic debate, self-in-relation theory and women's voice theory tend to dominate the discourse and training workshops in feminist therapy.

2. The present chapters are part of this collective effort and were developed and published in earlier form, before I had the benefit of reading several of these contributions.

3. Judging by number of articles, few contributions on the psychology of women or men are submitted to (or survive the review processes of) most psychoanalytic journals. Those which are published, however, by and large center on fantasies and feelings about genital anatomy. The recent "Supplement" to the *Journal of the American Psychoanalytic Association* (Richards and Tyson, 1996) is a welcome exception here. Tyson's "Introduction" explicitly addresses the way that, historically within psychoanalysis, female psychology has been reduced to female sexuality, and many of the contributions to the issue do not center directly on female body experience and its psychodynamic transformations. Among those which do, we find, in addition to articles that address genital anatomy and anxiety, investigations of menopause (Bemesderfer, 1996)

and pregnancy and motherhood (Raphael-Leff, 1996; Balsam, 1996; and Furman, 1996). Psychoanalytic journals with avowedly feminist editorial boards have of course also been the exceptions.

4. My claims here may be obsolete in a few years, as I suspect that both clinical treatment and psychoanalytic theories of gender will recognize more complexity and diversity. The taken-for-granted, moreover, may be even harder to challenge in the cases of gay and lesbian sexualities, their causes, dynamics, normativity, and normality.

5. Elizabeth Abel (1990) provides a stunning example of this possibility, as she shows how writers about race and class draw from and modify psychoanalytic claims and as she herself uses psychoanalytic interpretive approaches (derived from both Lacanian psychoanalysis and object-relations theory) to create race- and class-specific oedipal and preoedipal readings of mothers, fathers, sons, and daughters in their various relationships. See also Abel, Christian, and Moglen, 1997.

6. As I note also in Chodorow, 1994, my impression, derived from mother-daughter accounts from a variety of racial and ethnic groups and from my clinical work with women from a variety of cultural and national backgrounds, is that across the spectrum, as *The Reproduction of Mothering* would predict, the mother-daughter relationship is extremely important emotionally to the daughter's sense of self. Prevalent in mother-daughter writings and among my patients from other countries is something that we might characterize as a search or longing for a mother. Women are preoccupied with "needing," desiring, relating to, separating from, agonizing about, or wanting to be with or be understood by their mother. This can be an actual mother, a literary mother or mothers, the "mothers" of one's culture, community mothers, or the idealized mother sought in individual biography. The daughter's selfhood is experienced as bound up with the mother's; her sense of femininity or womanhood and her sexuality evolve in reaction to or continuation with her mother's (mother in all the senses just enumerated). At the same time, it is also my impression that there are cultural variations in prevalent conscious (and perhaps unconscious) constructions of the mother-daughter relationship. There may, for example, be more sympathy and ability to see both individual and community mothers as separate and to understand their situations and constraints, and therefore less blame of the mother (that is, less fantasizing about the perfect mother [Chodorow and Contratto, 1972]) among black than among white women (if we take their writings as exemplary).

7. On Latino cultures, see Alarcon, 1985; Espin, 1984; and Moraga, 1986. Espin

and Moraga describe the direct teaching in Latino and Chicano culture of male superiority and female inferiority and the psychological effects of that teaching on daughters. Moraga provides a particularly poignant vignette: her mother has called to tell her how much she misses her. Moraga begins to weaken and respond, and, at that very moment, she hears another phone in the background. It is her brother, and her mother hangs up on her. Alarcon and Moraga also describe a kind of sadness that I would relate to what I am calling weeping for the mother, though Moraga's sadness, like that of S, whom I describe later, is more attenuated by anger than is the sadness described by Alarcon.

CHAPTER 5: SELVES AND EMOTIONS AS PERSONAL AND CULTURAL CONSTRUCTIONS

1. I am thinking here in very general terms, of almost definitional or foundational assumptions in fields like sociology, anthropology, cultural studies, postmodernism, and poststructuralism. Constructionists who do not hold holistic, deterministic views of culture or of how cultural meanings are invoked or appropriated likewise include a wide range of thinkers—anthropologists who consider themselves practice-theorists and postmodernists, sociological symbolic interactionists and social constructionists, and so forth. Within sociology, Swidler (1986) provides the classic claim for culture as an available web of meaning or "tool kit."

2. For a sociological exception that takes seriously the emotions and self of the researcher as well as the subjects researched, see Krieger, 1991.

3. The general outlines of my historical account and the analytic distinctions I make appear pretty consistently in quite a number of writers (most recently, see Ingham, 1996). Various terms both illuminate and confuse the account. Thus, the term "ethnopsychology" is sometimes used to refer to the investigation of indigenous psychological theories—that is, how members of a culture conceptualize and describe human psychology (what the self is, what a person is, how the emotions are characterized, how people behave in certain situations, and so on). According to this terminology, the anthropology of self and feeling studies ethnopsychology. The contemporary study of cultural psyches (or formerly of culture and personality) is also called psychodynamic ethnography (Marcus and Fischer, 1986), psychocultural anthropology, and person-centered ethnography (LeVine, 1982). Finally, the term "cultural psychology" is sometimes used to refer to studies in which the analytic domain of investigation is psychology rather than cultural meanings and forms of thought, as in ethnopsychology. Cultural psychology according to this definition could include classical culture and per-

sonality studies, studies using psychoanalytic methods, studies based on projective or other personality tests, or any other method that investigates elements of psyche, self, or personality in members of other cultures or as typical of other cultures (for a summary account, see Czordas, 1994, p.332). However, others (e.g., Ingham, 1996, 6, following Stigler, Schweder, and Herdt, 1990) use the term "cultural psychology" to refer to an ethnopsychology that emphasizes language and intellect rather than more psychodynamic aspects of the psyche.

4. Paul (1987) notes Leach's overinsistence on rejecting the psychological, and LeVine (1996) also claims that Geertz, Turner, and other nonpsychoanalytic anthropologists drew covertly upon psychoanalysis. M. Z. Rosaldo (1984) suggests, persuasively, that such concepts as Turner's liminality, Lévi-Strauss's mediation, and Douglas's anomaly were attempts to reintroduce energy and affect into structuralism. As my argument later would indicate, however, they do so without putting back the person who experiences this energy and affect. They thus imply a dynamic or motivational theory—that anomalies, tensions, contradictions, and so forth somehow need or drive toward mediation and resolution—but because they eschew psychology, they cannot elaborate such a theory even as an account of the dynamics of culture.

5. Spiro in particular has written an article focusing on each of these authors' works. On Geertz, see Spiro, 1993; on Rosaldo, see Spiro, 1984; and on Lutz, see Spiro, n.d.

6. Ingham similarly argues that both Geertz's Parsons-derived cultural determinism and postmodernism-poststructuralism have shaped antipsychological trends in contemporary anthropological studies of subjectivity.

7. My discussion here bears some relation to other discussions and critiques of Geertz. Czordas (1994) and Spiro (1993) point out a distinction between normative or symbolic cultural conceptions of the person or self and a psychological investigation of experiential selfhood (reflective and nonreflective mental representations and constitutions of selfhood or sense in individuals of being an "I" or subject). Both review the different psychological and sociological theories that make such distinctions beginning with James and Mead. They claim that Geertz is addressing only cultural conceptions while implying that this completely subsumes, is isomorphic with, or determines experiential selfhood. I follow both Czordas and Spiro in problematizing the reduction of experience to cultural conception, but I have developed my argument less by pointing to theoretical and empirical distinctions between person, self, and individual than by working with the contradictions and leakiness in Geertz's argument and ethnographic case examples.

In addition, Spiro develops an extended critique of (virtually, an attempt to entirely demolish) Geertz, in which he reviews numerous ethnographic cases, Western juridical, psychological, and folk theories of personhood, and other culturalist theories of person and self, in order to argue that the Western conception of the self is not strange in the context of world cultures. Western conceptions often express an unbounded self in relation with others, and many non-Western conceptions describe a bounded, dynamic center of awareness and motivation.

8. Anthropologists D'Andrade (1995, n.d.), Ingham (1994), and Spiro (1984, n.d.), provide forceful critiques of the culturalist-poststructuralist anthropology of self and feeling. I agree with many of their criticisms. Ingham takes an overall position similar to mine, insisting on the mutual entanglements and effects of subjectivity (desire, emotion, motivation, unconscious thought, personality) and the sociocultural. He suggests (directing his attention especially to Schweder, e.g., 1991) that culturalist-poststructuralist works put forth an oversocialized view of humans: "They either ignore subjectivity or reduce it to culture or social context" (p.8). D'Andrade and Spiro, in contesting constructionist claims that emotions are not internal states, give more emphasis to the obvious physiological, biological, or bioinstinctual elements in emotional experience and expression and the strong evidence for universality in basic emotional responses (which allows us to recognize someone from another culture as happy, sad, or angry and to expect that unwanted loss will bring a negative emotion like sadness or anger rather than joy).

This definition of the situation in terms of a polarized contest between culture and biology has, I think, hindered the anthropological debate: Spiro and D'Andrade's stress on biopsychology plays too easily into culturalist critiques in a way that a more fully psychodynamic constructionist view does not. Although I do not contest the claim that physiological or psychobiological processes play a role in emotions, in what follows my point is to argue, against both exclusively culturalist and exclusively psychobiological viewpoints, for a sui generis realm of personal meaning. Spiro (1984) alludes to such a realm—"imagination and fantasy" that might respond to or "transcend" the biological, social, and cultural (330)—but he does not develop this insight.

D'Andrade incisively dissects the discursive constructionists' syllogism: "The psychological theory of the cultural determinists runs as follows: First, it is asserted that experience is determined by one's culture. This is thought to be because humans respond not to external things as such, but to the meanings that things have for them, and that this meaning comes from one's culture. Culture is taken to consist of symbols, or of discourse which is made up of symbols in use. Symbol and discourse create meaning, and meaning constructs experience. Emotion, as one of the things one experiences, is therefore culturally constructed. Finally, since symbols have no necessary relation to things, a culture can symbolize anything in any way. Hence emotions and other cultural things have no necessary relation to biology, sensation, or other 'outside of meaning' events, and are entirely determined by culture" (n.d., 13).

9. Robert LeVine (in an E-mail exchange with the author in 1996 or 1997) suggests that Rosaldo's specific contribution was to take ethnopsychology out of psychological anthropology and into symbolic anthropology. Briggs (1970) and Levy (1973), who demonstrate in minute detail how cultural notions of emotion and self are shaped but who also pay attention to psychodynamics, could also be considered ethnopsychologists, or anthropologists of self and feeling. Briggs's *Never in Anger* (1970), which I discuss in Chapter 6, is probably the founding work of the anthropology of emotions. In contrast to Rosaldo and Lutz, who wish to class emotions as part of a network of discursive signifiers, these ethnographies of emotions (along with later works like Hollan and Wellencamp, 1994) tend to assume that there is a sui generis referential realm of the emotional, even if its construction varies from culture to culture.

10. Several books and articles have been dedicated to Shelly, and her strong influence continues. Even now, well over fifteen years since her death, younger scholars are preparing a book of essays on her work (Lugo and Maurer, forthcoming).

11. Another wonderful example of leakiness concludes Lutz and Abu-Lughod's (1990) collection of self-designated, nonpsychological, discursive studies of emotion. Trawick describes the poignant hymn sung by Cevi, a Tamil untouchable woman, about and to a local goddess of an even lower-status untouchable caste. Although she calls her account "Untouchability and the Fear of Death in a Tamil Song," and although she draws on a Lacanian-derived universalist psychological account to explain the song's themes, it is clear that Trawick is giving an account of a song that has individual, personal meaning for its singer. The song talks not about Tamil women, sisters, or daughters in general, not about untouchability in general, not about the Law of the Father and the body of the mother in general, but about the particularities of an individual woman's feelings and actions, her own individually constructed sense of self, sadness, and resistance, and her own personal construction of cultural expectation, in her own particular family and caste.

12. Ortner (1996, 116–117) also notes how the complexity of Rosaldo's thinking

leads her to make apparently contradictory claims and to see many layers in theoretical and empirical reality.

13. I have chosen to examine what I consider the strongest exemplars of a symbolic anthropology of self and feeling, but I would argue that some more psychodynamically informed ethnopsychological or culture and personality treatments reveal similar problems. The anthropologist-psychiatrist Robert Levy, for example, went to Tahiti to study the traditionally "private" aspects of experience—those "related to his body, his feelings, his sense of self, his needs for personal definition and integration, his understanding of what is going on around him as it involves himself" (1973, xix)—but throughout his text, he tends to accept native descriptions and categorizations of emotional experience as the totality of those experiences.

14. Levy (1973), for example, describes the behavior of mourners in Tahiti and pays much less attention to what people say about loss or to the private, individual behavior that he observes or hears reports of but that is not part of official mourning. He notes that those who have strong feelings are exceptions to the general cultural pattern, but he does not investigate these exceptions.

15. It is a testimony to the tenacity and insistence of poststructuralist discourse that in the entire Lutz and Abu-Lughod collection (1990), in which several writers cite Shelly Rosaldo as founder of the emotion-as-discourse school, no one cites Renato Rosaldo's article, first published in 1984, which so passionately and persuasively demonstrates the limitations of such a position. It is also notable that after his powerful account, Rosaldo himself returns to a more exclusive cultural determinism in the rest of his book.

CHAPTER 6: THE PSYCHE IN THE FIELD

1. LeVine (1996) notes that psychoanalytic anthropological positions mirror those in anthropology as a whole. Universalists oppose relativists, idealists oppose materialists, biological determinists oppose cultural environmentalists, and positivists oppose hermeneutic interpretivists. There are also divisions between those who interpret cultural texts, stories, myths, and rituals and those who study individuals; between those who study children directly and those who reconstruct childhood from observations of adults or of cultural artefacts; and between those whose goal is to defend Freud and those who seek to challenge and revise his work. Almost all of these debates can also be found in some form within psychoanalysis.

2. Not only is the debate polarized, but it also seems uncommonly charged,

perhaps because it addresses such foundational assumptions within anthropology. Indeed, it seems rather risky to put oneself in a position that either Paul or Spiro, on the side of bioevolution, or perhaps Schweder, on the side of culture, might want to criticize. These writers are astoundingly knowledgeable, thorough, and masterful, but they often also lay waste those with whom they disagree. I find myself in the position of agreeing with many of the critiques of cultural determinism put forth by bioevolutionary psychoanalytic anthropologists (especially Spiro, whom I cite extensively in Chapter 5 and who also suggests a formulation that includes a sui generis realm of unconscious meaning) while disagreeing with the reasons for these critiques.

3. Hochschild's sociology of emotions, which also focuses on the relations between emotions and culture, demonstrates that particular emotions are appropriate in particular cultural contexts and that actors evaluate themselves according to the felt contextual appropriateness of their emotions. Her methodology, however, leads in the opposite direction from that of the anthropologists, in such a way that her focus is not only on how moral emotions enforce norms and control behavior but also on the costs, in anxiety, conflict, and splitting, of coping with cultural rules. Because Hochschild is especially attuned to the difficulties people face as they attempt to follow cultural rules and personal "feeling rules," she takes the dissonance between cultural expectation and individual conformity for granted theoretically and examines it empirically. She thereby illuminates precisely the arena of personal and cultural meaning—how any individual constructs, for instance, a not too conflictual or contradictory marital or parental identity that nonetheless fulfills, cultural norms of emotion and self well enough, and how feeling is deeply internal even as it gains energy from a culturally inflected sense of self. She documents how individual experience results from the conflicts about or assaults on the self that arise from following or not following cultural feeling rules. Methodologically, after developing her theoretical repertoire of concepts like emotion work and feeling rules in *The Managed Heart* (1983), she turns in *The Second Shift* (1989) to individual case studies, showing how a variety of individual people negotiate personal and cultural meaning and indicating, through her attention to anxiety, guilt, and conflict, the emotional difficulty of these negotiations.

4. Some of the complexities of terminology and ways of making analytic distinctions in these fields have been mentioned in Chapter 5; see note 3.

5. Scheper-Hughes (1992, 164) notes that Brazilian Portuguese erotic language also links sex to eating and cites researchers on the poverty-stricken Brazilian Northeast who claim that sex may be a substitute for the gratification of hunger.

6. I note, as I did earlier, the fuzzy boundaries between psychoanalytic and nonpsychoanalytic anthropologists in the study of sexuality. Turner, who did not acknowledge the influence of Freud until late in his writing career, is of course also the symbolic anthropologist who modeled most compellingly for contemporary anthropology the complexity and emotional power of symbols of bodies and bodily fluids in ritual practices.

7. Obeyesekere is evaluating psychoanalysis against the cultural viewpoint of the actor, and nonpsychoanalytic Weberians make similar points. Fields (1985), for example, argues that an ethnographer should not impose radical distinctions between conceptions of a real world and of a spirit or witchcraft world when these equally motivate behavior and sustain understanding.

8. For other accounts that suggest a maternal and preoedipal origin for kinder and more compassionate aspects of the superego and for the internal capacity to distinguish good from evil in ways that go beyond culture, see Schafer, 1960, and Sagan, 1993. On maternality in the psyche in India, see Kurtz, 1992.

9. LeVine (1984) illustrates well the contemporary anthropologist's dilemma on this score. He describes the difficult ethnographic search for shared meanings in the face of disagreement among informants and variant accounts and emphasizes the importance of group consensus about meaning as a fundament of human community; yet he also stresses the multiplicity and variability of meanings both within a single person and among different people with different relations to cultural symbols.

10. Herdt (1987), Grolnick, (1987), and Kracke (1994) note the transitional character of personal symbols. See also Stromberg (1993) on personal symbols in Christian conversion narratives.

One of my own first forceful understandings of the transitional character of culture arose in a seminar in 1981, in which the late Paul Riesman, an anthropologist, gave an autobiographical example. When you are playing a quartet, he said, the music is before you, you are interacting with three other people, and you are holding an instrument built by someone, with a particular shape, musical range, and so forth. All given from without. But when you play, your instrument is part of you; you give it personal life. Also, you create the music, with particular conscious and unconscious meanings and your own particular emotional infusion. In your omnipotence and fantasy (and in the potential space in which each of you plays with the others) you each create your own instrument and music.

11. As I noted earlier, Hochschild (1983, 1989) provides both the theory and one of the most extended accounts of the disjunctions between culture and psyche and the costs of emotion work for members of the culture. One wonders if her

freedom to do so is another side of the sociology-anthropology divide: she is not criticizing another culture when she documents the personal costs of the feeling rules in our own. I have not focused in these chapters on the sociology of emotions, because it does not directly address the question of cultural meaning. In terms of the anthropologies I investigate, sociologists of emotions would agree with the anthropologists of self and feeling that different cultures create different rules about self and feeling. They differ from these anthropologists, however, in implying the existence of a true or authentic self that can be harmed by following the feeling rules of the culture. At the same time, the sociology of emotions is explicitly nonpsychological or nonpsychoanalytic, so that it does not acknowledge the psychological theory that it implicitly assumes.

12. Obeyesekere does not claim that the work of culture is entirely constituted by the symbolic transformation of unconscious images into culture, although that particular work is the focus of his book. As a psychoanalytic Weberian, he does take issue with the structuralist view that culture can be formed or transformed without a subject's doing the transforming (1990, xix).

13. Winnicott compares symbolizing and fantasizing under conditions of relative health or illness. Conscious fantasy, unlike dreaming and true symbolic functioning, can be devoid of meaning and depth and a way to avoid being psychically alive (see Winnicott, 1971, chap. 2).

14. The direct quotes in what follows are taken from Briggs's important article, "Mazes of Meaning" (1991), though I have in mind her larger work on Chubby Maata, put forth in many articles and culminating in *Inuit Morality Play* (1998). I read that book in manuscript but do not have final page numbers and exact formulations ready to hand.

15. A good example of the particularities of difference can also be found by comparing the two daughters in Briggs's *Never in Anger* family: both eventually learn to act appropriately like self-contained Inuit children, but it is clear that the nuances of compliance and resistance, and the nuances of parental reaction, differ in each case.

16. There is a certain rereading of history in some of these formulations. Much as with early psychoanalytic views of transference and later of countertransference, the involvement of the self as an instrument of knowing and the mutual construction of the ethnographic encounter were historically denied by many anthropologists or seen as unfortunate but necessary intrusions into ethnographic work (the result of being not well enough trained, as the analyst experiencing countertransference was not well enough analyzed).

17. Devereux's *From Anxiety to Method in the Social Sciences* (1967) first ad-

dressed the anthropological denial of feelings in the field. He claims (in an account that could easily be extended to psychoanalysts' rigid and defensive use of technique and neutrality) that much of the activity of the social scientist generates anxiety and conflict, because social science involves unpredictable interpersonal encounters and experiences with the unfamiliar. Social scientists have developed formalized, de rigueur scientific methods as a way to distance themselves from and defend against this conflict and anxiety. Anthropologists in addition have invested in the concept of cultural relativism in order to ward off and repress their horror and anxiety at some observed practices (say, genital mutilation, cannibalism, or headhunting). Devereux's argument—that the anthropologist's real emotional reactions to particular cultural practices or to the cross-cultural experience must be attended to—remains powerful and persuasive.

CHAPTER 7: CODA ON CULTURE

1. This last is of course the focus of the longest and most highly charged cross-cultural psychoanalytic debate: the debate about the universality of the Oedipus complex that begins with Malinowski. For pivotal statements, see A. Parsons, 1964; Spiro, 1982, 1992; Obeyesekere, 1990; Johnson and Price-Williams, 1996. On cultural variations in parenting and their consequences, see Kurtz, 1991, 1992; Okonogi, 1978, 1979; Whiting et al., 1958.

2. Parsons's remarkable work deserves much more attention than I give it here. In her short life of thirty-three years, and during a period when cultural difference was hardly on the analytic agenda, she managed to address an extraordinary array of questions concerning cross-cultural differences in psychopathology, culturally specific oedipal constellations and family patterns, the meaning of the clinical relationship to people from different cultures, and the need for culturally attuned psychiatric treatment. She also wrote a complex article on psychoanalytic training for academic researchers (1969d), focusing both on structural and psychodynamic factors in the resistance of the analytic establishment and on candidates' own complex personal and academic motivations and desires.

3. Any psychoanalytic reader can find striking national specificities among psychoanalytic theories (in the contemporary period, French, English, American, Argentinian, and so forth), yet it seems to be mainly non-European and non-American analysts who emphasize the ways in which psychoanalytic claims are embedded in cultural assumptions.

4. A similar claim is currently made about the need for heterosexual psychoanalysts to understand the homophobic culture and homoanxious families in which gays and lesbians grow up and live (see, e.g., Blechner, 1996).

5. Such projective processes, of course, provide another example of what Freud (1930, 114) called the narcissism of minor differences—those differences which, on a larger political scale, also help create and sustain some of the most pressing problems of genocide, war, and aggression in the contemporary world.

CHAPTER 8: PSYCHOANALYTIC VISIONS OF SUBJECTIVITY
1. Of course, many cultural, social, and literary critics have also found psycho-analysis central to their liberatory and visionary understandings and critiques.
2. Discomfort with emotion and feeling is not new in Western thought (see Hochschild, 1983; Jaggar, 1989; Lutz, 1988; Nussbaum, 1990) and has certainly shaped many academic disciplines as well as norms of science and rationality (see Keller, 1985).
3. It is always both gratifying and a bit uncanny to find how much one's own ideas seem to develop in parallel with those of one's contemporaries (culture and individuality again). This project has taken many years to reach completion, and I now find, as I complete it, that these writers (perhaps especially Mitchell, 1993b, 1998) have been inspired by many of the same earlier theorists and have formulated their accounts very much as I have formulated mine.

I have puzzled also about the generation of the 1950s, especially after recently designing a course on psyche, culture, and society and finding that (after Freud) almost the entire syllabus was drawn from this era. It has occurred to me that there may be an historical alternation between liberatory and transformative visions that focus more on the outside and those which turn their focus more inward. It also seems possible that during periods of ideological and political repression such as the 1950s (and the 1930s), visions of internal life can serve both in themselves and as closeted political critiques (*Eros and Civilization* makes use of Freud's premises to develop a theory of alienation and does not mention Marx by name).
4. This preference must stem partly from my own self-construction (see also, in appreciation of Loewald, Fogel, 1991; Fogel et al., 1996; Lear, 1990, 1996; Mitchell, 1993b and 1998). I am drawn to the philosophically trained Loewald's clearly spelled-out arguments, whereas many others are attracted to Winnicott's preference for paradox and elliptical and allusive language. Readers can readily incorporate Winnicott's writings into a (loosely connected) Independent per-spective that values psychoanalytic attention to the meaning of life, whereas it has been harder for readers to see American theorists like Loewald (and Erik-son), whose main reference point and predominant self-identity were within ego

psychology, as part of an alternate (if also loosely connected) theoretical and visionary development.

5. Although he writes about the structure of id, ego, and superego and discusses many aspects of superego and ego formation, Loewald, like Obeyesekere, seems intuitively to favor Freud's first topography.

6. Mitchell follows Loewald: "Psychoanalysis today is . . . the hope of fashioning a personal reality that feels authentic and enriching. . . . grounded in personal meaning, not rational consensus. The bridge supporting connections with others is not built out of a rationality superseding fantasy and imagination, but out of feelings experienced as real, authentic, generated from the inside, rather than imposed externally, in close relationship with fantasy and the imagination" (1993b, 21).

7. I believe I paraphrase here Janine Chasseguet-Smirgel's plenary address to the American Psychoanalytic Association, San Francisco, May 1989.

8. Again, we find a reflection of these formulations in the current generation of analysts. Ogden claims, "One cannot change the past, one cannot change who one's mother or father is, one cannot change the fact that specific psychological catastrophes have occurred. One can change the way in which one views, understands, and experiences these aspects of oneself" (1991, 364).

9. In a related vein, Caper claims that a Kleinian focus on the patient's psychic reality is contradictory to a focus on the intersubjective pair, the analyst's subjectivity, or the analytic third. He suggests that the intersubjective focus makes it difficult or impossible to resolve who is contributing what to the encounter: "It locates the experience of the analysis as it exists in the patient's psychic reality somewhere *between* the patient and analyst, in such a form that the respective contributions of each cannot be resolved. This seems to be a way of denying that the transference can be analyzed" (1997, 30).

10. Many object-relations and relational analysts are concerned about acknowledging the pervasive importance of aggression in psychic life, even while they reject the drive theory. See Mitchell, 1993a; Fonagy, Moran, and Target, 1993.

11. Schachtel's distinction makes sense of Winnicott's (1951) subtle comparison of two brothers and their first possessions which is otherwise difficult to comprehend. One brother, free of depressive tension and anxiety, could playfully create his teddy bear as a transitional object; the other could use his teddy bear only as a comforter, as a direct replacement for his mother.

REFERENCES

Abel, Elizabeth. 1990. "Race, Class, and Psychoanalysis? Opening Questions."
In Marianne Hirsch and Evelyn Fox Keller, eds., *Conflicts in Feminism*, 184–
204. London: Routledge.

Abel, Elizabeth, Barbara Christian, and Helene Moglen. 1997. *Female Subjects in
Black and White: Race, Psychoanalysis, Feminism.* Berkeley: University of California Press.

Abu-Lughod, Lila, and Catherine Lutz. 1990. "Introduction: Emotion, Discourse, and the Politics of Everyday Life." In Catherine Lutz and Lila Abu-Lughod, eds., *Language and the Politics of Emotion*, 1–23. Cambridge: Cambridge University Press.

Adler, Gerald, and Daniel H. Buie. 1979. "Aloneness and Borderline Psychopathology: The Possible Relevance of Child Development Issues. *International Journal of Psycho-Analysis* 60: 83–96.

Adorno, Theodor W., Else Frenkel-Brunswik, Daniel J. Levinson, and R. Nevitt Sanford. 1950. *The Authoritarian Personality.* New York: Harper.

Akhtar, Salman. 1995. "Immigration and Identity." *Journal of the American Psychoanalytic Association* 43: 1051–1084.

Alarcon, Norma. 1985. "What Kind of a Lover Have You Made Me, Mother: Towards a Theory of Chicanas' Feminism and Cultural Identity Through Poetry." In Audrey T. McCluskey, ed., *Perspectives on Feminism and Identity in Women of Color,* 85–110. Bloomington: Indiana University Press.

Altman, Neil. 1995. *The Analyst in the Inner City: Race, Class, and Culture Through a Psychoanalytic Lens.* Hillsdale, N.J.: Analytic Press.

Amati-Mehler, Jacqueline, Simona Argentieri, and Jorge Canestri. 1993. *The Babel of the Unconscious: Mother Tongue and Foreign Languages in the Psychoanalytic Dimension.* New York: International Universities Press.

Anderson, Robin, ed. 1992. *Clinical Lectures on Klein and Bion.* London: Tavistock.

Anzaldúa, Gloria. 1990. *Making Face, Making Soul/Haciendo Caras: Creative and Critical Perspectives by Women of Color.* San Francisco: Aunt Lute.

Applegarth, Adrienne. 1976. "Some Observations on Work Inhibition in Women." *Journal of the American Psychoanalytic Association* 24 (suppl.): 251–269.

Arlow, Jacob A. 1969. "Unconscious Fantasy and Disturbances of Conscious Experience." *Psychoanalytic Quarterly* 38: 1–27.

Balint, Alice. 1939. "Love for the Mother and Mother-Love." In Michael Balint, *Primary Love and Psycho-Analytic Technique,* 91–108. New York: Liveright.

Balint, Michael. 1968. *The Basic Fault.* London: Tavistock.

Balsam, Rosemary. 1996. "The Pregnant Mother and the Body Image of the Daughter." *Journal of the American Psychoanalytic Association* 44 suppl.: 401–427.

Bassin, Donna, Margaret Honey, and Ann M. Kaplan, eds. 1994. *Representations of Motherhood.* New Haven, Conn.: Yale University Press.

Bateson, Gregory. 1936. *Naven.* Stanford: Stanford University Press. 2d ed. 1958.

Belenky, Mary F., Blythe M. Clinchy, Nancy R. Goldberger, and Jill M. Tarule. 1986. *Women's Ways of Knowing: The Development of Self, Voice, and Mind.* New York: Basic.

Bem, Sandra. 1993. *The Lenses of Gender.* New Haven, Conn.: Yale University Press.

Bemesderfer, Sandra. 1996. "A Revised View of Menopause." *Journal of the American Psychoanalytic Association* 44 suppl.: 351–369.

Benedict, Ruth. 1934. *Patterns of Culture.* New York: Houghton Mifflin.

Benjamin, Jessica. 1988. *The Bonds of Love: Psychoanalysis, Feminism, and the Problem of Domination.* New York: Pantheon.

——. 1995. *Like Subjects, Love Objects.* New Haven, Conn.: Yale University Press.

——. 1996. "In Defense of Gender Ambiguity." *Gender and Psychoanalysis* 1: 27–43.

Bion, Wilfred. 1959. "Attacks on Linking." In Elizabeth Bott Spillius, ed., *Melanie Klein Today: Developments in Theory and Practice,* vol. 1, 87–101. London: Routledge, 1988.

——. 1961. "A Theory of Thinking." In Elizabeth Bott Spillius, ed., *Melanie Klein Today: Developments in Theory and Practice,* vol. 1, 178–186. London: Routledge, 1988.

——. 1967. "Notes on Memory and Desire." In Elizabeth Bott Spillius, ed., *Melanie Klein Today: Developments in Theory and Practice,* vol. 2, 17–21. London: Routledge, 1988.

Bird, Brian. 1972. "Notes on Transference: Universal Phenomenon and Hardest Part of Analysis." *Journal of the American Psychoanalytic Association* 20: 267–301.

Birksted-Breen, Dana. 1996. "Phallus, Penis, and Mental Space." *International Journal of Psycho-Analysis* 77: 649–657.

——. 1999. "Melanie Klein's 'The Oedipus Complex in the Light of Early Anxieties.'" In Donna Bassin, ed., *Female Sexuality: Contemporary Engagements,* 281–286. Northvale, N.J.: Jason Aronson.

Blechner, Mark. 1996. "Psychoanalysis in and out of the Closet." In Barbara Gerson, ed., *The Therapist as a Person,* 223–239. Hillsdale, N.J.: Analytic Press.

Bloch, Ruth H. 1993. "A Culturalist Critique of Trends in Feminist Theory." *Contention* 2: 79–106.

Bock, Philip K., ed. 1994. *Psychological Anthropology.* Westport, Conn.: Praeger.

Bollas, Christopher. 1987. *The Shadow of the Object: Psychoanalysis of the Unthought Known.* New York: Columbia University Press.

——. 1989. *Forces of Destiny: Psychoanalysis and Human Idiom.* Northvale, N.J.: Jason Aronson.

——. 1992. *Being a Character.* New York: Hill and Wang.

Bowlby, John. 1969–1980. *Attachment and Loss.* 3 vols. New York: Basic.

Breen, Dana, ed. 1993. *The Gender Conundrum.* London: Routledge.

Breuer, Josef, and Sigmund Freud. 1893–1895. *Studies on Hysteria.* In *Standard*

Edition of the Complete Psychological Works of Sigmund Freud, James Strachey, ed. London: Hogarth Press, 1953–1974 (hereafter, *SE*), 2.

Briggs, Jean L. 1970. *Never in Anger: Portrait of an Eskimo Family.* Cambridge: Harvard University Press.

——. 1987. "In Search of Emotional Meaning." *Ethos* 15: 8–15.

——. 1991. "Mazes of Meaning: The Exploration of Individuality in Culture and of Culture Through Individual Constructs." In L. Bryce Boyer and Ruth M. Boyer, eds., *Psychoanalytic Study of Society* 16:111–153.

——. 1998. *Inuit Morality Play: The Emotional Education of a Three-Year Old.* New Haven, Conn.: Yale University Press.

Britton, Ronald. 1992. "Keeping Things in Mind." In Robin Anderson, ed., *Clinical Lectures on Klein and Bion,* 102–113. London: Tavistock.

Britton, Ronald, Michael Feldman, and Edna O'Shaughnessy. 1989. *The Oedipus Complex Today: Clinical Implications.* London: Karnac Books.

Brown, Norman O. 1959. *Life Against Death: The Psychoanalytical Meaning of History.* New York: Vintage.

Brown, Lyn Mikel, and Carol Gilligan. 1992. *Meeting at the Crossroads: Women's Psychology and Girls' Development.* Cambridge: Harvard University Press.

Butler, Judith. 1990. *Gender Trouble: Feminism and the Subversion of Identity.* London: Routledge.

——. 1995. "Melancholy Gender—Refused Identification." *Psychoanalytic Dialogues* 5: 165–180.

——. 1997. "Response to Lynne Layton's 'The Doer Behind the Deed: Tensions and Intersections Between Butler's Vision of Performativity and Relational Psychoanalysis." *Gender and Psychoanalysis* 2: 515–520.

Caper, Robert. 1988. *Immaterial Facts.* Northvale, N.J.: Jason Aronson.

——. 1997. "Psychic Reality and the Interpretation of Transference." *Psychoanalytic Quarterly* 66: 18–33.

Chasseguet-Smirgel, Janine. 1985. *Creativity and Perversion.* London: Free Association Books.

——. 1986. *Sexuality and Mind.* New York: New York University Press.

Chodorow, Nancy, 1978. *The Reproduction of Mothering.* Berkeley: University of California Press.

——. 1979. "Gender, Relation, and Difference in Psychoanalytic Perspective." In *Feminism and Psychoanalytic Theory,* 99–113. New Haven, Conn.: Yale University Press; Cambridge, England: Polity Press.

——. 1986. "Toward a Relational Individualism: The Mediation of Self Through

Psychoanalysis." In *Feminism and Psychoanalytic Theory,* 154–162. New Haven, Conn.: Yale University Press; Cambridge, England: Polity Press.

——. 1989a. *Feminism and Psychoanalytic Theory.* New Haven, Conn.: Yale University Press; Cambridge, England: Polity Press.

——. 1989b. "Psychoanalytic Feminism and the Psychoanalytic Psychology of Women." In *Feminism and Psychoanalytic Theory,* 178–198. New Haven, Conn.: Yale University Press; Cambridge, England: Polity Press.

——. 1989c. "Seventies Questions for Thirties Women: Gender and Generation in a Study of Early Women Psychoanalysts." In *Feminism and Psychoanalytic Theory,* 199–218. New Haven, Conn.: Yale University Press; Cambridge, England: Polity Press.

——. 1993. "Perspectives on the Use of Case Studies: All It Takes Is One." In Philip Cowan et al., eds., *Family Self and Society: Toward a New Agenda for Family Research,* 453–462. Hillsdale, N.J.: Lawrence Erlbaum.

——. 1994. *Femininities, Masculinities, Sexualities: Freud and Beyond.* Lexington: University Press of Kentucky; London: Free Association Books.

——. 1999. "From Subjectivity in General to Subjective Gender in Particular." In Donna, Bassin, ed., *Female Sexuality: Contemporary Engagements,* 241–250. Northvale, N.J.: Jason Aronson.

Chodorow, Nancy J., and Susan Contratto. 1982. "The Fantasy of the Perfect Mother." In *Feminism and Psychoanalytic Theory,* 79–96. New Haven, Conn.: Yale University Press; Cambridge, England: Polity Press.

Coates, Susan W. 1997. "Is It Time to Jettison the Concept of Developmental Lines? Commentary on de Marneffe's Paper 'Bodies and Words.' " *Gender and Psychoanalysis* 2: 35–53.

Cohen, Mabel Blake. 1952. "Counter-Transference and Anxiety." *Psychiatry* 15: 501–539.

Collins, Patricia Hill. 1990. *Black Feminist Thought: Knowledge, Consciousness, and the Politics of Empowerment.* London: Routledge.

Crapanzano, Vincent. 1980. *Tuhami: Portrait of a Moroccan.* Chicago: University of Chicago Press.

D'Andrade, Roy. 1995. *The Development of Cognitive Anthropology.* Cambridge: Cambridge University Press.

——. n.d. "Towards a Theory of Emotion and Culture." Unpublished paper presented at the first Mellon Symposium, "Emotion: Culture, Psychology, Biology," Emory University, 1993.

De Marneffe, Daphne. 1997. "Bodies and Words: A Study of Young Children's Genital and Gender Knowledge." *Gender and Psychoanalysis* 2: 3–33.

Devereux, George. 1967. *From Anxiety to Method in the Behavioral Sciences.* Paris: Mouton.

Dimen, Muriel. 1991. "Deconstructing Difference: Gender, Splitting, and Transitional Space." *Psychoanalytic Dialogues* 1:335–352.

——. 1996. Discussion of the symposium "The Relational Construction of the Body." *Gender and Psychoanalysis* 1: 385–401.

Dodds, E. R. 1951. *The Greeks and the Irrational.* Berkeley: University of California Press.

Doi, Takeo. 1971. *The Anatomy of Dependence.* Tokyo: Kodansha International.

——. 1990. "The Cultural Assumptions of Psychoanalysis." In James W. Stigler, Richard A. Schweder, and Gilbert Herdt, eds., *Cultural Psychology: Essays on Comparative Human Development,* 446–453. Cambridge: Cambridge University Press.

Donington, Robert. 1990. *Opera and Its Symbols: The Unity of Words, Music, and Staging.* New Haven, Conn.: Yale University Press.

DuBois, Cora. 1944. *The People of Alor.* Minneapolis: University of Minnesota Press.

Dundes, Alan. 1984. *Life Is Like a Chicken Coop Ladder: A Portrait of German Culture Through Folklore.* New York: Columbia University Press.

——. 1997. *Flowering Tree and Other Indian Oral Tales.* Berkeley: University of California Press.

Emde, Robert N. 1991. "Positive Emotions for Psychoanalytic Theory: Surprises from Infancy Research and New Directions." *Journal of the American Psychoanalytic Association,* 39 (suppl.): 5–44.

Emde, Robert N., and James F. Sorce. 1983. "The Rewards of Infancy: Emotional Availability and Maternal Referencing." In Justin D. Call, Eleanor Galenson, and Robert Tyson, eds., *Frontiers of Infant Psychiatry,* vol. 2, 17–30. New York: Basic.

Erikson, Erik H. 1950. *Childhood and Society.* 2d ed. 1963. New York: Norton.

——. 1958. *Young Man Luther: A Study in Psychoanalysis and History.* New York: Norton.

——. 1959. "Ego Development and Historical Change." In *Psychological Issues* Monograph 1: *Identity and the Life Cycle,* 18–49. New York: International Universities Press.

——. 1964. "Identity and Uprootedness in Our Time." In *Insight and Responsibility,* 81–107. New York: Norton.

Espin, Olivia. 1984. "Cultural and Historical Influences on Sexuality in Hispanic/Latin Women: Implications for Psychotherapy." In Carol Vance, ed.,

Pleasure and Danger: Exploring Female Sexuality, 149–164. New York: Monthly Review Press.

Ewing, Katherine. 1987. "Clinical Psychoanalysis as an Ethnographic Tool." *Ethos* 15: 16–39.

Fairbairn, W. R. D. 1940. "Schizoid Factors in the Personality." In *An Object-Relations Theory of the Personality,* 3–27. New York, Basic, 1952.

———. 1952. *An Object-Relations Theory of the Personality.* New York: Basic.

Fast, Irene. 1984. *Gender Identity: a Differentiation Model.* Hillsdale, N.J.: Lawrence Erlbaum.

Fields, Karen E. 1985. *Revival and Rebellion in Colonial Central Africa.* Princeton N.J.: Princeton University Press.

Fogel, Gerald I., ed. 1991. *The Work of Hans Loewald: An Introduction and Commentary.* Northvale, N.J.: Jason Aronson.

Fogel, Gerald I., Phyllis Tyson, Jay Greenberg, James T. McLaughlin, and Ellen R. Peyser. 1996. "Special Panel Report on Hans Loewald." *Journal of the American Psychoanalytic Association* 44: 863–924.

Fonagy, Peter, George S. Moran, and Mary Target. 1993. "Aggression and the Psychological Self." *International Journal of Psycho-Analysis* 74: 471–485.

Freud, Anna. 1965. *Normality and Pathology in Childhood: Assessments of Development.* London: Hogarth Press and the Institute of Psychoanalysis.

Freud, Sigmund. 1900–1901. *The Interpretation of Dreams.* In *Standard Edition of the Complete Psychological Works of Sigmund Freud,* James Strachey, ed. London: Hogarth Press, 1953–1974 (hereafter, *SE*), 4 and 5.

———. 1901. *The Psychopathology of Everyday Life.* In *SE* 6.

———. 1905a. *Fragment of an Analysis of a Case of Hysteria* ("Dora"). In *SE* 7.

———. 1905b. *Jokes and Their Relation to the Unconscious.* In *SE* 8.

———. 1905c. *Three Essays on the Theory of Sexuality.* In *SE* 7.

———. 1909a. *Analysis of a Phobia in a Five-Year-Old Boy* ("Little Hans"). *SE* 10.

———. 1909b. *Notes upon a Case of Obsessional Neurosis* (The "Rat Man"). In *SE* 10.

———. 1911. "Formulations on the Two Principles of Mental Functioning." In *SE* 12.

———. 1912. "The Dynamics of Transference." In *SE* 12.

———. 1913. *Totem and Taboo. SE* 13.

———. 1915. "Observations on Transference Love (Further Recommendations on the Technique of Psycho-Analysis III)" In *SE* 12.

———. 1917. "Mourning and Melancholia." In *SE* 14.

———. 1918. *From the History of an Infantile Neurosis* (The "Wolf Man"). In *SE* 17.

——. 1923. "Two Encyclopaedia Articles." In *SE* 18.

——. 1924. *The Ego and the Id.* In *SE* 19.

——. 1926a. *Inhibitions, Symptoms, and Anxiety.* In *SE* 20.

——. 1926b. "Psycho-Analysis." In *SE* 20.

——. 1930. *Civilization and Its Discontents.* In *SE* 21.

——. 1931. "Female Sexuality." In *SE* 21.

——. 1937. "Analysis Terminable and Interminable." In *SE* 23.

——. 1939. *Moses and Monotheism.* In *SE* 23.

Friedman, Lawrence. 1996. "The Loewald Phenomenon." *Journal of the American Psychoanalytic Association* 44: 671–672.

Fromm-Reichmann, Frieda. 1950. *Principles of Intensive Psychotherapy.* Chicago: University of Chicago Press.

Frye, Marilyn. 1990. "The Possibility of Feminist Theory." In Deborah Rhode, ed., *Theoretical Perspectives on Sexual Difference,* 174–184. New Haven, Conn.: Yale University Press.

Furman, Erna. 1996. "On Motherhood." *Journal of the American Psychoanalytic Association* 44 suppl.: 429–447.

Gabbard, Glen O., and Sallye M. Wilkinson. 1996. "Nominal Gender and Gender Fluidity in the Psychoanalytic Situation." *Gender and Psychoanalysis* 1: 463–481.

Garfinkel, Harold. 1967. *Studies in Ethnomethodology.* Englewood Cliffs, N.J.: Prentice Hall.

Geertz, Clifford. 1973. *The Interpretation of Cultures.* New York: Basic.

——. 1974. " 'From the Native's Point of View': On the Nature of Anthropological Understanding." In Richard A. Schweder and Robert A. LeVine, eds., *Culture Theory: Essays on Mind, Self, and Emotion,* 123–136. Cambridge: Cambridge University Press, 1984.

Gerson, Samuel. 1996. "A Shared Body of Language." *Gender and Psychoanalysis* 1: 345–360.

Gill, Merton, and Hoffman, Irwin Z. 1982. *Analysis of the Transference.* New York: International Universities Press.

Gilligan, Carol. 1982. *In a Different Voice: Psychological Theory and Women's Development.* Cambridge: Harvard University Press.

Gilligan, Carol, Annie Rogers, and Deborah Tolman. 1991. *Women, Girls, and Psychotherapy: Reframing Resistance.* Binghamton, N.Y.: Haworth Press.

Goldberger, Nancy, Jill M. Tarule, Blythe M. Clinchy, and Mary F. Belenky. 1996. *Knowledge, Difference, and Power: Essays Inspired by Women's Ways of Knowing.* New York: Basic.

Goldner, Virginia. 1991. "Toward a Critical Relational Theory of Gender." *Psychoanalytic Dialogues* 1: 249–272.

Gregor, Thomas. 1985. *Anxious Pleasures: the Sexual Lives of an Amazonian People*. Chicago: University of Chicago Press.

Grolnick, Simon. 1987. "Reflections on Psychoanalytic Subjectivity and Objectivity as Applied to Anthropology." *Ethos* 15: 136–143.

Guntrip, Harry. 1969. *Schizoid Phenomena, Object Relations, and the Self.* New York: International Universities Press.

Gussow, Mel. 1997. "Interview with Studs Terkel." *New York Times,* 17 June 1997: B1 and B6.

Hallowell, Alfred Irving. 1955. *Culture and Experience*. Philadelphia: University of Pennsylvania Press.

Harris, Adrienne. 1991. "Gender as Contradiction: A Discussion of Freud's 'The Psychogenesis of a Case of Homosexuality in a Woman." *Psychoanalytic Dialogues* 1: 197–224.

———. 1996. "Animated Conversation: Embodying and Gendering." *Gender and Psychoanalysis* 1: 361–383.

Harris, Adrienne, Owen Renik, Susan B. Parlow, Louise J. Kaplan, Kareen Ror Malone, Harriet Kimble Wrye, and Judith K. Welles. 1996. "Commentaries on *The Narration of Desire.*" *Gender and Psychoanalysis* 1: 483–529.

Heilbrun, Carolyn G. 1988. *Writing a Woman's Life*. New York: Ballantine Books.

Heimann, Paula. 1950. "On Counter-Transference." *International Journal of Psycho-Analysis* 31: 81–84.

Herdt, Gilbert H. 1981. *Guardians of the Flutes: Idioms of Masculinity*. New York: McGraw-Hill.

———. 1987. *The Sambia: Ritual and Gender in New Guinea*. New York: Holt, Rinehart, and Winston.

Hochschild, Arlie Russell. 1983. *The Managed Heart*. Berkeley: University of California Press.

———. 1989. *The Second Shift*. New York: Viking.

Hoffman, Irwin Z. 1983. "The Patient as Interpreter of the Analyst's Experience." *Contemporary Psychoanalysis* 19: 389–422.

Hollan, Douglass W., and Jane C. Wellenkamp. 1994. *Contentment and Suffering: Culture and Experience in Toraja*. New York: Columbia University Press.

Horkheimer, Max. 1936. *Critical Theory*. New York: Herder and Herder, 1972.

Ingham, John M. 1996. *Psychological Anthropology Reconsidered*. Cambridge: Cambridge University Press.

Irigaray, Luce. 1985. *This Sex Which Is Not One*. Ithaca, N.Y.: Cornell University Press.

Jacobs, Theodore J. 1991. *The Use of the Self: Countertransference and Communication in the Analytic Situation*. Madison, Conn.: International Universities Press.

Jay, Nancy. 1992. *Throughout Your Generations Forever: Sacrifice, Religion, and Paternity*. Chicago: University of Chicago Press.

Jaggar, Alison M. 1989. "Love and Knowledge: Emotion in Feminist Epistemology." In Alison M. Jaggar and Susan R. Bordo, eds., *Gender/Body/Knowledge: Feminist Reconstructions of Being and Knowing*, 145–171. New Brunswick, N.J.: Rutgers University Press.

Johnson, Allen, and Douglass Price-Williams. 1996. *Oedipus Ubiquitous: The Family Complex in World Folk Literature*. Stanford, Calif.: Stanford University Press.

Jordan, Judith, Alexandra Kaplan, Jean Baker Miller, Irene Stiver, and Janet Surrey. 1991. *Women's Growth in Relation*. New York: Guilford Press.

Joseph, Betty. 1985. "Transference: The Total Situation." In Michael Feldman and Elizabeth Bott Spillius, eds., *Psychic Equilibrium and Psychic Change: Selected Papers of Betty Joseph*, 156–167. London: Routledge, 1989.

———. 1987. "Projective Identification: Some Clinical Aspects." In Michael Feldman and Elizabeth Bott Spillius, eds., *Psychic Equilibrium and Psychic Change: Selected Papers of Betty Joseph*, 168–180. London: Routledge, 1989.

Kakar, Sudhir. 1990. "Stories from Indian Psychoanalysis: Context and Text." In James W. Stigler, Richard A. Schweder, and Gilbert Herdt, eds., *Cultural Psychology: Essays on Comparative Human Development*, 427–445. Cambridge: Cambridge University Press, 1984.

———. 1995. "Clinical Work and Cultural Imagination." *Psychoanalytic Quarterly* 64: 265–281.

Kandiyoti, Denise. 1988. "Bargaining with Patriarchy." *Gender and Society* 2: 274–90.

Kardiner, Abram. 1939. *The Individual and His Society: The Psychodynamics of Primitive Social Organization*. New York: Columbia University Press.

Kaywin, Ralph. 1993. "The Theoretical Contributions of Hans W. Loewald." *Psychoanalytic Study of the Child* 48: 99–114.

Keller, Evelyn Fox. 1985. *Reflections on Gender and Science*. New Haven, Conn.: Yale University Press.

Kestenberg, Judith. 1968. "Outside and Inside, Male and Female." *Journal of the American Psychoanalytic Association* 16: 457–520.

———. 1982. "The Inner-Genital Phase." In David Mendel, ed., *Early Feminine Development: Contemporary Psychoanalytic Views*, 81–125. New York, Spectrum.

Klein, George S. 1973. "Two Theories or One?" in *Psychoanalytic Theory*, 41–71. New York: International Universities Press, 1976.

Klein, Melanie. 1928. "Early Stages of the Oedipus Conflict." In *Love, Guilt, and Reparation, and Other Works*, 186–198. New York: Delta, 1975.

———. 1930. "The Importance of Symbol-Formation in the Development of the Ego." In *Love, Guilt, and Reparation, and Other Works*, 219–232. New York: Delta, 1975.

———. 1935. "A Contribution to the Psychogenesis of Manic-Depressive States." In *Love, Guilt, and Reparation, and Other Works*, 262–289. New York: Delta, 1975.

———. 1940. "Mourning and its Relation to Manic-Depressive States." In *Love, Guilt, and Reparation, and Other Works*, 344–369. New York: Delta, 1975.

———. 1945. "The Oedipus Complex in the Light of Early Anxieties." In *Love, Guilt, and Reparation, and Other Works*, 370–419. New York: Delta, 1975.

———. 1946. "Notes on Some Schizoid Mechanisms." In *Envy and Gratitude and Other Works*, 1–24. New York: Delta, 1975.

———. 1952. "The Origins of Transference." In *Envy and Gratitude and Other Works*, 48–56. New York: Delta, 1975.

———. 1957. "Envy and Gratitude." In *Envy and Gratitude and Other Works*, 176–235. New York: Delta, 1975.

———. 1963. "On the Sense of Loneliness." In *Envy and Gratitude and Other Works*, 300–313. New York: Delta, 1975.

———. 1975a. *Love, Guilt, and Reparation, and Other Works, 1921–1945*. New York: Delta.

———. 1975b. *Envy and Gratitude and Other Works, 1946–1963*. New York: Delta.

Kluckhohn, Clyde. 1944. *Navaho Witchcraft*. Boston: Beacon.

Knoblauch, Steven H. 1996. "The Play and Interplay of Passionate Experience: Multiple Organizations of Desire." *Gender and Psychoanalysis* 1: 323–344.

Kohut, Heinz. 1971. *The Analysis of the Self: A Systematic Aproach to the Psychoanalytic Treatment of Narcissistic Personality Disorders*. New York: International Universities Press.

Kracke, Waud. 1978. *Force and Persuasion: Leadership in an Amazonian Society*. Chicago: University of Chicago Press.

———. 1979. "Dreaming in Kagwahiv: Dream Beliefs and Their Intrapsychic Uses in an Amazonian Indian Culture." *Psychoanalytic Study of Society* 8: 119–172.

———. 1987a. "Encounter with Other Cultures." *Ethos* 15: 58–81.

———. 1987b. " 'Everyone Who Dreams Has a Bit of Shaman': Cultural and Personal Meanings of Dreams—Evidence from the Amazon." *Psychiatry Journal of the University of Ottowa* 12: 65–72.

———. 1987c. "Myths in Dreams, Thoughts in Images: An Amazonian Contribution to the Psychoanalytic Theory of Primary Process." In Barbara Tedlock, ed., *Dreaming: Anthropological and Psychological Interpretations*, 31–54. Cambridge: Cambridge University Press.

———. 1991. "Languages of Dreaming: Anthropological Approaches to the Study of Dreaming in Other Cultures." In Jayne Gackenbach and Anees A. Sheikh, eds., *Dream Images: A Call to Mental Arms*, 203–224. Amityville, N.Y.: Baywood.

———. 1994. "Reflections on the Savage Self: Introspection, Empathy, and Anthropology." In Marcelo Suarez-Orozco, George Spindler, and Louise Spindler, *The Making of Psychological Anthropology II*, 195–222. Orlando, Fla.: Harcourt Brace.

Kracke, Waud, and Gilbert Herdt. 1987. "Introduction: Interpretation in Psychoanalytic Anthropology." *Ethos* 15: 3–7.

Krieger, Susan. 1991. *Social Science and the Self: Personal Essays on an Art Form.* New Brunswick, N.J.: Rutgers University Press.

Kurtz, Stanley. 1991. "Polysexualization: A New Approach to Oedipus in the Trobriands." *Ethos* 19: 68–101.

———. 1992. *All the Mothers Are One: Hindu India and the Cultural Reshaping of Psychoanalysis.* New York: Columbia University Press.

Lacan, Jacques. 1982. *Feminine Sexuality,* Juliet Mitchell and Jacqueline Rose, eds. New York: Norton.

Layton, Lynne. 1997. "The Doer Behind the Deed." *Gender and Psychoanalysis* 2: 131–155.

Lear, Jonathan. 1990. *Love and Its Place in Nature.* New York: Farrar, Straus & Giroux.

———. 1996. "The Introduction of Eros: Reflections on the Work of Hans Loewald." *Journal of the American Psychoanalytic Association* 44: 673–698.

Leary, Kimberlyn. 1995. "Interpreting in the Dark: Race and Ethnicity in Psychoanalytic Psychotherapy." *Psychoanalytic Psychology* 12: 127–140.

———. 1997. "Race in Psychoanalytic Space." *Gender and Psychoanalysis* 2: 157–172.

LeVine, Robert A. 1982. *Culture, Behavior, and Personality: An Introduction to the Comparative Study of Psychosocial Adaption.* 2d ed. Chicago: Aldine.

———. 1984. "Properties of Culture: An Ethnographic View." In Richard A.

Schweder and Robert A. LeVine, eds., *Culture Theory: Essays on Mind, Self, and Emotion*, 67–87. Cambridge: Cambridge University Press, 1984.

——. 1996. "Psychoanalysis." In David Levinson and Melvin Ember, eds., *Encyclopedia of Cultural Anthropology*, vol. 3, 1036–1042. New York: Henry Holt.

Levy, Robert I. 1973. *Tahitians: Mind and Experience in the Society Islands.* Chicago: University of Chicago Press.

——. 1983. "Introduction: Self and Emotion." *Ethos* 11: 128–134.

——. 1984. "Emotion, Knowing, and Culture." In Richard A. Schweder and Robert A. LeVine, eds., *Culture Theory: Essays on Mind, Self, and Emotion*, 214–237. Cambridge: Cambridge University Press, 1984.

Lewin, Kurt, and Dorwin Cartwright. 1964. *Field Theory in Social Science: Selected Theoretical Papers.* New York: Harper & Row.

Little, Margaret I. 1951. "Counter-Transference and the Patient's Response to It." *International Journal of Psycho-Analysis* 32: 32–40.

——. 1981. *Transference Neurosis and Transference Psychosis.* Northvale, N.J.: Jason Aronson.

——. 1990. *Psychotic Anxieties and Containment: A Personal Record of an Analysis with Winnicott.* Northvale, N.J.: Jason Aronson.

Loewald, Hans W. 1951. "Ego and Reality." In *Papers on Psychoanalysis*, 3–20. New Haven, Conn.: Yale University Press, 1980.

——. 1960. "On the Therapeutic Action of Psychoanalysis." In *Papers on Psychoanalysis*, 221–256. New Haven, Conn.: Yale University Press, 1980.

——. 1962. "Internalization, Separation, Mourning, and the Superego." In *Papers on Psychoanalysis*, 257–276. New Haven, Conn.: Yale University Press, 1980.

——. 1972. "Freud's Conception of the Negative Therapeutic Reaction with Some Comments on Instinct Theory." In *Papers on Psychoanalysis*, 315–325. New Haven, Conn.: Yale University Press, 1980.

——. 1975. "Psychoanalysis as an Art and the Fantasy Character of the Psychoanalytic Situation." In *Papers on Psychoanalysis*, 352–371. New Haven, Conn.: Yale University Press, 1980.

——. 1978a. "Primary Process, Secondary Process, and Language." In *Papers on Psychoanalysis*, 178–206. New Haven, Conn.: Yale University Press, 1980.

——. 1978b. "Instinct Theory, Object Relations, and Psychic Structure Formation." In *Papers on Psychoanalysis*, 207–218. New Haven, Conn.: Yale University Press, 1980.

——. 1978c. *Psychoanalysis and the History of the Individual.* New Haven: Yale University Press.

——. 1979. "The Waning of the Oedipus Complex." In *Papers on Psychoanalysis,* 384–404. New Haven, Conn.: Yale University Press, 1980.

——. 1980. *Papers on Psychoanalysis.* New Haven, Conn.: Yale University Press.

——. 1986. "Transference-Countertransference." *Journal of the American Psychoanalytic Association* 34: 275–287.

Lugo, Alejandro, and Bill Maurer. Forthcoming. *The Legacy of Michelle Rosaldo: Politics and Gender in Modern Societies.* Ann Arbor: University of Michigan Press.

Lutz, Catherine A. 1988. *Unnatural Emotions: Everyday Sentiments on a Micronesian Atoll and Their Challenge to Western Theory.* Chicago: University of Chicago Press.

Lutz, Catherine A., and Lila Abu-Lughod, eds. 1990. *Language and the Politics of Emotion.* Cambridge: Cambridge University Press; Paris: Editions de la Maison des Sciences de l'Homme.

Maccoby, Eleanor E., and Jacklin, Carol Nagy. 1974. *The Psychology of Sex Difference.* Stanford, Calif.: Stanford University Press.

MacCormack, Carol P., and Marilyn Strathern. 1980. *Nature, Culture, and Gender.* Cambridge: Cambridge University Press.

McDougall, Joyce. 1986. *Theatres of the Mind: Illusion and Truth on the Psychoanalytic Stage.* London: Free Association Books.

Mahler, Margaret. 1972. "On the First Three Subphases of the Separation-Individuation Process." In Peter Buckley, ed., *Essential Papers on Object Relations,* 222–232. New York: New York University Press, 1986.

Mahler, Margaret S., Fred Pine, and Anni Bergman. 1975. *The Psychological Birth of the Human Infant.* New York: Basic.

Mahoney, Maureen, and Barbara Yngvesson. 1992. "The Construction of Subjectivity and the Paradox of Resistance: Reintegrating Feminist Anthropology and Psychology. *Signs* 18: 44–73.

Malcolm, Ruth Reisenberg. 1986. "Interpretation: The Past in the Present." In Elizabeth Bott Spillius, ed., *Melanie Klein Today: Developments in Theory and Practice,* vol. 2, 73–89. London: Routledge, 1988.

Marcus, George E., and Michael M. J. Fischer. 1986. *Anthropology as Cultural Critique: An Experimental Moment in the Human Sciences.* Chicago: University of Chicago Press.

Marcuse, Herbert. 1956. *Eros and Civilization: A Philosophical Inquiry into Freud.* Boston: Beacon.

——. 1970. *Five Lectures: Psychoanalysis, Politics, and Utopia.* Boston: Beacon.

———. 1964. *One Dimensional Man: Studies in the Ideology of Advanced Industrial Society.* Boston: Beacon.

Martin, Emily. 1987. *The Woman in the Body: A Cultural Analysis of Reproduction.* Boston: Beacon.

Martin, Jane Roland. 1994. "Methodological Essentialism, False Difference, and Other Dangerous Traps." *Signs* 19: 630–657.

Marx, Karl. 1845–1846. *The German Ideology, Part I.* In Robert C. Tucker, ed., *The Marx-Engels Reader,* 2d ed. New York: Norton, 1978.

Mayer, Elizabeth Lloyd. 1985. " 'Everybody Must Be Just Like Me': Observations on Female Castration Anxiety." *International Journal of Psycho-Analysis* 66: 331–347.

———. 1995. "The Phallic Castration Complex and Primary Femininity: Paired Developmental Lines Toward Female Gender Identity." *Journal of the American Psychoanalytic Association* 43: 17–38.

Mead, George Herbert. 1934. *Mind, Self, and Society.* Chicago: University of Chicago Press.

Mead, Margaret. 1928. *Coming of Age in Samoa.* New York: William Morrow.

———. 1935. *Sex and Temperament in Three Primitive Societies.* New York: William Morrow.

Mernissi, Fatima. 1994. *Dreams of Trespass: Tales of Harem Girlhood.* Reading, Mass.: Addison-Wesley.

Milner, Marion. 1936. *A Life of One's Own.* London: Chatto & Windus.

———. 1957. *On Not Being Able to Paint.* New York: International Universities Press.

———. 1969. *The Hands of the Living God.* London: Hogarth.

———. 1987. *The Suppressed Madness of Sane Men: Forty-Four Years of Exploring Psychoanalysis.* London: Tavistock.

Mitchell, Stephen A. 1993a. "Aggression and the Endangered Self." *Psychoanalytic Quarterly* 62: 351–382.

———. 1993b. *Hope and Dread in Psychoanalysis.* New York: Basic.

———. 1996. "Gender and Sexual Orientation in the Age of Postmodernism: The Plight of the Perplexed Clinician." *Gender and Psychoanalysis* 1: 45–73.

———. 1998. "From Ghosts to Ancestors: The Psychoanalytic Vision of Hans Loewald." *Psychoanalytic Dialogues* 8: 825–855.

Mitscherlich, Alexander. 1969. *Society Without the Father: A Contribution to Social Psychology.* New York: Schocken.

Money, John, and Anke A. Ehrhardt. 1972. *Man and Woman, Boy and Girl.* Baltimore, Md.: Johns Hopkins University Press.

Moraga, Cherrie. 1986. "From a Long Line of Vendidas: Chicanas and Feminism." In Teresa de Lauretis, ed., *Feminist Studies Critical Studies,* 173–190. Madison: University of Wisconsin Press.

Nussbaum, Martha. 1990. *Love's Knowledge: Essays on Philosophy and Literature.* New York: Oxford University Press.

Obeyesekere, Gananath. 1981. *Medusa's Hair: An Essay on Personal Symbols and Religious Experience.* Chicago: University of Chicago Press.

——. 1990. *The Work of Culture: Symbolic Transformation in Psychoanalysis and Anthropology.* Chicago: University of Chicago Press.

Ogden, Thomas H. 1986. *Matrix of the Mind: Object Relations and the Psychoanalytic Dialogue.* Northvale, N.J.: Jason Aronson.

——. 1989. "Misrecognitions and the Fear of Not Knowing." In *The Primitive Edge of Experience,* 195–221. Northvale, N.J.: Jason Aronson.

——. 1991. "Interview." *Psychoanalytic Dialogues* 1: 361–376.

——. 1994. *Subjects of Analysis.* Northvale, N.J.: Jason Aronson.

——. 1995. "Analysing Forms of Aliveness and Deadness in the Transference-Countertransference." *International Journal of Psycho-Analysis* 76: 695–709.

Okonogi, Keigo. 1978. "The Ajase Complex of the Japanese (1)." *Japan Echo* 5: 88–105.

——. 1979. "The Ajase Complex of the Japanese (2)." *Japan Echo* 6: 104–118.

Ortner, Sherry B. 1995. "Resistance and the Problem of Ethnographic Refusal." *Comparative Studies in Society and History* 37: 173–193.

——. 1996. *Making Gender: The Politics and Erotics of Culture.* Boston: Beacon.

O'Shaughnessy, Edna. 1981. "W. R. Bion's Theory of Thinking and New Techniques in Child Analysis." In Elizabeth Bott Spillius, ed., *Melanie Klein Today: Developments in Theory and Practice,* vol. 2, 177–190. London: Routledge, 1988.

——. 1992. "Psychosis: Not Thinking in a Bizarre World." In Robin Anderson, ed., *Clinical Lectures on Klein and Bion,* 89–101. London: Tavistock.

Parsons, Anne. 1964. "Is the Oedipus Complex Universal? The Jones-Malinowski Debate Revisited." In *Belief, Magic, and Anomie: Essays in Psychosocial Anthropology,* 3–66. New York, Free Press.

——. 1969a. *Belief, Magic, and Anomie: Essays in Psychosocial Anthropology.* New York, Free Press.

——. 1969b. "Cultural Barriers to Insight and the Structural Reality of Transference." In *Belief, Magic, and Anomie: Essays in Psychosocial Anthropology,* 295–333. New York: Free Press.

——. 1969c. "Expressive Symbolism in Witchcraft and Delusion." In *Belief, Magic, and Anomie: Essays in Psychosocial Anthropology,* 177–203. New York, Free Press.

——. 1969d. "On Psychoanalytic Training for Research Purposes." In *Belief, Magic, and Anomie: Essays in Psychosocial Anthropology*, 334–357. New York: Free Press.

Parsons, Talcott. 1952. "The Superego and the Theory of Social Systems." In *Social Structure and Personality*, 17–33. New York: Free Press, 1970.

Paul, Robert A. 1982. *The Tibetan Symbolic World.* Chicago: University of Chicago Press.

——. 1987. "The Question of Applied Psychoanalysis and the Interpretation of Cultural Symbolism." *Ethos* 15: 82–103.

——. 1989. "Psychoanalytic Anthropology." *Annual Review of Anthropology* 18: 177–202.

——. 1996. *Moses and Civilization: The Meaning Behind Freud's Myth.* New Haven, Conn.: Yale University Press.

Person, Ethel S. 1995. *By Force of Fantasy.* New York: Basic.

Personal Narratives Group, eds. 1989. *Interpreting Women's Lives.* Bloomington: Indiana University Press.

Phillips, Adam. 1993. "Playing Mothers: Between Pedagogy and Transference." In *On Kissing, Tickling, and Being Bored*, 101–108. Cambridge: Harvard University Press.

Poland, Warren. 1992. "Transference: An Original Creation." *Psychoanalytic Quarterly* 61: 185–205.

Poole, Fitz John Porter. 1987. "Personal Experience and Cultural Representation in Children's 'Personal Symbols' Among Bimin-Kuskusmin." *Ethos* 15: 104–135.

——. 1990. "Images of an Unborn Sibling: The Psychocultural Shaping of a Child's Fantasy Among the Bimin-Kuskusmin of Papua New Guinea." In L. Bryce Boyer and Ruth M. Boyer, eds., *Psychoanalytic Study of Society* 15: 105–177.

——. 1991. "Cultural Schemas and Experiences of the Self Among the Bimin-Kuskusmin of Papua New Guinea." In L. Bryce Boyer and Ruth M. Boyer, eds., *Psychoanalytic Study of Society* 16: 55–85.

——. 1994. "Socialization, Enculturation, and the Development of Personal Identity." In Tim Ingold, ed., *Companion Encyclopedia of Anthropology*, 831–860. London: Routledge.

Prager, Jeffrey. 1998. *Presenting the Past: Psychoanalysis and the Sociology of Misremembering.* Cambridge: Harvard University Press.

Pratt, Minnie Bruce. 1984. "Identity: Skin, Blood, Heart." In Elly Bulkin, Minnie Bruce Pratt, and Barbara Smith, *Yours in Struggle: Three Feminist Perspec* *tives on Anti-Semitism and Racism,* 9–63. Brooklyn, N.Y.: Long Haul Press.

Rabinow, Paul. 1977. *Reflections on Fieldwork in Morocco.* Berkeley: University of California Press.

Racker, Heinrich. 1953. "Contribution to the Problem of Countertransference." *International Journal of Psycho-Analysis* 34: 313–324.

——. 1957. "The Meanings and Uses of Countertransference." *Psychoanalytic Quarterly* 26: 303–357.

Raphael-Leff, Joan. 1996. "Pregnancy—Procreative Process, the 'Placental Paradigm,' and Perinatal Therapy." *Journal of the American Psychoanalytic Association* 44 suppl.: 373–399.

Reich, Annie. 1951. "On Counter-Transference." *International Journal of Psycho-Analysis* 32: 25–31.

Renik, Owen. 1993a. "Analytic Interaction: Conceptualizing Technique in Light of the Analyst's Irreducible Subjectivity." *Psychoanalytic Quarterly* 57: 553–571.

——. 1993b. "Countertransference Enactment and the Psychoanalytic Process." In Mardi J. Horowitz, Otto F. Kernberg, and Edward M. Weinshel, *Psychic Structure and Psychic Change: Essays in Honor of Robert S. Wallerstein,* 135–158. Madison, Conn.: International Universities Press.

Richards, Arnold D., and Phyllis Tyson, eds., 1996. *The Psychology of Women: Psychoanalytic Perspectives. Journal of the American Psychoanalytic Association* 44 (suppl.).

Riesman, Paul. 1977. *Freedom in Fulani Social Life: An Introspective Ethnography.* Chicago: University of Chicago Press.

Roiphe, Herman, and Eleanor Galenson. 1981. *Infantile Origins of Sexual Identity.* New York: International Universities Press.

Rosaldo, Michelle Z. 1980. *Knowledge and Passion: Ilongot Notions of Self and Social Life.* Cambridge: Cambridge University Press.

——. 1983. "The Shame of Headhunters and the Autonomy of Self." *Ethos* 11: 135–151.

——. 1984. "Toward an Anthropology of Self and Feeling." In Richard A. Schweder and Robert A. LeVine, eds., *Culture Theory: Essays on Mind, Self, and Emotion,* 137–157. Cambridge: Cambridge University Press, 1984.

Rosaldo, Renato. 1989. "Grief and a Headhunter's Rage." In *Culture and Truth: The Remaking of Social Analysis,* 1–21. Boston: Beacon.

Sagan, Eli. 1993. "Cultural Diversity and Moral Relativism." Brandeis University: Women's Studies Program Working Papers Series #4.

Sandler, Joseph, and Anne-Marie Sandler. 1984. "The Past Unconscious, the

Present Unconscious, and the Interpretation of the Transference." *Psychoanalytic Inquiry* 4: 367–399.

———. 1994. "The Past Unconscious and the Present Unconscious." *Psychoanalytic Study of the Child* 49: 278–292.

Schachtel, Ernest G. 1947. "On Memory and Childhood Amnesia." In *Metamorphosis,* 279–322. New York: Basic, 1959.

———. 1954. "The Development of Focal Attention and the Emergence of Reality." In *Metamorphosis,* 251–278. New York: Basic, 1959.

Schafer, Roy. 1960. "The Loving and Beloved Superego in Freud's Structural Theory." *Psychoanalytic Study of the Child* 15: 163–188.

———. 1974. "Some Problems in Freud's Psychology of Women." *Journal of the American Psychoanalytic Association* 22: 459–485.

———. 1976. *A New Language for Psychoanalysis.* New Haven, Conn.: Yale University Press.

———. 1982. "The Relevance of the 'Here and Now' Transference Interpretation to the Reconstruction of Early Development." *International Journal of Psycho-Analysis* 63: 77–82.

———. 1983. *The Analytic Attitude.* New York: Basic.

———. 1992. *Retelling a Life: Narration and Dialogue in Psychoanalysis.* New York: Basic.

———. 1997. *The Contemporary Kleinians of London.* Madison, Conn.: International Universities Press.

Scheper-Hughes, Nancy. 1992. *Mother-Love and Child Death in Northeast Brazil.* Berkeley: University of California Press.

Schorske, Carl E. 1979. *Fin-de-Siècle Vienna: Politics and Culture.* New York: Random House.

Schweder, Richard A. 1984. "Introduction." In Richard A. Schweder and Robert A. LeVine, eds., *Culture Theory: Essays on Mind, Self, and Emotion,* 1–24. Cambridge: Cambridge University Press.

———. 1991. *Thinking Through Cultures: Expeditions in Cultural Psychology.* Cambridge: Harvard University Press.

Schweder, Richard A., and Robert A. LeVine, eds. 1984. *Culture Theory: Essays on Mind, Self, and Emotion.* Cambridge: Cambridge University Press.

Scott, Joan Wallach. 1988. *Gender and the Politics of History.* New York: Columbia University Press.

Segal, Hanna. 1957. "Notes on Symbol Formation." In Elizabeth Bott Spillius, ed., *Melanie Klein Today: Developments in Theory and Practice,* vol. 1, 160–177. London: Routledge, 1988.

——. 1985. "The Klein-Bion Model." In Arnold Rothstein, ed., *Models of the Mind: Their Relationships to Clinical Work.* Madison, Conn.: International Universities Press.

Settlage, Calvin F. 1980. "Psychoanalytic Developmental Thinking in Current and Historical Perspective." *Psychoanalysis and Contemporary Thought* 3: 139–170.

——. 1993. "Therapeutic Process and Developmental Process in the Restructuring of Object and Self Constancy." *Journal of the American Psychoanalytic Association* 41: 473–492.

Shapiro, Sue A. 1996. "The Embodied Analyst in the Victorian Consulting Room." *Gender and Psychoanalysis* 1: 297–322.

Sharpe, Ella. 1930. "The Technique of Psycho-Analysis. Seven Lectures." In *Collected Papers on Psycho-Analysis,* 9–106. New York, Brunner/Mazel, 1978.

Slater, Philip Elliot. 1968. *The Glory of Hera: Greek Mythology and the Greek Family.* Boston: Beacon.

Smith-Rosenberg, Carroll. 1985. *Disorderly Conduct: Visions of Gender in Victorian America.* New York: Oxford University Press.

Spain, David H. 1988. "Taboo or Not Taboo: Is That the Question?" *Ethos* 16: 285–301.

——. 1994. "Entertaining (Im)possibilities: Chance and Necessity in the Making of a Psychological Anthropologist." In Marcelo M. Suarez-Orozco, George Spindler, and Louise Spindler, *The Making of Psychological Anthropology II,* 104–31. Orlando, Fla.: Harcourt Brace.

Spillius, Elizabeth Bott, ed. 1988. *Melanie Klein Today: Developments in Theory and Practice,* 2 vols. London: Routledge.

Spiro, Melford E. 1984. "Some Reflections on Cultural Determinism and Relativism with Special Reference to Emotion and Reason." In Richard A. Schweder and Robert A. LeVine, eds., *Culture Theory: Essays on Mind, Self, and Emotion.* 323–346. Cambridge: Cambridge University Press, 1984.

——. 1987. *Culture and Human Nature.* Chicago: University of Chicago Press.

——. 1992. "Oedipus Redux." *Ethos* 20: 358–376.

——. 1993. "Is the Western Conception of the Self 'Peculiar' Within the Context of the World Cultures?" *Ethos* 21: 107–153.

——. n.d. "On a Feminist/Constructionist View of Emotions." Unpublished paper.

Stacey, Judith. 1990. *Brave New Families.* New York: Basic.

Stein, Arlene. 1997. *Sex and Sensibility: Stories of a Lesbian Generation.* Berkeley: University of California Press.

Stein, Ruth. 1995. "Analysis of a Case of Transsexualism." *Psychoanalytic Dialogues* 4: 257–289.

Steiner, Ricardo. 1995. "Hermeneutics or Hermes-Mess?" *International Journal of Psycho-Analysis* 76: 435–445.

Stern, Daniel. 1985. *The Interpersonal World of the Infant.* New York: Basic.

Stigler, James W., Richard A. Schweder, and Gilbert Herdt. 1990. *Cultural Psychology: Essays on Comparative Human Development.* Cambridge: Cambridge University Press.

Stocking, George W., Jr., ed. 1986. *History of Anthropology,* Vol. 4: *Malinowski, Rivers, Benedict, and Others.* Madison: University of Wisconsin Press.

Stoller, Robert. 1968. *Sex and Gender,* vol. 1. New York: Science House.

——. 1985. *Presentations of Gender.* New Haven, Conn.: Yale University Press.

Stoller, Robert J., and Gilbert Herdt. 1982. "The Development of Masculinity: A Cross-Cultural Contribution." *Journal of the American Psychoanalytic Association* 30: 29–59.

Stromberg, Peter G. *Language and Self-Transformation: A Study of the Christian Conversion Narrative.* Cambridge: Cambridge University Press.

Suarez-Orozco, Marcelo M., George Spindler, and Louise Spindler, 1994. *The Making of Psychological Anthropology II.* Orlando, Fla.: Harcourt Brace.

Sutherland, John D. 1994. *The Autonomous Self: The Work of John D. Sutherland,* Jill Savage Scharff, ed. Northvale, N.J.: Jason Aronson.

Swidler, Ann. 1986. "Culture in Action: Symbols and Strategies." *American Sociological Review* 51: 273–286.

Tower, Lucia. 1956. "Countertransference." *Journal of the American Psychoanalytic Association* 4: 224–255.

Trawick, Margaret. 1990. "Untouchability and the Fear of Death in a Tamil Song." In Catherine A. Lutz and Lila Abu-Lughod, eds., *Language and the Politics of Emotion,* 186–206. Cambridge: Cambridge University Press; Paris: Editions de la Maison des Sciences de l'Homme.

Trevarthan, Colwyn. 1979. "Communication and Cooperation in Early Infancy: A Description of Primary Intersubjectivity." In Margaret Bullowa, ed., *Before Speech: The Beginning of Interpersonal Communication,* 321–347. Cambridge: Cambridge University Press.

——. 1980. "The Foundations of Intersubjectivity: Development of Interpersonal and Cooperative Understanding in Infants. In Jeremy M. Anglin, ed., *The Social Foundations of Language and Thought: Essays in Honor of Jerome Bruner,* 316–342. New York: Norton.

Turner, Victor. 1967. *Forest of Symbols.* Ithaca, N.Y.: Cornell University Press.

———. 1978. "Encounter with Freud: The Making of a Comparative Symbologist." In George Spindler and Louise Spindler, eds., *The Making of Psychological Anthropology*, 556–583. Berkeley: University of California Press.

Tyson, Phyllis. 1982. "A Developmental Line of Gender Identity, Gender Role, and Choice of Love Object." *Journal of the American Psychoanalytic Association* 30: 61–86.

———. 1991. "Some Nuclear Conflicts of the Infantile Neurosis in Female Development." *Psychoanalytic Inquiry* 11: 582–601.

Tyson, Phyllis, and Robert Tyson. 1990. *Psychoanalytic Theories of Development.* New Haven, Conn.: Yale University Press.

Whiting, Beatrice B., and John W. M. Whiting. 1975. *Children of Six Cultures.* Cambridge: Harvard University Press.

Whiting, Beatrice, ed. 1963. *Six Cultures: Studies of Child-Rearing.* New York: John Wiley.

Whiting, John W. M., Richard Kluckhohn, and Albert Anthony. 1958. "The Function of Male Initiation Rites at Puberty." In Eleanor E. Maccoby, Theodore M. Newcomb, and Eugene L. Hartley, eds., *Readings in Social Psychology*, 359–370. New York: Holt.

Winnicott, D. W. 1949. "Hate in the Countertransference." In *Collected Papers: Through Paediatrics to Psycho-Analysis*, 194–203. London: Tavistock, 1958.

———. 1951. "Transitional Objects and Transitional Phenomena." In *Collected Papers: Through Paediatrics to Psycho-Analysis*, 229–242. London: Tavistock, 1958.

———. 1956. "Primary Maternal Preoccupation." In *Collected Papers: Through Paediatrics to Psycho-Analysis*, 300–305. London: Tavistock, 1958.

———. 1958. "The Capacity to Be Alone." In *Maturational Processes and the Facilitating Environment*, 29–36. New York: International Universities Press, 1965.

———. 1960. "The Theory of the Parent-Infant Relationship." In *Maturational Processes and the Facilitating Environment*, 37–55. New York, International Universities Press, 1965.

———. 1965. *The Maturational Processes and the Facilitating Environment.* New York: International Universities Press.

———. 1971. *Playing and Reality.* New York: Basic.

———. 1989. *Psycho-Analytic Explorations.* Cambridge: Harvard University Press.

Wrye, Harriet Kimble. 1996. "Bodily States of Mind: Dialectics of Psyche and Soma in Psychoanalysis." *Gender and Psychoanalysis* 1: 283–296.

Wrye, Harriet Kimble, and Judith K. Welles. 1994. *The Narration of Desire: Erotic Transferences and Countertransferences.* Hillsdale, N.J.: Analytic Press.

INDEX

Abu-Lughod, Lila, 153, 159–160, 288n11, 289n15

Akhtar, Salman, 232–233

Anthropology: cultural determinism of, 4, 130, 136, 220, 283n7; and emotions, 4, 177–178, 288n9, 293n17; and cultural meaning, 130–134, 141; and psychoanalytic theory, 131, 133–136, 141, 206, 219–220, 274, 286n4; and intersubjective interaction, 134–135, 204–205, 266; and individuality versus generalization, 135–138; and transference, 135, 207–209, 212; and culture, 139–140, 172–173; of culture and personality, 139–140, 170, 179, 227; and structural theory, 142, 214. *See also* Anthropology of self and feeling; Psychoanalytic anthropology; and other specific fields of anthropology

Anthropology of self and feeling: and emotions, 65, 129, 149, 152–162, 164, 166–167, 170–171, 176–177, 185, 288n9, 288n11, 289n13, 289n15; and cultural determinism, 130, 143, 160,

Identity, 4, 5, 102–103, 144–147, 228–232, 271. *See also* Gender identity

Internal-external relationship, 6, 47, 51, 52–54, 56–57, 60, 260

Interpersonalism, 17, 61, 64, 98–99, 261, 264, 280n11

Introjection: and subjectivity, 1, 21; and personal meaning, 3, 5, 8, 14, 22, 41, 61, 63, 65, 88, 91; and transference, 15, 19, 215; and developmental theory, 46–47, 52, 59; and psychic reality, 164; and psychoanalytic anthropology, 215; and cultural meaning, 230; and introjective identification, 276n1

Joseph, Betty, 44, 278n7, 279n7

Kakar, Sudhir, 119, 224–225, 233

Kardiner, Abram, 137, 140

Klein, Melanie: and transference, 13, 16, 17–18, 21, 47, 54–55, 208, 263, 276–277n1; and developmental theory, 20–21, 42, 46–48, 52, 56–57, 63, 281n13; and projection, 22, 204, 276n1; and object-relations theory, 53; and fantasy, 54, 193; and observed gender, 105; and penis envy, 107; and emotions, 185; and symbolization, 200

Kleinian theory: and personal meaning, 3, 51; and transference, 44, 47–48, 247, 253, 260; and developmental theory, 47–48, 53–55, 281n13; and gender, 87, 100, 283n5; and body, 117; and unconscious, 249; and Erikson, 254; and symbolization, 262; and psychic reality, 263, 295n9; general theory of, 275–276n1; and countertransference, 277n7

Kracke, Waud, 181–182, 192–193, 198–199, 207–210, 212, 226

Lacanian theory, 70–71, 78, 94, 100, 134, 243, 282n3, 288n11

Language: and developmental theory, 58–61, 64–65; and emotions, 58, 72, 152; and fantasy, 58, 72, 202; and gender meaning, 70, 112; and feminism, 71; and gender identity, 72, 115–116; and personal meaning, 76; and psychic reality, 77; and structuralism, 142; and M. Rosaldo, 150–151, 154. *See also* Linguistic meaning

Lear, Jonathan, 23, 277n5

LeVine, Robert, 188, 203, 288n9, 289n1, 291n9

Lévi-Strauss, Claude, 138, 286n4

Levy, Robert I., 178, 184–188, 190–191, 194, 203, 288n9, 289n13, 289n14

Linguistic meaning, 70–71, 76, 78, 101, 143–144, 170, 251. *See also* Language

Linguistic pragmatics, 142, 144, 150, 154, 159, 160

Loewald, Hans: and incompatibility between theories, 3; and transference, 13, 18–19, 21–22, 27, 45, 207, 244–248, 263; and ego psychology, 26, 48, 52, 204, 263, 277n4, 280n10, 281n13, 294–295n4; and developmental theory, 46, 52–53, 56–57, 59, 260, 269–270, 281n15; and object-relations theory, 52–53, 55, 280n10, 280–281n11; and past-present relationship, 73; and language, 202; and unconscious, 239; and goals of psychoanalysis, 242, 243, 244; and fantasy, 247–248, 273; and self, 257–258; and ego integrity, 258; and countertransference, 278n7